The Cutting Edge of Tourism Series

Series Editors
Sue Berry, Brighton Business School, University of Brighton
Howard Hughes, Department of Hotel Catering and Tourism Management, Manchester Metropolitan University

As the tourism industry becomes more sophisticated, professionals and academic researchers need to look ahead and consider the industry's approach to product design, marketing and management. Among the subjects to be covered in this series are the challenges facing policy development in the three sectors – public, private and not for profit; the issues surrounding the development of federal structures both within the public sector (e.g. the European Union) and in the industry; and the reconciliation of profit versus the conservation and enhancement of the environment on which tourism depends, but which without income cannot be sustained.

International City Tourism

Analysis and Strategy

Klaus Grabler, Gunther Maier, Josef A. Mazanec and Karl Wöber

Edited by Josef A. Mazanec

PINTER
LONDON AND WASHINGTON

First published 1997 by
Pinter
A Cassell imprint

Wellington House, 125 Strand, London WC2R 0BB, England

PO Box 605, Herndon, VA 20172, USA

British Library Cataloguing-in-Publication Data

International city tourism: analysis and strategy. – (The
cutting edge of tourism)
1. Tourist trade   2. Urban economics
I. Grabler, Klaus   II. Mazanec, Josef A.
338.4'791'091732
ISBN 1–85567–392–4

Library of Congress Cataloging-in-Publication Data

International city tourism: analysis and strategy/by Klaus Grabler
. . . [et al.]; edited by Josef A. Mazanec.
p. cm. — (The cutting edge of tourism series)
Includes bibliographical references and index.
ISBN 1–85567–392–4
1. Tourist trade. 2. Cities and towns. I. Grabler, Klaus.
II. Mazanec, Josef A. III. Series
G155.A1I4995   1997
338.4'791—dc20   96–42574
                                                          CIP

Typeset by Textype Typesetters, Cambridge
Printed and bound in Great Britain by Biddles Ltd., Guildford and King's Lynn

Contents

List of figures

List of tables

List of place name codes used in figures and tables

AAH	Aachen	GRZ	Graz
AGB	Augsburg	GVA	Geneva
ALV	Andorra	HAG	The Hague
AMS	Amsterdam	HAM	Hamburg
ATH	Athens	HEL	Helsinki
AVN	Avignon	INN	Innsbruck
BAD	Baden-Baden	IST	Istanbul
BCN	Barcelona	LBC	Lübeck
BER	Berlin	LIS	Lisbon
BNJ	Bonn	LNZ	Linz
BOD	Bordeaux	LON	London
BRE	Bremen	LUX	Luxembourg
BRG	Bruges	MAD	Madrid
BRN	Berne	MAN	Manchester
BRU	Brussels	MCM	Monte Carlo
BSL	Basle	MHG	Mannheim
BTS	Bratislava	MIL	Milan
BUD	Budapest	MLA	Malta
CAG	Cagliari	MRS	Marseilles
COL	Cologne	MUC	Munich
CPH	Copenhagen	NCE	Nice
CWL	Cardiff	NTE	Nantes
DBN	Dublin	OSL	Oslo
DIJ	Dijon	PAR	Paris
EAS	San Sebastian	POT	Potsdam
EBU	Saint-Etienne	PRG	Prague
EDI	Edinburgh	QFB	Freiburg
FMO	Munster	QGL	St Gallen
FRA	Frankfurt	QGN	Tarragona
GLA	Glasgow	QHD	Heidelberg

Introduction: Information requirements for the strategic management of city tourism

Josef A. Mazanec

This book is about marketing an urban destination to tourism-generating countries. It rests on the premise that, in terms of strategic reasoning, this effort is not fundamentally different from marketing a branded product to consumer target groups. The managers of a municipal tourist board are in charge of promoting inbound tourism into an urban destination. Like their colleagues in any other service industry they have to decide on which urban tourism products should be offered to which segments of the international tourist demand. This implies analytical and subsequent planning exercises called 'product positioning' and 'market segmentation' (Day, 1990; Calantone and Mazanec, 1991).

Positioning and segmentation issues are strategic decisions that precede action planning for individual marketing instruments such as designing promotional messages or choosing advertising media and distribution channels. An action plan for image advertising for a city, for example, is developed along the guidelines of a positioning strategy and accompanied by coordinated product planning of tour operators and other private and public service providers. The monitoring of the market segments assists in maintaining a reasonable ratio of promotional input to segment response. Segmentation itself is a dynamic process. Resourceful managers are identifying and 'inventing' new market segments by experimenting with new tourist attributes more imaginative than gender, age, or household size and income.

Strategic marketing cannot function without a major investment into market research and data analysis. An in-depth 'marketing audit' (McDonald, 1995) is the step to start with. If a city tourism marketing manager decides to pursue a rather sophisticated planning approach, e.g. aiming at consumer lifestyle groups as market segments (Mazanec and Zins, 1994), the need for costly data will increase tremendously. But there is a trade-off. A more comprehensive cause–effect model providing more information about reality also enhances the scope for managerial influence. Analysing data guards the whole marketing planning process from setting objectives to examining the reasons for being off target. Unlike many other managerial capabilities it can be trained. It contributes to streamlining strategic thinking and it may inspire problem-solving creativity.

The chapters of this book focus on the analytical preparation for strategic decision-making. Part I outlines the responsibilities of the major European city tourist offices and their working conditions. Part II illustrates the contemporary volume and directions of travel flows into European cities. Part III touches upon micro models of tourist behaviour. It addresses several explanatory variables that are crucial in tackling positioning and segmentation problems. Part IV recognizes the tourist cities as competitors in a fragmented market where it is imperative to know who the 'real' rivals are.

Switching to the demand side on aggregate level Part V looks into the evaluation of tourism generating countries. In today's managerial routine this analytical step employs some variant of a 'portfolio model'. Part VI introduces one particular aspect of the marketing mix by highlighting the role of the hyper-information highway in distributing text, sound and vision related to urban destinations. Finally, the Appendix complements the analytical procedures used in the case examples for those readers seeking a more rigorous treatment of some data processing tools.

References

Calantone, R. and Mazanec, J. A. (1991) Marketing management and tourism. *Annals of Tourism Research* **18**, 101–19.

Day, G. S. (1990) *Market Driven Strategy, Processes for Creating Value.* New York: Free Press.

McDonald, M. (1995) *Marketing Plans, How to Prepare Them, How to Use Them*, 3rd edn. Oxford: Butterworth-Heinemann.

Mazanec, J. A. and Zins, A. (1994) Tourist behaviour and the new European life style typology. In W.F. Theobald (ed.) *Global Tourism: The Next Decade.* Oxford: Butterworth-Heinemann, 199–216.

Part I

Local tourism organizations in European cities

Karl Wöber

Decision-making in tourism planning and development is most critical at the local level, especially in urban areas. In recent years many urban communities have come to recognize that tourism is more important than originally thought. This increased awareness of tourism's potential to create employment, stimulate the economy and generate wealth was not noticed solely by any single organization or authority. Perhaps the most important aspect of urban tourism planning and promotion is that it is neither owned nor directed by a single authority or enterprise. In most cities the various functions are performed by individuals and municipal and private enterprises (e.g. chambers of commerce, local tourist councils, voluntary groups, local authorities and agencies which have become involved in tourism). These groups have the potential to develop new attractions, products, facilities and services for tourism in their local areas. They can also initiate these projects and mobilize others to commit resources for effective marketing. Magee (1995) identified a danger of overfragmentation of the development and marketing effort, arguing that a minimum level of coordination is necessary to avoid inefficient use of scarce resources and ineffective promotions which serve to confuse rather than attract tourists.

At the national level this coordination task is usually carried out by the national tourist office (NTO), which is also the most important instrument in the implementation of governmental tourism policy. Unfortunately most cities do not have similar institutional structures to plan for the growth and development of tourism (Gunn, 1988; Haywood, 1988). To a certain extent, however, city tourist offices (CTOs) tend to fulfil a similar role at an urban community level. Whereas the structures of NTOs are extensively analysed and reported (IUOTO, 1966; WTO, 1975, 1979; Wahab *et al.*, 1976; Akehurst *et al.*, 1993; Choy, 1993; Baum, 1994; Morrison *et al.*, 1995), very little is known about the objectives, functional responsibilities, instruments and funding of CTOs.

Page (1995) summarizes the results of a survey carried out by the US Travel Service covering 142 US cities with populations exceeding 100,000 in 1978 (see also Pearce, 1992). The primary functions of the services provided by the surveyed organizations included design and production of information material, administration of tourist information kiosks, maintenance of public tourist attractions, advertising, promotion, public relations, convention planning and technical assistance, maintenance of hotel-based computer reservation systems and tourism research. While half of the interviewed CTOs stated that they contracted out their tourism activities to agencies (e.g. convention and visitor bureaux and Chambers of Trade), only 16 per cent dealt with tourism activities directly through their offices and units, while another 16 per cent indicated that they were not involved in promoting urban tourism. A substantial number of cities reported that they undertook promotional activities in partnership with the private sector.

In Europe, Greene Belfield-Smith (1991), the Tourism and Leisure Consultancy Division of Touche Ross, conducted a survey of 39 CTOs covering issues such as funding, cooperation with other cities and private industry, and the monitoring of productivity in terms of tourism generated. While 80 per cent of CTOs in their study monitored the performance of the industry, only two of the cities monitored their own performance as a marketing organization.

In 1992 the Federation of European Cities' Tourism Offices conducted a pilot survey of 43 European member cities which covered funding, evaluation of tourism policy, resources and city tourism statistics (FECTO, 1992). Similar to the US results reported by Law (1993), large tourist-oriented cities commanded generous promotional budgets. Vienna was one of the best financed and most aggressive cities with an annual budget of ECU 10.7 million to operate its tourist and convention department. Paris had a budget of ECU 5.4 million, followed by Amsterdam (ECU 4.3 million) and Zurich (ECU 3.4 million).

Questions regarding policy objectives and statistics were answered completely; however, the quality of responses varied on questions concerning financing and funding at the urban level and the process of budgetary formulation. Specifically, calculations of key indicators such as the annual budget per full-time employee and the annual budget per number of bednights lacked comparability among the participating CTOs.

In general, it is difficult to compare and analyse urban community organizations responsible for tourism affairs because they face enormous differences in their organizational structures and the services they provide. The main differences appear to be determined by local fiscal stability, leadership, tradition and legal responsibility. As FECTO's Research and Statistics Working Group assumed that all CTOs share at least some common functional responsibilities, they decided to carry out an extended survey in 1995 to compare urban policies in all member cities, in particular, to gain comparative knowledge about the successful functions and instruments of local management authorities.

A pilot survey and interviews with eight executives of CTOs from eight different European countries with different organizational structures (Budapest, Dublin, Edinburgh, Heidelberg, Lisbon, Nice, Tarragona, and Vienna) resulted in a comprehensive list of alternative functions and services. The final questionnaire was targeted at 77 major European CTOs which were either FECTO members or other important tourism cities in terms of size or tourism volume. Sixty-one of these cities sent back the requested tourism statistics and 45 CTO managers answered the questions concerning their respective organizations.

Functions and services of city tourist offices

Promotion is often believed to be one of the most important tasks of tourism organizations (Wahab *et al.*, 1976). Every city tourist office spends remarkable amounts on tourism promotion. Tourism promoters are carrying out more and more research and increasing their levels of sophistication in order to meet new market needs. Travel behaviour and segmentation are studied to refine promotional techniques and approaches. Table 1.1 summarizes the response of the interviewed city tourism managers

Table 1.1 Target groups specially promoted by European CTOs

Target groups promoted by CTOs (multiple response allowed)	Percentage of all CTOs surveyed
Travellers in groups (organized)	92%
Day trip and weekend visitors	88%
Leisure travellers	86%
Single travellers (not organized)	86%
Visitors to congresses, fairs and exhibitions	84%
Conference and event organizers	84%
Business travellers	68%
Pensioners	60%
Youth	52%
Families travelling with children	50%
Long-term holiday makers	46%

Source: 50 leading CTO managers answering on a dichotomous scale (FECTO survey, 1995, unpublished survey report).

regarding the target groups of their organizations' promotional efforts.

The responses to the question about policy instruments are summarized in Table 1.2. The range of instruments deployed to implement tourism

Table 1.2 Services and functions of European CTOs

Variable names used in analysis	Services and functions provided by CTO (multiple response allowed)	Percentage of all CTOs surveyed
FAIRNAT	Participation in national fairs or exhibitions	100%
FAIRINT	Participation in international fairs or exhibitions	96%
INFOPHONE	Information by phone or fax	96%
INFOINT	Regular info-material to intern. press and tour operators	94%
PRINT	Design and production of printmedia	94%
INFONAT	Regular info-material to national press and tour operators	92%
PRINTFRE	Free dispatch of print media	90%
PRESSCON	Press conferences	84%
INFOOFIC	Help for visitors in information offices	82%
INCENTIV	Incentives for journalists (e.g. invitations)	80%
PACKAGES	Development of packages	76%
PRINTMED	Selling of printmedia, books	69%
WALKING	Guided walking tours	69%
SIGHTSEE	Sightseeing tours	65%
HOTCITON	Hotel bookings in the city *after* arrival	63%
SOUVENIR	Selling of souvenirs	61%
HOTREGON	Hotel booking services in the city's region *after* arrival	59%
BUSTOUR	Bus tours	57%
THEATRE	Selling of concert, theatre tickets	55%
PUBLTIC	Selling of tickets for public transport in the city	53%
SECTOR	Encouraging cooperation different sectors	53%
PRINTSAL	Sale of publications by mail	49%
HOTREGBE	Hotel booking services in the city's region *before* arrival	47%
HOTCITBE	Hotel booking services in the city *before* arrival	45%
RESEARCH	Research planning and statistics	45%
ELECINFO	Electronic information services	43%
CONVENT	Convention bureau services	41%
DEVELOP	Development of tourist facilities, attractions	41%
ACCOMBE	Booking services of other accommodation facilities *before* arrival	39%
PACKAGBE	Booking services of packages (accommodation and transport)	37%
ACCOMON	Booking services of other accommodation facilities *after* arrival	37%
HOTCOUON	Booking services of hotels nationally *after* arrival	31%
ELECBOOK	Electronic booking services	29%
HOTCOUBE	Booking services of hotels nationally *before* arrival	27%
TRAINING	Training, business advice	24%
TRAINTIC	Selling of tickets for trains	20%
MANAGEM	Maintenance/management of attractions	18%
QUALITY	Quality certification of accommodations or restaurants	18%
CARRENT	Car rentals	16%
HOTINTON	Booking services of hotels internationally *after* arrival	12%
GRANTS	Capital grants to tourism enterprises	12%
HOTINTBE	Booking services of hotels internationally *before* arrival	10%
SUPERVIS	Regulation and supervision of tourism enterprises	10%
AIRTIC	Selling of air-travel tickets	2%
EMPLOY	Employment services	2%

Source: 45 leading CTO managers answering on a dichotomous scale (FECTO survey, 1995, unpublished survey report).

planning is determined by objectives of tourism policy. As the success of managerial effort is usually judged by certain criteria or ratios, the CTO managers were asked to list these key indicators in an open question. While 80 per cent of CTOs monitored the performance of the industry or specific promotion activities, only two of the cities indicated that they used any form of evaluation of effectiveness of their office as a marketing organization. Most offices used either visitor expenditures or number of visitors or bednights as a productivity measure. Only a few organizations indicated that the number of enquiries handled by their offices or the awareness of their cities was used as a measure of productivity.

The primary task of tourist information centres is to provide tourists with the necessary information about places of interest, tourist resources, accommodation, prices of services, means of transportation, tourist circuits, etc. The most labour-intensive method of disseminating information, namely the usage of phone or fax, is still the primary means used by most CTOs (96 per cent).

Printed matter is also an important communication medium between the service provider and the market. The free dispatch of print media (90 per cent) and the provision of regular information material to international (94 per cent) and national (92 per cent) press are the dominant services. The design and production of print media is undertaken by 94 per cent of all CTOs. Most of them prepare one or more brochures in one language, usually their mother tongue, and then translate them into leading foreign languages to be distributed to the major tourist markets (for criticism on this unprofessional and naive method see Wahab *et al.*, 1976).

Maintaining good relations with tour operators and travel agents in the tourist-generating countries is of great importance. All CTOs participate in national fairs and exhibitions, with almost every office (96 per cent) conducting this service on an international level as well.

Most CTOs invite a certain number of travel editors, writers, travel agents, carriers' staff and tour operators in each of the important generating markets to visit their cities each year for demonstration purposes (80 per cent). These groups of tourism professionals are multipliers and it is of prime importance to stimulate their interest in selling the city. To do this most effectively the incentive tours should be well organized and comprehensive in giving the travel agent the atmosphere of the city.

The distribution of travel literature, as far as timing, quantity and channels are concerned, is also of great importance. Some CTOs prefer to sell their information booklets, maps and tourist guides in their information centres (69 per cent), others distribute them free of charge, together with normal promotional literature.

While 76 per cent of CTOs get involved in product development, only a few become involved in the actual planning of tourist attractions (41 per cent). Several CTOs manage various aspects of tourism enterprises (e.g.

guided walking tours, 69 per cent; provision of bus tours, 57 per cent; selling of sightseeing tours, 65 per cent, selling of print media or books, 69 per cent; selling of concert and theatre tickets, 55 per cent; selling of tickets for public transport in the city, 53 per cent), but only 18 per cent maintain or manage tourist attractions.

Many CTOs perform like professional travel agencies. Booking services of hotels in the city after the guests' arrival was mentioned by 63 per cent (including the neighbouring region, 59 per cent) of all tourism managers. CTOs' booking services are generally organized manually, with facilities for electronic bookings relatively rare (43 per cent electronic information services and only 29 per cent electronic booking services).

A minority of CTOs are involved in inspection of tourist-related operations (quality certification of accommodations or restaurants, 18 per cent; allocation of capital grants to tourism enterprises, 12 per cent) and when undertaken, it is usually because of legal obligation.

Dimensions of CTO services and functions

The nature of the variations in the responses and the researchers' experiences during the data collection procedure hinted at the possibility that the underlying dimensions of CTO services and functions may differ in a systematic way. To test this hypothesis a factor analysis of the 46 services was performed using the principal component extraction and varimax rotation method.[1] Factors with an eigenvalue exceeding 1.89 were considered significant.[2] A CTO service or function with the factor loading exceeding 0.4 was regarded as part of a given factor (see Table 1.3). For city tourism organizations, the important service factors suggested in this study include the following items:

1. provider of supplementary tourism services
2. management and consultancy bureau
3. progressive booking office with strong city orientation
4. retail office for the city and the neighbouring region
5. guest-oriented promotional organization
6. professional travel agency
7. industry-oriented promotional organization
8. simple information office.

As can be seen, the eight extracted service factors explain 60.7 per cent of the total variance, of which the first factor, provider of supplementary tourism services, explains 16.8 per cent. This type of tourist office (category 1) offers services directly to the tourist primarily on a commercial basis. These services cover sale of souvenirs, tickets for local public transport, print media, books, sightseeing tours, theatre and concert tickets. Even promotional publications are sold on request. Using factor score plots it is

Table 1.3 Rotated factor matrix

Variable names (services and function)	1	2	3	4	5	6	7	8
PRINTMED	0.74951		0.17289	0.10785			-0.12729	-0.17603
SOUVENIR	0.72496		0.24262	0.31528	-0.14704			
THEATRE	0.71759	0.15151	0.31576				-0.13620	
SIGHTSEE	0.69789		0.13577	0.32460	-0.15383			
PUBLTIC	0.63954	0.17159	0.16412	0.23273			0.16182	0.19616
PRINTSAL	0.54471	0.15713	-0.22355					0.37918
CONVENT	0.48692	-0.13592	-0.30435	0.23705			0.20746	0.17271
PACKAGBE	0.46994	-0.11438			-0.44135	0.29647	0.21459	0.39849
CARRENT	0.44256	0.43189	0.14666		0.15335	0.40092		
EMPLOY	0.11323	0.72861		-0.21177			-0.12596	
GRANTS	0.16617	0.67940			0.21818	0.23491		
SUPERVIS	-0.13674	0.60203	0.13649		-0.11990	-0.38557		
DEVELOP		0.58892		0.25836	0.12042		0.14813	0.17805
MANAGEM	-0.15043	0.55619	-0.17062	0.14978		0.25282		
FAIRINT		-0.53089	-0.21700	0.15246	0.49322		0.14545	0.14086
TRAINTIC	0.24451	0.43479	0.24037	0.18127	-0.13530	0.14796	0.20778	0.14211
TRAINING	0.14229	0.41675	0.14304	-0.12458	0.13136	-0.21329	0.40150	
HOTCOUBE	0.12644	0.17854	0.76381		-0.12588	0.35875		
HOTCOUON	0.22922	0.23296	0.70427			0.26845	0.21613	
HOTCITON	0.19433	-0.21716	0.67913					
HOTCITBE	0.12001		0.63706	0.21414		0.19351		
ELECINFO		0.43059	0.45051			-0.23000		
ELECBOOK	0.40074	0.30718	0.40140			0.16499	-0.25379	
HOTREGBE	0.15615		0.27069	0.75494			0.12366	
ACCOMON	0.11126			0.75096	0.17163	-0.17127		0.14086
HOTREGON	0.14210	-0.13266	0.28336	0.71140				
WALKING	0.40200	-0.16134	-0.10889	0.63511		0.12574		-0.15027
ACCOMBE		0.21004		0.59130	0.21963	0.27133		0.13256
BUSTOUR	0.21229	-0.10510	-0.20067	0.59100	-0.24976	0.33445	-0.20260	0.12996
PRINTFRE			0.16141	-0.14699	0.78706			
PRINT	-0.19367		-0.20312	0.15604	0.71577	0.13547		
INFONAT			-0.22717		0.62419		0.34761	0.37193
INFOINT	0.14779	-0.10739	-0.43462	-0.20937	0.44866	0.26737	0.33468	
HOTINTBE		0.11887	0.17873	0.25203		0.74483	0.13062	
HOTINTON			0.29317	0.13032	0.22054	0.64794		0.11395
AIRTIC		0.18366	0.14273			0.58387		0.10391
QUALITY		0.11268	0.10756		0.21796	-0.51251		0.27946
PRESSCON			0.11050				0.73994	
INCENTIV	-0.17304	-0.34024		-0.14392			0.69947	
RESEARCH		0.43006			0.14140		0.58925	
SECTOR	0.19627	0.36438		0.23062	-0.23760	0.10208	0.47738	-0.16640
INFOPHON	-0.10086		0.16103	0.10147				0.81207
INFOOFIC	0.17967	0.12834	-0.27378	-0.11251	0.32178		-0.11152	0.70793
PACKAGES	0.18070	-0.22312	0.11869	0.27516	-0.26191			0.57448
Variance explained	16.8%	9.5%	8.9%	6.4%	5.3%	5.0%	4.5%	4.3%
Cumulated	16.8%	26.3%	35.2%	41.7%	47.0%	52.0%	56.5%	60.7%

Note: Only factor loadings of 0.10 and above reported.

easy to identify cities with this type of CTO organization. Cities showing high loadings on factor 1 are Heidelberg, Amsterdam, Stuttgart and St Gall.

Category 2 tourist offices take greater responsibility for managerial and policy tasks within the community. Typical services covered by corresponding CTOs are provision of employment services, allocation of capital grants and regulation and supervision of tourism enterprises. Furthermore, the management and maintenance of attractions, training and business advice to local tourism enterprises are primary tasks of CTOs with factor 2 orientation. A high negative loading on the very common service participation in international fairs or exhibitions is unusual. There are only a few cities with this organizational structure, among them Dublin and Athens.

Category 3 and 4 tourist offices offer primary hotel booking services within the city and sometimes in the neighbouring regions. Although these offices provide retail functions, the majority work on a non-profit basis. The provision of modern electronic information and booking services (e.g. travel kiosks) are typical features of factor 3-oriented cities which include Paris, Toulon and Frankfurt. More conservative supplementary services like the organization of bus and walking tours are covered by factor 4; cities with a strong correlation with factor 4 include Lyon, Bratislava, Berne and Würzburg.

Tourist offices with a strong correlation to factor 6 display all features of a professional profit-oriented travel agency. They operate internationally and are usually connected to a computer reservation system for air travel ticketing. CTOs with this clear commercially oriented business strategy are Graz, Geneva, Madrid and Aachen.

CTOs of categories 5, 7 and 8 offer purely promotional services. The differences between factors 5 and 7 can be described as either more guest- or industry-oriented. Factor 5 stands for the free dispatch of information and promotional material both within and outside the country, primarily directly to the guest. Cities with a strong correlation with factor 5 are Prague, Copenhagen and Vienna. Factor 7 covers more indirect, but also typical, promotional activities like organizing press conferences and providing incentives for journalists or travel agents. CTOs which typically provide these kind of functions are Edinburgh, Bordeaux and Lyon. Finally factor 8 clearly covers tasks of simple information services for guests during their stay in the city. The majority of CTOs are fulfilling this function, whereas Barcelona, Edinburgh and Rome are outstanding.

Reasons for different organizational structures and tasks of CTOs

The purpose of this study was to investigate variations in the organizational structures and primary services offered by European CTOs. The study revealed that these differences are significant. Eight types of organizational structures could be identified by factor analysis. Given that the organizational structures and tasks of National Tourist Offices are relatively homogeneous (Akehurst *et al.*, 1993), the reasons for the differences in the organizational structures in urban tourism are unclear. Hypotheses concerning the differences in size of the city (as a usable substitute for an indicator of capital flexibility), importance of tourism, guest-mix structure and national dependency are obvious. Consequently, correlation and variance analysis of the eight previously defined factors with these variables have been performed (Table 1.4).

Table 1.4 Reasons for the different tasks European city tourism organizations provide

Factor	Size of the city (n=77)†	Tourism importance (n=61)†	Foreign tourism intensity (n=61)†	Nationality (n=77)‡
1	-0.114	-0.011	-0.059	1.52
2	0.031	0.245	0.286	6.17**
3	0.334**	0.179	0.235	0.70
4	-0.001	-0.226	-0.258*	1.01
5	-0.011	-0.433**	0.159	0.53
6	-0.100	-0.068	0.011	0.95
7	-0.085	0.009	0.023	1.38
8	-0.068	-0.379**	0.090	0.75

† Pearson correlation coefficient.
‡ ANOVA F-ratio.
* Significant at < 0.05 level.
** Significant at < 0.01 level.

The data in Table 1.4 illustrate the relative importance of city size, importance attached to tourism, the amount of foreign tourism and national origin in explaining the services and functions provided by European city tourism organizations.

The only national differences that could be identified related to factor 2 (management and consultancy services and tasks). Cities in eastern Europe and Great Britain show considerably more identification with this CTO category (German cities in particular do not). Furthermore, significant correlation between factor 3 and the city's size (population) indicates that maintaining a modern booking office with extensive electronic facilities is still a privilege of major cities and federal capitals. Strong negative correlations between the ratio of tourism importance and factor 5 (guest-oriented promotional organization, r = -0.433) and factor 8 (simple information office, r = -0.379) indicate that CTOs in tourism development areas start with more guest-oriented services, which cover informational and promotional tasks. The foreigner's share in the guest mix did not show any statistically significant influence on the CTO services.

Notes

[1] The item 'participation in national fairs or exhibition' has been excluded from the analysis, as it did not provide any discriminating function.
[2] Solution with the best interpretation capability (60.7 per cent of the total variance explained).

References

Akehurst, G., Bland, N. and Nevin, M. (1993) Tourism policies in the European Community member states. *International Journal of Hospitality Management* **12**, 33–66.

Baum, T. (1994) The development and implementation of national tourism policies. *Tourism Management* **15**, 185–92.

Choy, D.J.L. (1993) Alternative roles of national tourism organizations. *Tourism Management* **14**, 357–65.

Greene Belfield-Smith, Touche Ross (1991) *A Survey of Tourist Offices in European Cities. For the European City Symposium, Manchester*. London: Greene Belfield-Smith.

Gunn, C.A. (1988) *Tourism Planning*, 2nd edn. New York: Taylor & Francis.

Haywood, K.M. (1988) Responsible and responsive approach to tourism planning in the community. *Tourism Management* **9**, 105–18.

Federation of European Cities' Tourist Offices (1992) *Evaluation of FECTO's Member Structure. Report for the General Assembly of FECTO*. Lisbon, Heidelberg: FECTO.

International Union of Official Travel Organizations (1966) *Aims, Functions and Fields of Competence of National Tourist Offices*. Geneva: IUOTO.

Law, C. M. (1993) *Urban Tourism: Attracting Visitors to Large Cities*. London: Mansell.

Magee, F. (1995) *The Structures of Tourism in Dublin*. MBS thesis, Dublin: University College.

Morrison, A.M., Braunlich, C.G., Kamaruddin, N. and Cai, L.A. (1995) National tourist offices in North America: an analysis. *Tourism Management* **16**, 605–17.

Page, S. (1995) *Urban Tourism*. London: Routledge.

Pearce, D.G. (1992) *Tourist Organizations*. London: Longman.

Wahab, S., Crampon, L.J. and Rothfield, L.M. (1976) *Tourism Marketing. A Destination-Oriented Programme for the Marketing of International Tourism*. London: Tourism International Press.

World Tourism Organization (1975) *Aims, Activities and Fields of Competence of National Tourist Organizations*. Geneva: WTO.

World Tourism Organization (1979) *Role and Structure of National Tourism Administrations*. Madrid: WTO.

Part II

An urban tourism database

2.1

A database on the travel demand for European urban tourism destinations

Karl Wöber

Harmonizing European city tourism statistics

Tourism marketing is becoming increasingly sophisticated as a result of greater importance attached to the reliability of information and the competent analysis of that information for the effective planning, monitoring and management of tourism enterprises (Bar-On, 1989).

Decisions concerning tourism-related investments in tourism developments such as infrastructure for major new tourist regions or individual resorts; transportation facilities; accommodation facilities, including new hotels, self-catering apartments and campsites; museums and theme parks are crucial because they are very cost intensive. In the planning phase of such new tourism investments, a careful consideration of potential customer benefits, technological expertise and the identification of a unique competitive positioning is necessary. To avoid investment failures the target market has to be clearly defined and its potential estimated and forecast.

Without doubt, the greatest commitment to tourism by the government and private sector is the promotion of tourism. Every tourism organization on a national, regional or city level spends considerable amounts of money on promotion. In general this involves four types of activities: advertising, publicity, public relations and incentives (Gunn, 1988). Decisions on promotional activities include the selection of geographical markets in which to promote, the selection of segments within those markets, the image to portray about the tourism destination or product, the medium to be used for the message, and the optimal timing and frequency of the campaign. Comprehensive budget allocation models are available to support the promotional planning process (Mazanec, 1986; Moutinho *et al.*, 1995). To feed these models extensive data input is necessary and regular use is impossible unless these systems are combined with a continuously maintained database (Wöber, 1994).

Governments and other official organizations and major enterprises in the tourism and transportation industry need statistical data on the present structure of the industry as well as on historical and future trends. Based on reliable information, strategies and operational plans are implemented, monitored and, where necessary, modified in response to feedback from the marketplace. However, the social, economic and environmental impact of tourism is an international issue which does not stop at national borders. For example, when the number of visitors to a city exceeds the number of residents, some social response is likely to be aroused, both negative and positive. Each community has developed its own agencies, policies, practices and traditions to monitor indicators which measure the environmental impact of travel and tourism. Obviously, such indicators must be comparable at national and international levels if the global impact of tourism is to be quantified and corresponding policies and safeguards are to be developed. Location-specific variations measuring the impact of tourism must be removed if tourism is to progress.

At the management level, planning processes for marketing projects are determined by specific objectives. These objectives should be both comprehensive and precise enough to be measured (and accomplished) within a given time frame. Statistical data on successes and failures of projects need to be collected and analysed.

In the reconciliation phase of a market planning process, tourism managers require data on the size and characteristics of different market segments and on the tourist requirements and profile. Latham (1989) identifies three main categories of statistics: volume, expenditure and profile of the tourist and his trip. Tourism volume statistics are typically measurements of arrivals, trips and tourist nights on the demand side and capacities on the supply side. Volume data often appear in total or split into categories such as country of origin or business versus leisure travel. The basic statistics of monetary flows are naturally compiled under the headings of income and expenditure. Statistics relating to the profile of the tourist include details of age, sex, occupation, income, origin, purpose of visit, mode of transport, type of accommodation and details of activities engaged in.

The major problems which are likely to be encountered when tourism managers are facing market planning processes are the availability and comparability of market research information (Table 2.1).

Table 2.1 Problems with tourism statistics are twofold

Problem	Instruments/actions	Possible errors
Availability	Evaluation and forecasting	Sample error, interviewer bias, missing values . . .
Comparability	Compilation and harmonization	Varying definitions, survey methods, aggregation techniques . . .

Evaluation and forecasting

Although the statistical measurement of tourism is a relatively recent activity, a considerable amount of data on tourism movements is already available at the national level. Most of this comes from public organizations, including national tourist administrations, governments and other statistical offices, who evaluate tourism statistics for their own country. There is a broad literature base available on the various methodologies for collecting tourism statistics and the planning, design and management of tourism surveys. The historical development of the statistical measurement of tourism is described in detail by Burkart and Medlik (1974) and also by Chadwick (1987).

It is possible to measure tourist activities in several ways, some of which will be appropriate for one purpose but not for another. The most frequently used tourism volume indicators are the number of visitors/travellers, the number of nights and the expenditures/receipts in a specific area within a certain period of time. However, there are different methodologies and definitions of these main indicators creating problems which have to be considered in any comparative study. For instance, the monetary impact of tourism may be measured on the supply side (receipts) or on the demand side (expenditures). For identifying and measuring the tourism revenue of a certain resort, region or country, both approaches have their own measurement problems. The evaluation of tourism receipts on the supply side needs to identify and separate tourism activities and expenditures from other recreational and business activities of individuals. Clearly, the identification and separation of tourism receipts from other receipts in establishments or service organizations providing services to both tourists and local residents is crucial and often impossible. The evaluation of tourism expenditures from the demand side is also unclear. The tourist who buys a package tour is usually unaware of the way the price is split between different service providers or different destinations. In addition there are expenditures he may not recognize as part of his trip or vacation. Finally there are different possibilities as to when the evaluation of the tourists' expenditures should take place (McIntosh and Goeldner, 1986). When the measurement is taken before the trip ends it is obvious that the data represent intended behaviour and are likely to differ from the actual. Data collected on the tourist's return home involve the problem of identifying and locating respondents as well as the problem of inaccurate recall. Data collected during travel show a mixture of both shortcomings. These methodological problems may occur in all survey-based research, but are particularly relevant in the measurement of tourism expenditures.

The definition of tourism expenditure may vary depending on the way in which the data are being used. For example, the destination country may only be interested in tourism earnings, payments made by visitors within the country and to the national carriers. Other bodies, depending on their standpoint, may also want data on expenditures in the country of residence before departure or after returning home (e.g. processing of films, credit card payments).

The most frequently used statistics in international tourism are the number of international or national visitor arrivals/departures during a given time period. A disadvantage of using this particular measure is that it does not take account of the visitor's length of stay, which is especially important for accommodation providers. To them a more satisfactory measure of volume is the number of total tourist nights, as it is a measure of overall demand.

Arrivals can be counted at borders or on arrival at accommodation establishments. Border surveys are mostly carried out at international points of entry where travellers must show their passports or other identification to the police or immigration official. In countries where visitors have to fill out an additional form on entry or departure, the border control usually represents the major source of tourism data. However, the procedures used at frontiers are often not satisfactory. Counting at frontiers does not provide an effective measure on length of stay, as explained above. Furthermore, frontier statistics usually do not distinguish between tourists who stay overnight and excursionists. From the city tourism management point of view, this source of information is rather uninteresting as it does not give any information about a specific city's performance.

Nights and/or arrivals registered by the accommodation providers are reported either voluntarily or by law. In most accommodation establishments guests have to fill out a form on arrival. In many areas hoteliers are obliged to send a monthly report on the number of persons who stayed at the accommodation. This information is frequently broken down by country of origin. It also enables the calculation of the average stay per guest in establishments of different category and in different resorts or regions of the country. The number of arrivals reported by accommodation providers will differ from those at frontiers because some travellers will not stay in such establishments or patronize more than one.

When hotels and other organizations are obliged to report these statistics, the coverage and the content of their reports are often incomplete. In many cases this error is due to the entrepreneurs' desire to avoid taxes which are determined by the number of guests registered or by revenue. In Austria, for example, a 30 per cent divergence between accommodation registration statistics and annual results of the European Travel Monitor survey has been regularly observed (ÖGAF, 1995). Where such reports are not required by law, voluntary occupancy surveys are sometimes carried out among a sample of establishments by the tourist board or some other organization. The main data derived from the person-nights and number of beds is bed occupancy. The occupancy data may be used internally by the hotel itself to monitor its operating performance. Occupancy data are also collected as part of the surveys on hotel profitability and operating ratios by consultancies such as Horwath & Horwath International (1980).

Further difficulties in collecting accommodation statistics are caused by

Table 2.2 Applied methodologies for monitoring 'arrivals' and 'nights' in 18 OECD countries

	Arrivals of foreign tourists at			Arrivals of foreign visitors at frontiers	Nights spent by foreign tourists in	
	Frontiers	Hotels and similar establishments	All means of accommodation		Hotels and similar establishments	All means of accommodation
Austria		✔	✔		✔	✔
Belgium					✔	✔
Denmark					✔	✔
Finland					✔	
France	✔	✔			✔	✔
Germany		✔	✔		✔	✔
Greece	✔					
Iceland	✔					
Ireland		✔	✔	✔	✔	✔
Italy		✔	✔	✔	✔	✔
Netherlands		✔	✔		✔	✔
Norway					✔	
Portugal	✔	✔	✔	✔	✔	✔
Spain		✔		✔	✔	
Sweden					✔	✔
Switzerland		✔	✔		✔	✔
Turkey		✔	✔	✔	✔	✔
United Kingdom				✔		✔

Source: Tourism policy and international tourism in OECD countries 1991–92. Paris: OECD, 1994.

unregistered accommodations like private households who rent out rooms to wild (off-site) campers. It is also impossible to estimate the number of tourists who stay with friends or relatives. Nights can be calculated as the product of tourist arrivals/departures and average length of stay. Thus errors in the values of the two terms of the product accumulate multiplicatively. Table 2.2 gives a summary of applied survey methodologies for national arrivals and nights by OECD countries.

For efficiency it is frequently necessary to use sampling techniques rather than to attempt collecting and processing all the data universally. The main difficulties in collecting reliable data from sample surveys involve the problem of identifying appropriate samples, the poor levels of response to enquiries and the collecting of data in a variety of languages and national settings. To assure a high quality of results it is essential that an experienced statistician is involved in designing the sample and carrying out the analysis. The interviewing has to be carried out by a carefully trained team whose work is properly supervised. The design, conduct and analysis of such surveys are therefore labour-intensive and costly.

Household surveys conducted in the originating countries are an easily accessible and useful source for evaluating a destination's popularity in the major generating markets. In many countries household surveys are sponsored by the government. Questions concerning the population's travel behaviour are often included in a more general survey together with other topics of social or economic importance (microcensus survey). Because of the limited questionnaire space, the questions usually cover only basic measures of tourism statistics, such as the number of trips, duration, destinations, means of travel, type of accommodation used and expenditure abroad.

When household surveys are sponsored and/or carried out by a commercial body, the subject matter of the survey is generally confined to tourism and thus more detailed. Travel surveys provide information which is of particular interest to commercial companies operating in the tourism market where it is collected. Results are often available only to subscribers. A main weakness of such surveys is that the sample sizes are often too small to give reliable and sufficiently detailed information. However, in recent years a number of studies of the European long haul market have been undertaken and these fill the gap to some extent.

Tourism data may also be obtained by analysing data published for a different purpose, for example, by using tour operators' brochures to analyse tourist costs and attractions in different countries. Fares or ticket statistics of major tourist attractions may provide data on visitor numbers. However, some of the information required by organizations involved in tourism can only be collected by putting questions directly to the guests. The core research interest of guest surveys is the evaluation of the tourists' perceptions of quality and price of the tourist products. Results include details of the customers' travel behaviour and supply information and guidelines for product optimization.

Quality research instruments like group discussions (focus groups) or individual in-depth interviews provide deeper insight. These methodologies are usually conducted for prototype product testing or for observing the customers' reaction to promotional stimuli and are usually carried out in laboratories with a relatively small number of respondents. General data such as the European Airports Traffic Report compiled and published annually by the Airports Council International (ACI, 1994) or the World Air Transport Statistics compiled and published by the International Air Transport Association (IATA, 1994), can provide a useful check against other sources of statistics.

Designing representative samples requires expert guidance. Even if the theoretical problems of sampling and its practical aspects can be overcome, serious doubts may still remain on the reliability of tourism data. In fact, the implementation of guest and/or travel surveys is often carried out partially or inadequately, and the definitions and classifications used vary considerably between the studies. A second important weakness is that there is little consistency between the different sample surveys in terms of survey techniques, definitions and presentation of analyses, so that comparability is greatly impaired (Devas, 1991). To date there have been few attempts to standardize the overall body of knowledge to improve the comparability of results gained through survey methods.

The main users of tourism statistics are governments, tourist organizations at national, regional and local levels, and providers of tourist services. The nature and form of the existing databases vary in accordance with the differing interests of users. Burkart and Medlik (1974) identify governments mainly interested in immigration control, in travel as an item in the balance of payments, in tourism as a source of employment and as a user of resources. On the other side, tourist organizations are more concerned with the marketing of their destinations and with their physical planning and development. The fundamental interest in tourism statistics of tourist offices coincides with that of the governments. The measuring of inbound traffic flows enables tourism managers at the national level to assess the magnitude and significance of tourism. Information requirements not covered by government surveys are often gathered by additional sample surveys.

As governments and national tourist offices are traditionally well organized and have similar interests in the scope of tourism statistics, the need for uniformity and comparability has been generally recognized by these two user groups.

Compilation and harmonization

As the collection of tourism statistics is an element of state responsibility, in most countries official statistics at the national level are collected by public statistical offices. The international compilation of these sources is organized by international organizations like the World Tourism Organization (WTO), International Air Transport Association (IATA) and the UN Statistical Office, regional organizations such as the Organization for Economic Cooperation and Development (OECD) and the Statistical Office of European Communities (Eurostat), and associations such as the Pacific Area Travel Association (PATA). They attempt to highlight differences in the data collection procedures and definitions and group the countries accordingly. Annual publications offered by some of them represent the main 'official' sources of international tourism statistics. The WTO *Yearbook of Tourism Statistics* has been published since 1947 under the titles *International Travel Statistics, World Travel Statistics, World Travel and Tourism Statistics* and its present title. The OECD publishes *Tourism Policy and International Tourism in OECD Member Countries,* sometimes referred to as the 'Blue Book'.

The *Yearbook of Tourism Statistics* (two volumes) provides a summary of the most important tourism statistics for about 150 countries and territories and can be supplemented by the WTO's *Compendium of Tourism Statistics* (published annually since 1985), a pocket-book designed to provide a condensed quick reference guide on the major tourism statistical indicators. The OECD 'Blue Book' is more restrictive in the sense that it covers only 25 countries, although these do include the main generating and receiving countries.

The collection and analysis of detailed statistics requires commitment of resources. The lack of comparability in the reported data is not only caused by differing survey methodologies but also by the measures themselves. The WTO has organized activities in response to this situation in the last ten years and has published recommendations for reducing the variations in gathering practice and terminology (WTO, 1981a, 1981b, 1983a, 1983b, 1983c, 1984a, 1984b, 1985a, 1985b). Figure 2.1 is a basic presentation advanced by the WTO and widely accepted, to show the overall definition and classification of tourists.

The recommendations on tourism statistics prepared by the WTO were adopted by the United Nations Statistical Commission at its twenty-seventh session in 1993. This was a first step in establishing internationally recognized standards in terms and definitions on tourism statistics. The Statistical Office of the European Communities (Eurostat) takes the UN/WTO recommendations as its basic reference and adapts them to the European context. During a joint Eurostat/DG XXIII meeting with professional associations held in Brussels on 19 January 1996, a

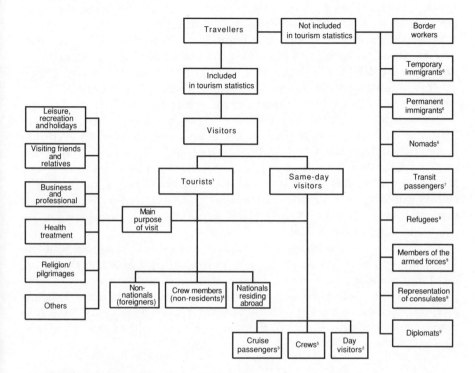

¹Visitors who spend at least one night in the country visited, but less than one year.
²Visitors who arrive and leave the same day for leisure, recreation and holidays; visiting friends and relatives; business and professional; health treatment; religion/pilgrimages and other tourism purposes, including transit day visitors en route to or from their destination countries.
³Persons who arrive in a country aboard cruise ships (as defined by the International Maritime Organization (IMO), 1965) and who spend the night aboard ship even when disembarking for one or more day visits.
⁴Foreign air or ship crews docked or in lay over and who use the accommodation establishments of the country visited.
⁵Crews who are not residents of the country visited and who stay in the country for the day.
⁶As defined by the United Nations in the Recommendations on Statistics of International.
⁷Who do not leave the transit area of the airport or the port, including transfer between airports or ports.
⁸As defined by the United Nations High Commissioner for Refugees, 1967.
⁹When they travel from their country of origin to the duty station and vice-versa (including household servants and dependants accompanying or joining them).

Figure 2.1 World Tourism Organization: classification of travellers

comprehensive reference document for the elaboration of comparable statistics was presented and discussed (Eurostat, 1996).

The recently presented Eurostat recommendations also consider certain aspects of tourism market segments (e.g. rural tourism). However, city tourism is not particularly mentioned. The list of variables and classifications for surveys of visitors and the resident population includes the evaluation of community size (V3 of the visitor profile variables) by the so-called 'NUTS' system. The NUTS classification system is a hierarchical one. The highest level, NUTS I, consists of 71 European community regions. The second level, NUTS II, is made up of 183 basic administrative regional units.[1] The third level, NUTS III, is derived by subdividing the basic regional units into 1044 subregional administrative units. Taking into account the existence of a further breakdown at national level, another nomenclature can be applied (for an explanation of the 'LOC' nomenclature, see Eurostat, 1992). Although this level is useful for the classification process delimiting rural areas, it obviously gives no clear definition of a city's borders or terms like 'urban tourism' or 'city tourism'.

With respect to city tourism, further problems arise when WTO and Eurostat definitions and recommendations are applied by national authorities and statistical offices. For instance, guidelines for the collection of arrivals at frontiers are not relevant to cities. Unfortunately, many statistical authorities use this methodology to measure tourism. Hence results published by these organizations (and compiled by international organizations such as WTO and OECD) do not allow a regional breakdown needed to monitor city tourism.

A CTO manager's primary task is the promotion of commercial tourism. Therefore nights and arrivals have to cover all sorts of accommodation, including pensions, self-catering apartments and camping as long as the guest is paying for it. Data covering friends and relatives tourism, which is a central element in the WTO definition, is typically disregarded by CTO's management, whereas domestic tourism is relevant to them and should be covered by the statistics.

Note

[1] Grouping only for twelve European member states (Belgium, Denmark, France, Germany, Greece, Ireland, Luxembourg, Netherlands, Portugal, Spain and United Kingdom).

References

Airports Council International (1994) *European Airports Traffic Report. Calendar Year 1993*. London: Coopers & Lybrand.

Bar-On, R. (1989) *Travel and Tourism Data: A Comprehensive Research Handbook on World Travel*. London: Euromonitor.

Burkart, A.J. and Medlik, S. (1974) *Tourism – Past, Present and Future*. London: Heinemann.

Chadwick, R.A. (1987) Concepts, definitions and measures used in travel and tourism research. In J.R.B. Ritchie and C.R. Goeldner (eds) *Travel, Tourism and Hospitality Research: A Handbook for Managers and Researchers*. New York: John Wiley & Sons, Inc., 101–16.

Devas, E. (1991) *The European Tourist – a Market Profile*, 5th edn. London: Tourism Planning and Research Associates.

Eurostat (1992) *Nomenclature of Territorial Units for Statistics*. Brussels: Eurostat.

Eurostat (1996) *Annex to the Council Recommendation for a Community Methodology on Tourism Statistics*. Document presented during a joint Eurostat/DG XXIII meeting with the professional associations on 'Tourism Statistics', 19 January 1996. Brussels: Eurostat.

Gunn, C.A. (1988) *Tourism Planning*, 2nd edn. New York: Taylor & Francis.

Horwath & Horwath International (1980) *Worldwide Lodging Industry*. New York: Horwath & Horwath International.

International Air Transport Association (1994) *World Air Transport Statistics 1993*. Number 38, 6/94. New York: IATA.

Latham, J. (1989) The statistical measurement of tourism. In C.P. Cooper (ed.) *Progress in Tourism, Recreation and Hospitality Management* vol. 1. London: Belhaven Press.

McIntosh, R.W. and Goeldner, C.R. (1986) *Tourism Principles, Practices, Philosophies*. New York: John Wiley & Sons.

Mazanec, J.A. (1986) Allocating an advertising budget to international travel markets. *Annals of Tourism Research* **13**, 609–34.

Moutinho, L., Rita, P. and Curry, B. (1995) *Expert Systems in Tourism Marketing*. London: Routledge, 137–55.

ÖGAF (1995) *Die Eignung der European Travel Monitor Nächtigungs- und Ausgabenstatistik für das Budgetoptimierungsmodell der Österreich Werbung*. Unpublished report for the Austrian National Tourist Office. Vienna: Austrian Society for Applied Research in Tourism.

Wöber, K.W. (1994) Tourism marketing information system. *Annals of Tourism Research* **21**, 396–9.

World Tourism Organization (annual) *Yearbook of Tourism Statistics* (2 volumes). Madrid: WTO.

World Tourism Organization (annual) *Compendium of Tourism Statistics*. Madrid: WTO.

World Tourism Organization (1981a) *Technical Handbook on the Collection and Presentation of Domestic and International Tourism Statistics*. Madrid: WTO.

World Tourism Organization (1981b) *Guidelines for the Collection and Presentation of Domestic and International Tourism Statistics*. Madrid: WTO.

World Tourism Organization (1983a) *Methodologies for Carrying Out Sample Surveys on Tourism*. Madrid: WTO.

World Tourism Organization (1983b) *Techniques for Preparing and Disseminating Tourism Statistics*. Madrid: WTO.

World Tourism Organization (1983c) *Definitions Concerning Tourism Statistics*. Madrid: WTO.

World Tourism Organization (1984a) *Domestic Tourism Statistics*. Madrid: WTO.

World Tourism Organization (1984b) *Survey of Surveys and Research in the Field of Tourism*. Madrid: WTO.

World Tourism Organization (1985a) *Methodological Supplement to World Travel and Tourism Statistics*. Madrid: WTO.

World Tourism Organization (1985b) *Measurement of Travel and Tourism Expenditure*. Madrid: WTO.

2.2

Introducing a harmonization procedure for European city tourism statistics

Karl Wöber

The previous section illustrated the measurement problems associated with tourism statistics. This is particularly relevant for European city tourism with its large numbers of highly mobile people living in close proximity and constantly entering, leaving and transiting neighbouring cities by car, train or plane. Furthermore, the simplification or elimination of documentation and of border controls inside the European Community, though highly desirable for the tourists and the governments, reduces the data sources available to tourism statistics.

Marketing research in urban tourism is usually based on accommodation statistics, results from sample surveys of guests, accommodation providers or other experts, or estimates achieved by grossing up procedures using other statistical sources (Figure 2.2). Even elementary tourism data like nights, arrivals, number of beds, number of accommodation establishments, occupancy rates or length of stay may vary significantly between cities. Much of the methodology used to compile tourism statistics centres on standard surveys involving questionnaires, interviews and observations. Although these methodologies are mostly well documented, the comparability of statistical measurement of city tourism has many shortcomings.

A comparable international city tourism database, however, requires

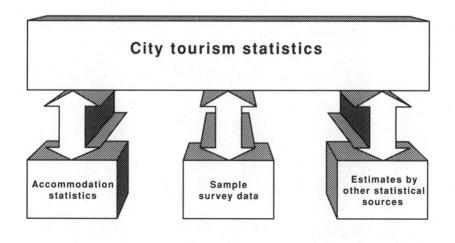

Figure 2.2 Classification of marketing research data in urban tourism

largely identical survey designs and methods. Many practical problems need to be resolved. There is even a need to standardize the meaning of many of the basic terms employed in describing city tourism. Terms such as city, tourist, hotel, excursionist, domestic and expenditure appear self-explanatory, but in fact have different meanings when used by different organizations.

To arrive at similar methodologies for all cities is a long-term objective which cannot be enforced by a single initiative. Therefore, it is necessary to combine different sources of data in order to provide better measurements. Unfortunately, international compilations of city tourism are rare (Van den Berg, 1995) and constantly lack comparability of the collected sources.

In 1995 the members of FECTO were asked for copies of official statistics from hotel and pension recordings or regular surveys. An additional questionnaire contained comments on the quality of the sources and supplementary information by the head of the local tourist board or by a representative of the marketing research department. The questionnaire was targeted at 77 major European city tourist offices which were either FECTO members or other important tourism cities. Sixty-one cities sent the requested tourism statistics and 46 CTO managers returned the supplementary questionnaire. The majority of European cities (72.8 per cent) receive their tourism statistics from official registration at accommodation establishments (see Table 2.3). Only in Glasgow is registration and notification voluntary. Estimates based on sample surveys among guests, accommodation operators or other tourism managers

Table 2.3 Sources of European city tourism statistics (FECTO 1995)

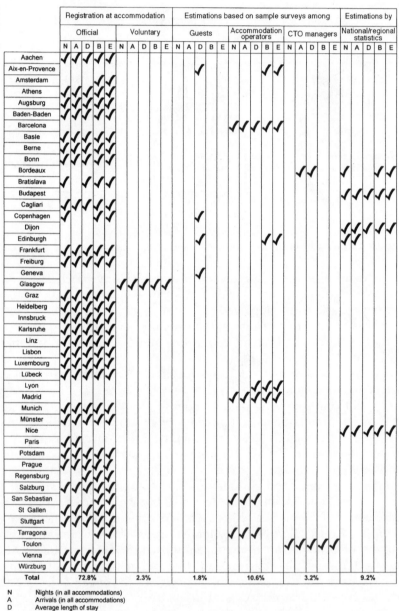

City	Registration at accommodation — Official					Voluntary					Sample surveys — Guests					Accommodation operators					CTO managers					National/regional statistics				
	N	A	D	B	E	N	A	D	B	E	N	A	D	B	E	N	A	D	B	E	N	A	D	B	E	N	A	D	B	E
Aachen	✓	✓	✓	✓	✓																									
Aix-en-Provence													✓				✓	✓												
Amsterdam			✓	✓																										
Athens	✓	✓	✓	✓	✓																									
Augsburg	✓	✓	✓	✓																										
Baden-Baden	✓	✓	✓	✓																										
Barcelona																✓	✓	✓	✓											
Basle	✓	✓	✓	✓																										
Berne	✓	✓																												
Bonn	✓	✓																												
Bordeaux																						✓	✓			✓			✓	✓
Bratislava	✓			✓	✓																									
Budapest																										✓	✓	✓	✓	✓
Cagliari	✓	✓		✓	✓																									
Copenhagen												✓																		
Dijon																										✓	✓	✓	✓	✓
Edinburgh												✓						✓	✓											
Frankfurt	✓	✓	✓	✓	✓																									
Freiburg	✓	✓	✓	✓																										
Geneva												✓																		
Glasgow						✓	✓	✓	✓	✓																				
Graz		✓	✓	✓	✓																									
Heidelberg	✓	✓	✓	✓																										
Innsbruck	✓	✓	✓	✓																										
Karlsruhe	✓	✓	✓	✓																										
Linz	✓	✓	✓	✓																										
Lisbon	✓	✓	✓																											
Luxembourg	✓	✓	✓																											
Lübeck	✓	✓																												
Lyon																	✓	✓	✓	✓										
Madrid												✓	✓			✓	✓	✓												
Munich	✓	✓	✓	✓																										
Münster	✓	✓																												
Nice																										✓	✓	✓	✓	✓
Paris	✓	✓																												
Potsdam	✓	✓	✓	✓																										
Prague	✓	✓	✓	✓																										
Regensburg	✓	✓	✓	✓																										
Salzburg	✓	✓	✓	✓																										
San Sebastian												✓	✓	✓																
St Gallen	✓	✓	✓	✓																										
Stuttgart	✓	✓	✓	✓																										
Tarragona												✓	✓	✓																
Toulon																					✓	✓	✓	✓	✓					
Vienna	✓	✓	✓	✓	✓																									
Würzburg	✓	✓	✓	✓																										
Total	72.8%					2.3%					1.8%					10.6%					3.2%					9.2%				

N   Nights (in all accommodations)
A   Arrivals (in all accommodations)
D   Average length of stay
B   Bed spaces
E   Number of accommodation establishments

generate 15.6 per cent of European cities' tourism statistics, whereas estimates based on other national or regional statistics provide 9.2 per cent of the key figures.

Nights and arrivals are the most commonly used figures for analysing the tourism industry and its development on the national, regional or city level. Of all participating cities, 93.5 per cent can provide time-series bednight statistics, and 83.9 per cent collect arrival statistics.

According to major differences in consumer behaviour and the simplicity of the approach, figures showing the proportion of visitors from the principal countries of origin are frequently available. Most cities compile monthly and annual detailed statistics by country of residence or by nationality (Table 2.4).

The principal tourism markets are France, Germany, Italy, the Netherlands, the United Kingdom and the USA. Around two thirds of the participating cities distinguish these countries in their guest mix statistics. Countries of origin of the lowest statistical consideration in European cities are the eastern European countries such as Hungary and Poland (both 34 per cent). Only neighbouring cities like Vienna, Prague and some German cities have recognized the importance of these markets.

Table 2.4 Availability of tourism statistics by country of origin for 61 European cities (FECTO 1995)

Country of origin	Nights in %	Arrivals in %
Australia/New Zealand	62.9	56.5
Austria	71.0	59.7
Belgium/Luxembourg	77.4	62.9
Canada	71.0	59.7
Denmark	75.8	59.7
Finland	62.9	58.1
France	87.1	71.0
Germany	83.9	74.2
Greece	62.9	58.1
Hungary	33.9	33.9
Italy	83.9	71.0
Japan	79.0	61.3
Netherlands	83.9	67.7
Norway	69.4	58.1
Poland	33.9	33.9
Portugal	50.0	45.2
Spain	77.4	61.3
Sweden	75.8	56.5
Switzerland	80.6	66.1
United Kingdom	85.5	69.4
USA	83.9	71.0
Other origins	83.9	71.0
Domestic tourists	90.3	74.2
All foreign tourists	88.7	77.4
All tourists	93.5	83.9

Due to the different structures of tourism authorities in the countries surveyed the FECTO working group had to agree on a standardization proposal. Similar to Frechtling (1976), who identified three principles which need to be observed in the formation of definitions and terminology, the working group decided that:

- definitions should meet the managerial needs in tourism statistics;
- definitions should conform to international guidelines (WTO/Eurostat) as much as possible;
- definitions should follow established usage as much as possible.

As a result of these principles a framework on city tourism statistics was developed (see Figure 2.3). This concept combines the WTO classification of international visitors (see previous section) with a proposal for the definition of the term city and the managerial interest in the various forms of 'city' tourism statistics.

Marketing analysis concerns the study of both the spatial and organizational structure of the city or region as a product as well as the characteristics, behaviour and needs of the identified users as consumers. Not only the identification of demand can provide basic difficulties for statisticians, but the definition of the supply side is also not self-evident. For instance, the word 'city' has two distinct meanings. It may either refer to an entity which offers functions, activities and an atmosphere, or it may refer to quite specific services or facilities. The usage of objective and perceived criteria for the definition of urban tourism was originally introduced by Ashworth and Voogd (1990). They illustrated, using the case of the Languedoc coast, that several distinct spatial scales exist.

A tourism product always exists within particular spatial borders which form a nested hierarchy of urban, regional or national supply. However, the spatial borders of the tourism product being purchased by the consumer may not correspond to the administrative boundaries of the city. The tourist's city may be confined to a small historic core area containing most of the city's recognizable sites and attractions. An urban product is what the market accepts as such, or: 'Every urban product is an assemblage of selected resources which in this case are bound together through interpretation, i.e. its presentation to customers through various communications media' (Ashworth and Voogd, 1990).

For the definition of a tourism city usually three different approaches exist:

- The visitor's perception, in which local users with the readiness to consume urban travel facilities (guests with typical travel motives such as shopping, culture, congress, etc.) decide on a particular resort. For instance, Nice, which is a typical French sea resort, may not be regarded as part of European city tourism, whereas Salzburg, which has approximately 60 per cent fewer inhabitants, clearly is.
- The city's self-image, or the attempt of the local tourism management to portray

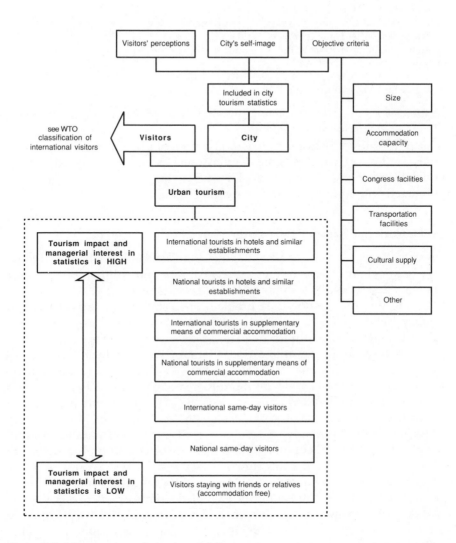

Figure 2.3 A framework on city tourism statistics

the city, is another important factor. Genoa, for example, a former industrial city with an historic harbour, is reviving its cultural heritage. This is an effort by the local tourism management to project the city as an important part of European city tourism.

• Finally objective criteria like community size, accommodation capacity and typical urban facilities have to be considered for defining the city tourism market.

The conditions for becoming a member in the Federation of European Cities' Tourist Offices passed by the General Assembly are:

- more than 100,000 inhabitants;
- more than 2000 rooms in commercial accommodations;
- one congress centre with at least 1000 seating capacity;
- an international airport within one hour's reach of the city centre;
- a major historical heritage;
- a minimum CTO budget of 250,000 ECU;
- regular important cultural events.

These criteria are not mandatory, but should be pursued by a city aspiring for membership in this organization.

The definition of urban tourism is extremely useful for competition analysis of a city, which will be demonstrated in Part 4. It implies that the competitive situation of a city as viewed from one or more target groups is compared with the actual situation existing in the town.

Framework of a harmonization procedure

As stated earlier, the two main difficulties statisticians face when comparing international city tourism data are availability and comparability where standardized procedures and rules have to be adopted.

Concerning the missing data problem (availability) two variants can be distinguished. First is missing data points in a time series. There are several reasons why this problem occurs, such as irregular surveys or an exceptional delay in the publication of survey results which excludes the data from an international collection. For this kind of missing data problem comprehensive forecasting methodologies exist. Simple extrapolation techniques are well suited and easy to apply. For arguments in favour of univariate versus econometric models see Witt and Witt (1992).

Second, a time series for a certain sort of information can be missing completely. Dublin's bednight statistics, for instance, are broken down for only ten countries of origin. Treating Norway and Sweden as one country of origin during the data collecting process causes additional problems. Strictly speaking, Dublin should be excluded from further market volume and market share analysis. However, an exclusion of Dublin would ignore a significant proportion of European city tourism when filling marketing planning models with data.

Even an incomplete dataset represents some information about the volume and the structure of a certain city. Missing time series are generally data of minor importance to the local city tourism management, and it is probably more feasible to make reliable assumptions rather than completely remove the data from further analysis.

There are several possibilities for estimating a missing time series in accordance with general calculation rules and hypothetical correlations.

Estimates based on general calculation rules
There are two formulae that provide a simple mechanism of estimating
missing data, based on information from different data sources.

$$\text{Average length of stay in all accommodations} = \text{Bednights in all accommodations} \Big/ \text{Arrivals in all accommodations}$$

$$\text{Occupancy rate (average rate per year)} = (\text{Bed capacity} \times 365) \text{ in all accommodations} \Big/ \text{Bednights in all accommodations}$$

In Copenhagen, for instance, bednight statistics are available through
accommodation registration, whereas information about the guest's average
length of stay is evaluated using a regular guest survey. As arrival figures
are not provided by the accommodation statistics, they may be calculated
by entering the guest survey data in the first formula above. Inaccuracies
that emerge as a result of sampling errors, differences in the scope of the
surveys (e.g. the guest survey may include private accommodation too) or
in the time scales have to be considered during interpretation and further
analysis.

Applying these general formulae for estimating missing time series may
lead to a set of 'if-then-else-rules' which can be programmed in any
standard computer language (for a flow diagram see Figure 2.4).

Estimates based on hypothetical correlations
In some cities the application of general calculation rules is not possible,
especially when for some countries of origin the time series data are missing
for several categories of information. Instead of eliminating these cities from
further analysis, estimates based on surrogate values might be appropriate.
For instance, values for the guest mix proportion, the occupancy rate or the
average length of stay may be too fragmented to be completed by general
calculation rules. The surrogate indicators can either be rates for a
neighbouring city, average rates for a subgroup of similar cities with
complete datasets within the country or average rates for the whole country.

If the monitoring system does not offer comparable cities within the
country (e.g. Dublin being the only Irish city in the dataset) or provides only
cities with similar missing time series (e.g. Italian cities do not count guests
from Poland separately), estimates might be better based on other external
variables. For instance, regression analysis offers guidelines for further
estimates by including additional tourism-related statistical variables, but
also other significant influence factors like geographical location or the
city's size.

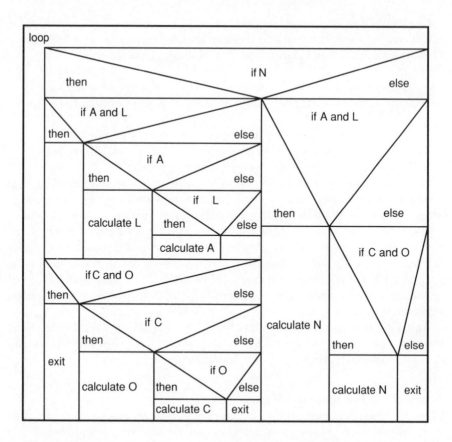

Note: N = nights, A = arrivals, L = average length of stay, C = number of beds, O = occupancy rate.

Figure 2.4 Procedure for calculating missing values by means of general tourism statistical formulae

Incomparability of the datasets may be caused by variations in definitions (e.g. by different questionnaire designs) and evaluation methodologies. Standardized methods of measurement and presentation are futile unless adopted by a significant number of cities. Cities with long-established and efficient statistical systems may be reluctant to make changes. In order to minimize the number of necessary changes, FECTO's proposal on guidelines for standards in city tourism statistics followed the most commonly used terms and definitions and was accepted during a Board meeting in Vienna in 1994 (Vienna Agreement).

According to the managers' interests (see Figure 2.3), nights and arrival statistics should cover all categories of accommodation, including pensions, self-catering apartments and camping sites as long as the guest is paying for it. This includes all kinds of private accommodation, except overnight stays with friends or relatives (where accommodation is free). In addition, the total figures should include domestic tourism, although gathering and reporting should be carried out separately. Inter-city comparable arrival statistics should not include day trips. Figures showing the number of accommodation establishments and bed capacities should represent an average number per year and the scope of the statistics should cover the territorial borders of the city and exclude the surrounding area.

For individual cities the amount of necessary modification can be determined by comparing the existing data and definitions with the standardization proposal. In 1995, leading CTO managers were asked whether their tourism statistics show deviations from FECTO's standardization proposal. As personal interviews with the tourism managers were too costly, the working group prepared a written questionnaire for the experts. This method was appropriate, because the main problem areas and deviations were relatively clear and the researchers could therefore prepare several well-structured questions in advance. The most frequently observed deviations are summarized in Table 2.5.

As expected the deviations in definitions include the interpretation of 'all commercial accommodation'. A deviation caused by different terms and scope or evaluation methodologies may affect figures on number of bednights, arrivals, accommodation establishments, bed capacities and also derived key figures like occupancy rates and average length of stay. The inclusion of day trips may affect the number of arrivals and possibly a calculated average length of stay.

The main reasons for the necessary modification and the average extent of deviations from the FECTO guidelines on city tourism statistics are listed in Table 2.6.

Table 2.5 Main deviations from FECTO's harmonization proposal

Reasons for deviation	Affects number of
Different definitions of commercial accommodation	Bednights, arrivals, accommodation establishments, bed capacities, average length of stay, occupancy rate
Inclusion of day trips	Arrivals, average length of stay
Existence of considerable seasonal differences and missing annual data	Accommodation establishments, bed capacities, occupancy rate
Exclusion of domestic tourism	Bednights, arrivals, average length of stay, occupancy rate
Different statistical definition of city (border problem)	Bednights, arrivals, accommodation establishments, bed capacities, average length of stay, occupancy rate

Table 2.6 Deviations from the FECTO agreement on city tourism statistics

Reasons for rectifications	Nights		Arrivals		Average duration of stay		Bed spaces		Accommodation establishments	
	Cases*	Extent†	Cases	Extent	Cases	Extent	Cases	Extent	Cases	Extent
Not all sorts of commercial accommodations included	21.2	14.0	19.2	14.1	15.4	n/a	15.4	21.4	17.3	15.2
Accommodation with friends and relatives included	7.7	1.0	7.7	1.0	3.8	n/a	7.7	1.0	7.7	1.0
Day trips included			1.9	50.0						
Statistics disregard seasonal deviations							1.9	15.0	1.9	15.0
Domestic tourism not included	23.1	n/a	21.2	n/a	7.7	n/a				
Territorial scope of statistics	7.7	5.7	7.7	5.7	5.8	n/a	5.8	7.3	7.7	8.0

* Percentage of cities that could provide statistics.
† Estimations by CTO managers (correction factor in %).

An expert system approach to support harmonization and correction

While quantitative methods have been quite successful in addressing systemic problems of a quantitative nature, they falter when a problem is mainly qualitative. Artificial intelligence and, specifically, expert systems use symbolic manipulation and are qualitative by nature (for an introduction of expert systems in the field of tourism research see Moutinho *et al.*, 1996).

An expert system consists of three major components (Zahedi, 1993): the production rules, the working memory and the conflict resolution mechanism (inference engine). One of the most common methods of knowledge representation in expert systems is in the form of the IF-THEN production rule, such as:

> IF a city's arrival statistics include day trips
> THEN the average length of stay is subject to examination.

When the conditions of a rule match the content of the working memory, the rule fires. When the firing of a rule is successful and generates an outcome, the result is added to the content of the working memory. The working memory acts like a pad or a blackboard on which the current state of reasoning is stored. The conflict resolution mechanism is needed when more than one rule becomes eligible for firing next. Here, for instance, the developer may attach priorities to the antecedents of rules in the knowledge base so that the rule with the highest priority should fire first.

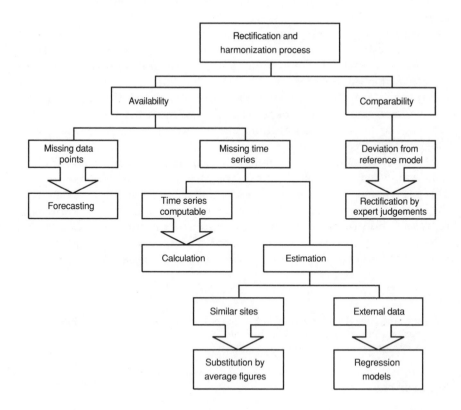

Figure 2.5 Framework of a harmonization and rectification system

The preceding knowledge acquisition process on the quality and comparability of European city tourism statistics leads to a number of production rules. Figure 2.5 shows a summary of all rectification and standardization procedures. According to different tasks the production rules vary in complexity and certainty. For instance, general calculation rules (Figure 2.4) will be relatively simple to formulate and, once fired, will give highly reliable results. On the other hand, production rules for the correction of incomparability based on expert judgement may show more constraints and lead to results with considerably more uncertainty.

Expert judgements are subjective, sometimes biased, inexact and uncertain. An expert system as a decision tool has the ability to accommodate the inexact nature of human knowledge processing. A number of methods have been developed to superimpose uncertainty on the logical structure of expert systems (for a comprehensive summary see Zahedi, 1993). Finally there are also theories, mainly in the field of fuzzy sets and fuzzy logic, which posit vagueness as their fundamental premise (see Zadeh, 1965, for the theory of fuzzy sets, or Negoita, 1985, who examines the utilization of fuzzy set theory for expert systems).

Expert systems normally do not provide an immediate answer to the user's query. Instead, the system asks the user questions regarding the particular application. In the present case the expert system is integrated in a database management system, where quantitative data and the accumulated knowledge of experts are stored. In such a system answers or reports can be generated automatically and, once established, operate independently from a user's input.

The most efficient way to combine an expert system and a conventional database system is to embed the expert system in the conventional program. This prevents the delay caused by switching between the expert system and the conventional program (for more about pros and cons of knowledge representation in symbolic and conventional programming see Wöber, 1994). For the prototype version of the harmonization and rectification system for European city tourism statistics this technique was appropriate.

Notes

[1] Nights, arrivals (in all accommodations); average length of stay; bed spaces; number of accommodation establishments.
[2] WTO recommendation: country of residence.

References

Ashworth, G.J. and Voogd, H. (1990) *Selling the City: Marketing Approaches in Public Sector Urban Planning*. London: Belhaven Press.

Frechtling, D.C. (1976) Proposed standard definitions and classifications for travel research, marketing travel and tourism. *Seventh Annual Conference Proceedings of the Travel Research Association*. Boca Raton: Travel Research Association, 59–74.

Moutinho, L., Rita, P. and Curry, B. (1996) *Expert Systems in Tourism Marketing*. New York: Routledge.

Negoita, C.V. (1985) *Expert Systems and Fuzzy Systems*. Menlo Park: Benjamin Cummings.

Van den Berg, L. (1995) Urban tourism at the break of the 21st century. *Conference Proceedings of the 1st Meeting of Central European Cities*. Ljubljana: Academia Turistica.

Witt, S. F. and Witt, C. A. (1992) *Modeling and Forecasting Demand in Tourism*. London: Academic Press.

Wöber, K. (1994) *Expertenschätzungen in touristischen Entscheidungsunterstützungs-systemen*. Vienna: Service Fachverlag.

Zadeh, L.A. (1965) Fuzzy sets. *Information and Control* 8, 338–53.

Zahedi, F. (1993) *Intelligent Systems for Business. Expert Systems with Neural Networks*. Belmont: Wadsworth.

2.3

International city tourism flows

Karl Wöber

Inbound tourism: flows into receiving cities

This section brings together, in the form of summary tables and graphs, the most recent data available on international tourist flows to FECTO member cities. All data presented in this chapter have been harmonized in accordance with the CTO managers' responses in the questionnaire described in section 2.2. However, in looking at the figures presented here, it should be remembered that there are still some deficiencies in the data. There is hope that these tables and graphs will stimulate further recommendations on improving the collection and presentation of tourism statistics and their wider use.

Main developments

Tourism is one of the most important industry sectors for nearly all European states. On the basis of the harmonization process described earlier it is now possible for the first time to calculate and monitor the market volume of city tourism in Europe. Table 2.7 presents the number of bednights and domestic share, arrivals, average length of stay, bed capacity and average annual occupancy rates for 65 European cities. A survey of urban tourism carried out by KPMG Consultants on behalf of the tourist office of the city of Amsterdam for 34 European cities is listed in the last two rows for comparability. According to Van den Berg (1995) the information gathered by KPMG gives only a rough idea as the quality of the data used for the analysis is doubtful (see also Costa *et al.*, 1993; Van den Berg *et al.*, 1994; Shachar, 1995).

Table 2.7 City tourism in Europe

	FECTO 1995*							KPMG 1993†	
	Nights§ 1993				Arrivals§ 1993	AS**	Bed capacity	OR≠	Nights§ 1991	Arrivals§ 1991
	Total§	D#	92–93	87–93						
Aachen	680	0.83	-0.02	0.22	261	2.6	4060	0.46		
Aix-en-Provence	1306	0.65			290	4.5				
Amsterdam	3618	0.06	-0.10	0.12	1670	2.2	27915	0.36	3786	1731
Antwerp									1026	247
Athens	5096	0.33			2097	2.4	33804	0.41		
Augsburg	431	0.71			233	1.8	3409	0.35		
Baden-Baden	750	0.79	-0.10	-0.11	242	3.1	4872	0.42		
Barcelona	7803	0.41	-0.02	-0.04	3195	2.4			4090	1819
Basle	639	0.30	-0.06	-0.09	318	2.0	4096	0.42		
Berlin	7292	0.75	-0.05	0.26	2985	2.4			6405	2542
Berne	442	0.39	-0.09	-0.11	236	1.9	2550	0.47	531	259
Bonn	1107	0.77	-0.04	0.44	477	2.3	6626	0.46		
Bordeaux	677	0.50			549	1.2				
Bratislava	847	0.42			385	2.2	7147	0.32		
Brussels	2960	0.05	-0.08	0.17	1366	2.2	24789	0.33	3035	2046
Budapest	4251	0.19	-0.06	-0.53	1472	2.9	40907	0.28	5032	1556
Cagliari	315	0.89	-0.03	-0.19	133	2.4				
Cologne									2515	571
Copenhagen	3212	0.27	0.01	0.07	1918	1.7	19140	0.46	3157	
Dijon	1021	0.59			777	1.3	4207	0.66		
Dublin	11233	0.23	0.18		2165	5.2				2522
Düsseldorf									1851	1010
Edinburgh	4187	0.28		0.00	1460	2.9	21521	0.53		1386
Florence									4160	1799
Frankfurt	3104	0.45	-0.04	0.04	1742	1.8	20132	0.42	3443	1863
Freiburg	554	0.76	-0.04	0.06	328	1.7	4005	0.38		
Geneva	1055	0.13	-0.01	-0.09	472	2.2	6903	0.42	2328	921
Graz	521	0.47	-0.09	0.01	254	2.1	4697	0.30		
Hamburg	3960	0.76	-0.02	0.26	2137	1.9	23000	0.47	4072	2157
Heidelberg	727	0.48	-0.09	0.05	446	1.6	4360	0.46		
Helsinki	1553	0.38	0.10	0.01	882	1.8			1292	710
Innsbruck	1211	0.20	-0.10	-0.07	691	1.8	9906	0.33		
Istanbul									2986	1365
Karlsruhe	559	0.79	-0.01	0.22	274	2.0	3907	0.39		

Table 2.7 cont'd

	FECTO 1995*							KPMG 1993†	
	Nights§ 1993			Arrivals§ 1993	AS**	Bed capacity	OR≠	Nights§ 1991	Arrivals§ 1991
	Total§	D#	92–93	87–93					
Lausanne	582	0.26	-0.03	-0.03	253	2.3	4049	0.39		
Linz	442	0.44	0.04	0.29	268	1.6	3383	0.36		
Lisbon	3116	0.34	-0.01	0.02	1416	2.2	22021	0.39		
London	85782	0.23	0.02	-0.17	16543	5.2			82600	14700
Luxembourg	1092	0.12	0.05	0.12	456	2.4	8858	0.34		
Lübeck	808	0.79	-0.09	0.33	360	2.2	5699	0.39		
Lucerne	845	0.19	-0.03		445	1.9	4402	0.53		
Lyon	4231	0.78			2489	1.7			2786	
Madrid	7186	0.58	-0.07	-0.12	4087	1.8	65284	0.30		
Mannheim	517	0.72	0.03	0.15	259	2.0	3812	0.37		
Milan	5339	0.55	-0.04	0.15	2360	2.3	40193	0.36	5579	2135
Munich	6095	0.60	-0.07	0.02	2923	2.1	35792	0.47	6608	3243
Münster	1141	0.95	0.07	0.57	323	3.5	6317	0.49		
Nice	8259	0.46			3477	2.4				
Oslo	1782	0.54	0.08	0.17	1012	1.8	12736	0.38	1573	9842
Paris	26443	0.29	-0.15	0.27	11772	2.2	133438	0.54	28269	12602
Potsdam	284	0.88	0.01		117	2.4	1679	0.46		
Prague	3515	0.20	-0.19	-0.12	1284	2.7	39000	0.25		
Regensburg	477	0.81	-0.01	0.89	249	1.9	3470	0.38		
Rome	11910	0.40	-0.04	-0.03	4896	2.4	84697	0.39	12019	2684
Salzburg	1644	0.22	-0.05	0.08	872	1.9	10540	0.43	1876	962
San Sebastian	590	0.75			311	1.9				
St Gallen	182	0.57	-0.03	-0.02	84	2.2	1225	0.41		
Stockholm	2985	0.60	0.14	-0.08	1696	1.8	19150	0.43		
Stuttgart	1277	0.69	0.06	0.14	639	2.0	9688	0.36		
Tarragona	3500	0.58			1842	1.9				
Toulon	6780	0.59			2542	2.7				
Venice	4236	0.26	0.05	0.14	2239	1.9	21375	0.54	2509	1111
Vienna	6614	0.13	-0.06	0.13	2766	2.4	37172	0.49	6718	2638
Würzburg	567	0.85	-0.03	0.04	336	1.7	3559	0.44		
Zurich					895		9787		2012	964
Total	269322				98666	2.8	869279	0.41	202258	66485

*Grabler and Wöber (1995).
†KPMG, Comparative Analysis of 34 European Cities, Amsterdam 1993; see also Costa *et al.* (1993).
§in 1000.
#Domestic share.
**Average length of stay.
≠Average occupancy rate (365 days).

The mix of domestic and foreign visitors varies widely among cities. Similar to the findings in the KPMG study, the more popular urban destinations report a larger share of foreign visitors. Obviously it is easier to operate on the domestic market than the foreign one. Not only are the promotion campaigns often cheaper for practical reasons, but the domestic market also tends to be better informed and thus easier to convince of the opportunities a city offers. A considerable proportion of domestic tourism in a city is not accessible by other competing cities. Most cities, therefore, prefer a high proportion of domestic tourism, but some cities, especially in the former Eastern countries, strongly serve the international travellers as they usually spend more than domestic tourists and bring desirable hard currency. Cities with a high proportion of domestic tourism are Münster (95 per cent), Cagliari (89 per cent), Potsdam (88 per cent), Würzburg (85 per cent), Aachen (83 per cent) and Regensburg (81 per cent). Cities with a particularly international guest mix are Brussels (5 per cent), Amsterdam (6 per cent), Luxembourg (12 per cent), Geneva (13 per cent), Vienna (13 per cent), Budapest (19 per cent) and Lucerne (19 per cent).

The average length of stay also varies widely among the cities in the survey. The average number of nights spent in European cities is 2.8, whereas London (5.2), Dublin (5.2) and Aix-en-Provence (4.5) deviate significantly.

In 48 European cities[1] 870,000 bed spaces were occupied for 150 days in 1993. This results in an average occupancy rate of 41 per cent. Cities with the lowest occupancy rate were Prague (25 per cent), Budapest (28 per cent), Graz (30 per cent) and Madrid (30 per cent). Exceptionally high occupancy rates have been observed in Dijon (66 per cent), Paris (54 per cent), Venice (54 per cent), Edinburgh (53 per cent) and Lucerne (53 per cent).

A classification of European cities according to their tourism performance cannot be based solely on the development of the overnight statistics. Other targets would have to be considered. Nevertheless the list of the most important tourism cities in Europe is headed by capital cities. London registered almost 86 million bednights in 1993. In the same year, Paris followed with more than 26 million. The total number of bednights in the other capital cities ranged from 440,000 in Berne to 12 million in Rome. For all cities, the Italian capital is followed by Dublin with 11.2 million bednights, then Nice (8.3), Barcelona (7.8), Berlin (7.3), Madrid (7.2), Toulon (6.8) and Vienna (6.6).

Considering the development between 1983 and 1993, German cities show a significant increase in their bednight figures. During this period the German unification in 1990 pushed up the total number of bednights in Regensburg (+89 per cent), Münster (+57 per cent), Bonn (+44 per cent) and Lübeck (+33 per cent). Of the other cities Linz (+29 per cent), Paris (+27 per cent) and Brussels (+17 per cent) enjoyed significant improvements, whereas Budapest (-53 per cent), Cagliari (-19 per cent), London (-17 per

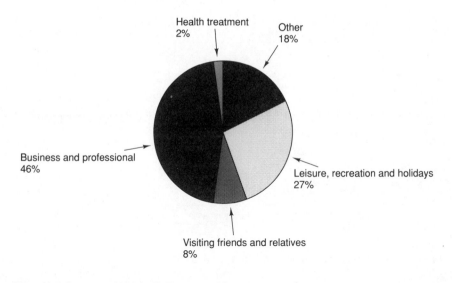

Figure 2.6 Purpose of visit in 35 European cities

cent), Prague (-12 per cent) and Madrid (-12 per cent) registered painful losses.

A breakdown by the major purpose of visit in 35 of all surveyed cities tells more about the European city tourism structure (Figure 2.6). As business and leisure travellers have markedly different perceptions related to their different motivations, the distinction between these two segments is of particular relevance. To business travellers such elements as international accessibility, the quality of exhibition halls and congress facilities, and the presence of internationally oriented economic activities are very important. Cities with few attractions but sufficient business elements may appeal to business travellers. From the cities' point of view business visitors are appreciated as their daily expenditure tends to be much higher than that which can be expected from leisure travellers.

A predominant portion of travellers to European cities arrive for professional reasons. Only about 27 per cent of the guests visit European cities for leisure and recreation. However, the mixture of leisure and business travel varies enormously from one city to another.

According to the OECD (1995), in 1993 tourism in Europe, expressed in terms of nights spent by foreign and domestic tourists in all means of accommodation in 15 leading destinations,[2] fell by 0.6 per cent to about 1430 million bednights. The slight overall decrease of overnight stays was the net result of countervailing tendencies. Losses recorded in Portugal (-4.7 per cent), Netherlands (-4.1 per cent), Austria (-2.6 per cent) and Germany (-2.0 per cent) were partially offset by the very strong performance in some Nordic countries and favourable figures for Spanish and Turkish tourism.

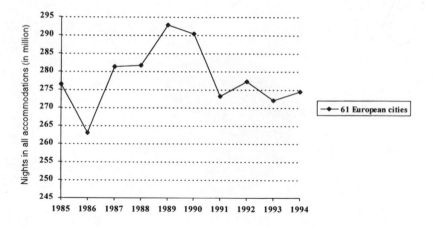

Figure 2.7 Urban tourism in Europe between 1985 and 1994

The losses were primarily affected by domestic tourism as the number of foreign tourists in all means of accommodation consolidated overall. According to Roth (1993) the stabilized major portion of European tourism is generated by holiday trips (66 per cent), followed by business trips (14 per cent) and by travellers who are visiting friends and relatives (8.6 per cent).

Until recently the volume and direction of travel flows in European city tourism have not been completely unknown but have been far from clear. There was little doubt that a high percentage of the tourism volume and a much higher percentage of the European business and professional travel volume were absorbed by European metropoles. But these assumptions could not be properly substantiated.

The number of bednights collected by FECTO and reported by Grabler and Wöber (1995) of 59 European cities adds up to 270 million. Adding data from six additional cities recorded by the KPMG study but not by FECTO gives a total of 284 million bednights, which represents about 20 per cent of the OECD statistics in 1993. Approximately 131 million bednights (46 per cent) were generated by business travellers, which represents more than 65 per cent of all trips in this segment.

Time series data for 61 of the cities evaluated show the development during the last decade and trends for the future (Figure 2.7). Surprisingly, between 1986 and 1989 most of the European cities enjoyed a significant upswing in their total number of bednights. The economic recession that was first felt heavily in 1990 and the Gulf Crisis led to a stagnation or decline of demand for many of the 61 cities from 1990 onwards. This mainly reflects a drastic reduction in British and US visitors. Judging from the figures provided by the OECD for the European tourist market, the growth in the European cities appears to lag somewhat behind the general tendency.

Outbound tourism: flows from generating countries

More insights can be gained by analysing the development of the most attractive markets. In the FECTO survey guest mix breakdowns are available for 21 European generating countries. Missing or incomplete information has been carefully rectified in accordance with the harmonization process introduced earlier. For better graphical presentation the markets have been classified according to their overall importance into large, medium and small generating countries.

Main developments

Figure 2.8 summarizes the development in the most important generators. Countries with a total of more than 10 million bednights are Germany, the United Kingdom, France, the USA, Italy and Spain. The German and recently also the Spanish market show promising development, whereas in the UK market 61 European cities recorded a considerable drop in demand between 1987 and 1990. In 1991 the US time series shows a significant drop. The economic recession and the Gulf crisis had a particular effect on these two markets. British and German cities which attract a larger proportion of tourists from these countries have been particularly affected.

Figure 2.9 summarizes the development in the generating countries of moderate importance. Countries with a total of between 4 and 10 million bednights in 61 European cities are Japan, Sweden, Australia (including New Zealand), Switzerland, the Netherlands, Austria and Canada.

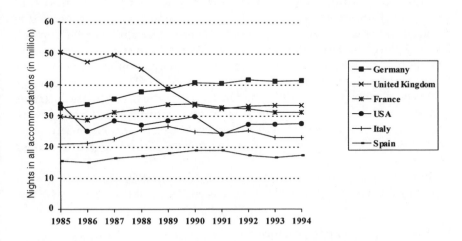

Figure 2.8 Trends in the European city tourism markets: large generating countries

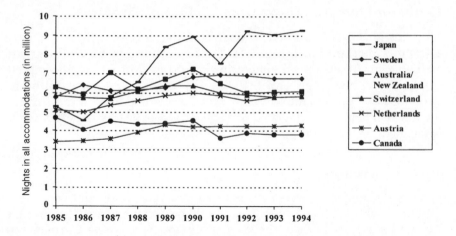

Figure 2.9 Trends in the European city tourism markets: medium generating countries

In recent years, the Japanese market has been one of the most dynamic for European cities, still maintaining its potential for further growth. In 1991, however, Japanese demand fell sharply: nights spent by Japanese guests declined by 15 per cent in the FECTO area. Other overseas markets like Australia and Canada reacted accordingly. On the other hand, other generating countries in this category stabilized over the period. Recently, all 61 European cities as a group noticed a slight increase in demand from the Dutch market.

Figure 2.10 summarizes the development for the less important generators. Countries with a total of up to 4 million bednights generated in 61 European cities are Greece, Belgium (including Luxembourg), Denmark, Norway, Portugal, Finland, Hungary and Poland. With regard to the smaller generating countries in the FECTO study, the sharp drop in demand of the East European markets arouses particular attention. The immediate desire to travel right after the Cold War led to a significant increase in travel demand in these countries, which have now returned to normal levels. Cities in neighbouring countries such as Austria and Germany were particularly affected by the considerable decrease in Hungarian or Polish demand.

Table 2.8 summarizes the overall development in all 21 generating countries during the last decade and between 1992 and 1993.

Incorporating other performance criteria

Inbound and outbound analysis automatically leads to a classification of cities into winner and loser categories as far as European urban tourism is concerned. However, the classification cannot be based exclusively on the

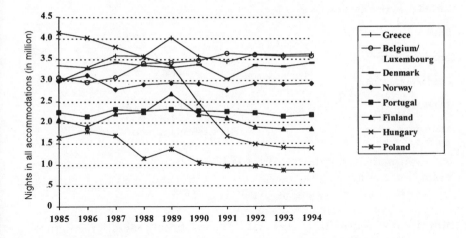

Figure 2.10 Trends in the European city tourism markets: small generating countries

Table 2.8 Development in 21 generating countries between 1985 and 1994, and 1992 and 1993

Country of origin	1985–94	1992–93
Japan	75.64%	-2.02%
Germany	26.97%	-1.12%
Austria	24.79%	0.17%
Sweden	17.21%	-2.39%
Belgium/Luxembourg	16.54%	-0.97%
Denmark	14.55%	-1.16%
Other origins	13.79%	-0.06%
Netherlands	13.76%	3.29%
Spain	12.92%	-3.29%
Italy	9.71%	-8.57%
Greece	7.72%	-0.58%
France	4.32%	-3.54%
Switzerland	-0.68%	-1.99%
All origins	-0.72%	-1.82%
Norway	-2.38%	-0.52%
Portugal	-3.04%	-4.25%
Australia/New Zealand	-3.25%	1.02%
Finland	-10.70%	-3.01%
USA	-19.28%	-0.63%
Canada	-19.44%	-2.27%
United Kingdom	-33.65%	0.67%
Poland	-47.65%	-10.37%
Hungary	-66.47%	-6.27%

Table 2.9 Performance criteria for classifying European cities

Criterion	Possible measuring devices
Growth in demand	Growth rate in total number of bednights, arrivals or tourist receipts
Capacity utilization	Occupancy rate
Competitiveness	Market share
Internationality	Proportion of foreign overnights
Seasonal distribution	Gini coefficient of monthly bednight statistics
Guest mix distribution	Gini coefficient of guest mix pattern

bednight statistics. Other tourism policy targets have to be considered. Examples of other success criteria which are based on statistical sources and are easy to monitor on a regular basis are given in Table 2.9.

Some of the criteria listed are certainly correlated (e.g. high capacity utilization and growth in demand). For an individual city it might be a trade-off between enlarging its international volume by penetrating a single but very attractive market and disturbing a well-balanced guest mix. The decision on the priority among the alternative strategies is a political one and will not be tackled here. (For a practical approach to this problem see Part V where multifactor portfolio models need managerial judgements for weighting a market chance index.)

For measuring the smoothness of seasonal or guest mix patterns the Gini coefficient has proved to be an ideal instrument. The Gini coefficient, which was initially applied to seasonality interpretation by Wanhill (1980), is a bounded measure of inequality in the range from 0 to 1. It can be used to indicate the skewness of a distribution. How to calculate the Gini coefficient is best illustrated by reference to the city of Lübeck (see Figure 2.11). Consideration of the degree of inequality begins with the joint cumulative distribution function of bednights and the months in which they arise. First the seasonal pattern for Lübeck has to be sorted in ascending order and then accumulated. If there is no seasonal effect the cumulative distribution function will be a straight line, the line of equality. The more unequal the seasonal distribution of bednights, the larger will be the area between the observed function and the line of equality. This is known as the concentration area and can be measured by an approximation formula named the Gini coefficient after its originator, Corrado Gini. The area is normalized to 1, thus giving the upper bound of the Gini coefficient. For complete inequality the Gini coefficient is 1, and for complete equality it is 0. For other measures as indicators of seasonality see also Yacoumis (1980).

For a permanent monitoring of multiple criteria, spider plots have proved to be an adequate graphical presentation. Figures 2.12, 2.13, 2.14 and 2.15 show five assessment criteria for selected European cities. Each leg of the spider plot represents the value of a success criterion relative to competitors (39 cities could provide information for all items). The centre of the plot is

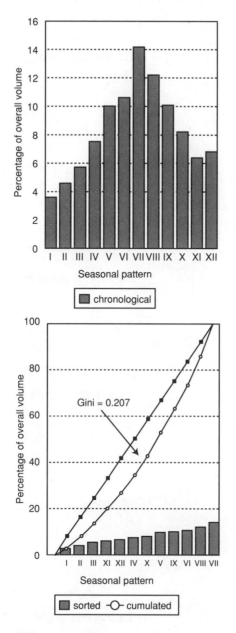

Figure 2.11 Gini coefficient for measuring seasonality in Lübeck

the minimum value and the outer diameter represents the maximum value. The dashed line represents the average number of all cities analysed and, where visible, indicates that the city's performance on this criterion is below average.

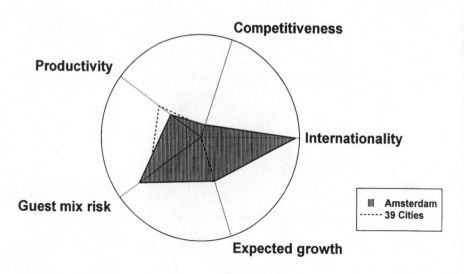

Figure 2.12 Spider plot for Amsterdam

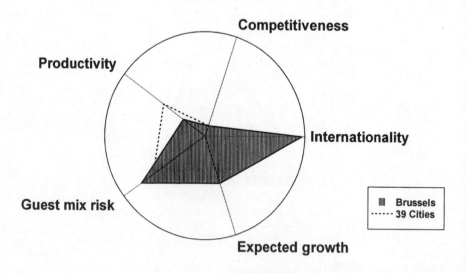

Figure 2.13 Spider plot for Brussels

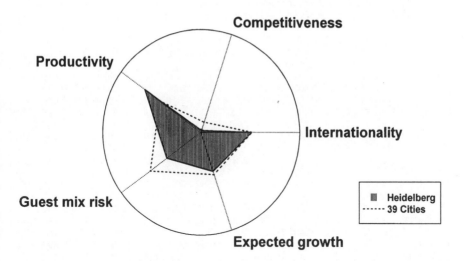

Figure 2.14 Spider plot for Heidelberg

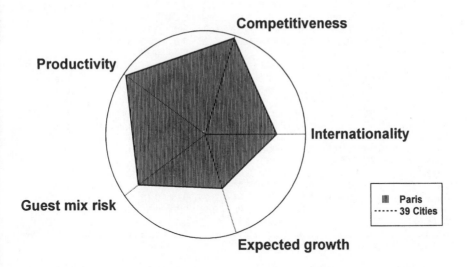

Figure 2.15 Spider plot for Paris

By displaying several plots simultaneously, differences and similarities among cities are easily emphasized. Paris, which is obviously very successful in the European tourism industry, still has some shortcomings concerning internationality, constant growth and equal guest mix distribution. Brussels and Amsterdam are international metropoles sharing

Table 2.10 Size of the success area when considering competitiveness, internationality, growth, guest mix distribution and capacity utilization for 39 European cities in 1993

City	A	B	C	D	E	A*	B*	C*	D*	E*	Area†	%§
Paris	0.71	9.812	0.54	0.452	0.27	0.75	1.00	1.00	0.89	0.56	1.610	71%
Vienna	0.87	2.456	0.49	0.380	0.13	0.92	0.25	0.91	0.75	0.46	0.863	38%
Venice	0.74	1.573	0.54	0.404	0.14	0.78	0.16	1.00	0.80	0.47	0.825	36%
Regensburg	0.19	0.177	0.38	0.453	0.89	0.20	0.02	0.70	0.89	1.00	0.785	35%
Hamburg	0.24	1.470	0.47	0.508	0.26	0.25	0.15	0.87	1.00	0.56	0.785	35%
Münster	0.05	0.424	0.49	0.499	0.57	0.05	0.04	0.91	0.98	0.77	0.785	35%
Rome	0.60	4.422	0.39	0.378	-0.03	0.63	0.45	0.72	0.74	0.35	0.738	33%
Amsterdam	0.94	1.343	0.36	0.429	0.12	0.99	0.14	0.67	0.84	0.46	0.737	33%
Brussels	0.95	1.099	0.33	0.437	0.17	1.00	0.11	0.61	0.86	0.49	0.734	33%
Munich	0.40	2.263	0.47	0.428	0.02	0.42	0.23	0.87	0.84	0.39	0.688	30%
Copenhagen	0.73	1.193	0.46	0.382	0.07	0.77	0.12	0.85	0.75	0.42	0.670	30%
Oslo	0.46	0.662	0.38	0.474	0.17	0.48	0.07	0.70	0.93	0.49	0.649	29%
Stockholm	0.40	1.108	0.43	0.503	-0.08	0.42	0.11	0.80	0.99	0.32	0.621	27%
Salzburg	0.78	0.610	0.43	0.368	0.08	0.82	0.06	0.80	0.72	0.43	0.607	27%
Lisbon	0.66	1.157	0.39	0.397	0.02	0.69	0.12	0.72	0.78	0.39	0.590	26%
Würzburg	0.15	0.211	0.44	0.498	0.04	0.16	0.02	0.81	0.98	0.40	0.578	26%
Milan	0.45	1.982	0.36	0.352	0.15	0.47	0.20	0.67	0.69	0.48	0.566	25%
Stuttgart	0.31	0.474	0.36	0.433	0.14	0.33	0.05	0.67	0.85	0.47	0.530	23%
Frankfurt	0.55	1.153	0.42	0.331	0.04	0.58	0.12	0.78	0.65	0.40	0.525	23%
Berne	0.61	0.164	0.47	0.409	-0.11	0.64	0.02	0.87	0.81	0.30	0.522	23%
Baden-Baden	0.21	0.278	0.42	0.495	-0.11	0.22	0.03	0.78	0.97	0.30	0.516	23%
Geneva	0.87	0.392	0.42	0.368	-0.09	0.92	0.04	0.78	0.72	0.31	0.515	23%
Karlsruhe	0.21	0.208	0.39	0.403	0.22	0.22	0.02	0.72	0.79	0.53	0.511	23%
Freiburg	0.24	0.206	0.38	0.435	0.06	0.25	0.02	0.70	0.86	0.42	0.490	22%
Luxembourg	0.88	0.405	0.34	0.271	0.12	0.93	0.04	0.63	0.53	0.46	0.483	21%
Linz	0.56	0.164	0.36	0.282	0.29	0.59	0.02	0.67	0.56	0.58	0.476	21%
Mannheim	0.28	0.192	0.37	0.389	0.15	0.29	0.02	0.69	0.77	0.48	0.476	21%
Innsbruck	0.80	0.450	0.33	0.386	-0.07	0.84	0.05	0.61	0.76	0.32	0.475	21%
Lausanne	0.74	0.216	0.39	0.346	-0.03	0.78	0.02	0.72	0.68	0.35	0.470	21%
Lübeck	0.21	0.300	0.39	0.330	0.33	0.22	0.03	0.72	0.65	0.61	0.464	21%
Heidelberg	0.52	0.270	0.46	0.303	0.05	0.55	0.03	0.85	0.60	0.41	0.459	20%
Prague	0.80	1.305	0.25	0.386	-0.12	0.84	0.13	0.46	0.76	0.29	0.447	20%
Basle	0.70	0.233	0.42	0.330	-0.09	0.74	0.02	0.78	0.65	0.31	0.439	19%
Madrid	0.42	2.668	0.30	0.330	-0.12	0.44	0.27	0.56	0.65	0.29	0.429	19%
St Gallen	0.43	0.068	0.41	0.327	-0.02	0.45	0.01	0.76	0.64	0.36	0.403	18%
Graz	0.53	0.193	0.30	0.318	0.01	0.56	0.02	0.56	0.63	0.38	0.371	16%
Bonn	0.23	0.411	0.46	0.143	0.44	0.24	0.04	0.85	0.28	0.68	0.291	13%
Aachen	0.17	0.252	0.46	0.187	0.22	0.18	0.03	0.85	0.37	0.53	0.285	13%
Budapest	0.81	1.578	0.28	0.339	-0.53	0.85	0.16	0.52	0.67	0.00	0.256	11%
Average	0.52	1.116	0.40	0.382	0.10	0.55	0.11	0.75	0.75	0.44	0.581	26%

A = internationality, B = competitiveness, C = capacity utilization, D = guest mix distribution, E = growth

* = normalized values.

† = $\frac{\sin\alpha}{2} (AB + BC + CD + DE + EA)$ with $\alpha = \frac{360}{5}$

§ = percentage of maximum area (2.262 for 5 parameters)

the problem of suboptimal capacity utilization. Heidelberg, which shows a high occupancy rate in the evaluation period, is not very competitive and has an unfavourable guest mix distribution. A comprehensive indicator for the overall success of a city can be expressed by calculating the area defined by the lines of the spider's legs. An advantage of this kind of success evaluation compared to the inspection of individual criteria is that a high value cannot be achieved unless several assessment criteria show a favourable result simultaneously.

A hypothetically optimal city leading in all assessment criteria would find itself in the form of an equilateral pentagon. Normalizing by equating this area to 1 permits simple comparisons as a percentage of optimal. It is implicitly assumed in this procedure that all performance criteria have the same weight in compiling the compact measure. A final summary for the present dataset is presented in Table 2.10.

Notes

[1] Not all cities could provide reliable information on bed capacity or occupancy rate.
[2] Austria, Belgium, Denmark, Finland, Germany, Greece, Italy, Netherlands, Norway, Portugal, Sweden, Switzerland, Turkey; Spain only hotels and similar establishments.

References

Costa, P., Manente, M. and van der Borg, J. (1993) *Traditional Cities: Problems and Perspectives*. Venice: Ciset.

Grabler, K. and Wöber, K.W. (1995) *City Tourism in Europe, Results of the 1995 FOTVE/FECTO Survey*. Unpublished research report. Vienna: Institute for Tourism and Leisure Studies, Vienna University of Economics and Business Administration.

OECD (1995) *Tourism Policy and International Tourism in OECD Countries 1992–1993. Special Feature 'Tourism and Employment'*. Paris: OECD.

Roth, P. (1993) Travelflows in Europe: a statistical summary. In W. Pompl and P. Lavery (eds) *Tourism in Europe. Structures and Developments*. Wallingford: CAB International.

Shachar, A. (1995) Metropolitan areas: economic globalisation and urban tourism. In A. Montanari and A.M. Williams (eds) *European Tourism. Regions, Spaces and Restructuring*. Chichester: John Wiley & Sons.

Van den Berg, L. (1995) Urban tourism at the break of the 21st century. In C. Kaspar and J. Planina (eds) *Tourism – The Basis of Intercity Cooperation*. Ljubljana: Academia Turistica.

Van den Berg, L., van der Borg, J. and Van der Meer, J. (1994) *Urban Tourism*. Rotterdam: EURICUR, Erasmus University.

Wanhill, S.R.C. (1980) Tackling seasonality: a technical note. *International Journal of Tourism Management* December, 243–5.

Yacoumis, J. (1980) Tackling seasonality: the case of Sri Lanka. *Journal of Tourism Management* June, 84–98.

2.4

Cities and the destination life cycle

Klaus Grabler

The life cycle concept

The concept of the destination life cycle goes back to the seminal work of Butler (1980). It was the first time the established concept of the product life cycle had been adopted in the field of tourism. The idea behind this concept is very simple and intuitively appealing; the applications and consequences, however, are heavily debated. In a biological analogy to the life and death of human beings the sales curves of products or product classes are separated into different stages beginning with the introduction of the product and ending with its disappearance from the market. (One step further in this analogy is the approach of the product evolutionary cycle by Tellis and Crawford (1981), which has not received attention in the literature.) The destination life cycle is a dynamic concept, representing the development of a destination through time and space (Ioannides, 1992). Identification of the forces behind this development and the key actors responsible would be helpful managerial information, but this information is not yet available. This section tries to explore some characteristics of different stages of the life cycle in the field of urban tourism. However, it is not meant as an introduction to the concept of the destination life cycle (this can be found in Cooper, 1992, 1994) with a detailed description of the different stages (see Cooper and Jackson, 1989), but highlights only those aspects that are important for the empirical study.

The strategical meaning of the concept implies that the life cycle is regarded as an exogenous or independent variable. This means that profits and marketing strategies are dictated by the stage of the life cycle rather than vice versa (Hooley, 1995; Cooper and Jackson, 1989). This, of course, has been contradicted often and is one of the most criticized points in the concept. Recently it has been shown that market position (e.g. market leader) is a better indicator for profit and strategies (Hooley, 1995). Nevertheless, the destination life cycle is used as an analytical strategic planning tool. It is a concept bearing meaning for the strategic marketing of destinations which is demonstrated by the treatment in nearly all textbooks on tourism (destination) marketing (compare Heath and Wall, 1992; Holloway and Plant, 1988; Law, 1993; Page, 1995).

✗ The two general managerial benefits of the life cycle concept are its use as a guide for strategic decision-making and as forecasting tool (Cooper and Jackson, 1989). The simple idea is that the managerial focus at earlier stages lies on the building of market shares, whereas in later phases it is a fight for maintaining these shares. The use as a forecasting tool depends heavily on the ability to isolate the forces that drive the flow of tourists to a specific destination. Most models in this context seem to work reasonably well in predicting the earlier stages, but fail in predicting stagnation and decline phases (Haywood, 1986). 'This is similar to the problem encountered by various growth curves, e.g., Gompertz and logistics' (Rink and Swan, 1979, p. 229). Both of these uses seem questionable given the criticism of the concept.

The sociological background underlying the product life cycle is the diffusion process and the associated adoption theory with the classification of the buyers according to their time of adoption (Brownlie, 1985). The life cycle approach therefore 'represents the supply side view of the diffusion model' (Haywood, 1986, p. 154). In the field of tourism the well known typologies of Plog or Cohen (see for example Lowyck *et al.*, 1992) seem to be closely connected, although 'the shift from higher to lower socio-economic groups, or "explorers" to "mass" tourists has not been a general pattern' (Choy, 1992, p. 31). Nevertheless, early visitors will normally differ in terms of novelty-seeking, income, sensitivity to price and values (Holloway and Plant, 1988, p. 127).

Of the different shapes a product life cycle can assume, the S-shape or classical pattern is the most dominant in the literature. This is justified given the empirical proof of this form, although it is only one of twelve types that have been identified (Rink and Swan, 1979). There is consensus that the shape of the curve depends heavily on external factors on the supply (policy, rate of development) as well as the demand side (tastes, preferences) (Cooper, 1992; Ioannides, 1992). Therefore it is common knowledge that this classical form is not suitable for all products and patterns called 'cycle-half-recycle' or 'growth decline plateau' have been detected (Rink and Swan, 1979).

The number of stages referred to in the marketing literature varies between four and six (Rink and Swan, 1979). The destination life cycle as introduced by Butler divides the development of destinations into six stages: exploration, involvement, development, consolidation, stagnation and decline/rejuvenation. The original product life cycle most often refers to four stages. The identification of the stages refers to the development of the nights or arrivals mirroring the tourist success of a destination.

The destination life cycle has been used primarily to describe the development of destinations. Almost all applications relate to island destinations (Cooper and Jackson, 1989; Choy, 1992; France, 1991; Weaver, 1990), due to the necessary long time series which only isles with an enormous tradition in tourism can provide. However, there is hardly any empirical work about the validity of the life cycle concept in tourism. Besides its use in the case of isles, the life cycle concept has found applications in the field of upcoming destinations (especially to illustrate the problem of day visitors; van den Berg *et al.*, 1993), the hospitality industry (Tse and Elwood, 1990) and in the explanation of the prevalent market form (Debbage, 1990).

The life cycle concept is predominantly used as a descriptional tool for the past development of a destination. The failure to use it as a prescriptive strategic marketing planning tool is one of the most often criticized points in this concept (Brownlie, 1985). This failure is due to the lack of empirical validation, the difficulties in the context of forecasting the transitions of the phases and especially the problems in exactly defining the stage a product or brand is in. However, there are approaches to measure all this by leading indicators such as the number of competitors or the levels of prices and profits (Cooper, 1992). Another common approach in defining the stage of a certain product is to define some rule of thumb in reference to a hypothesized normal distribution of night/arrival data (normally to take the variance as classification rule as suggested by Haywood, 1986, and Rink and Swan, 1979).

Operationalizing the destination life cycle for urban tourism

Urban tourism data are not available for long time series. A descriptive long-term destination life cycle of urban tourism similar to the applications in the field of island tourism cannot be drawn given the sparse data. The database reaches back to the middle of the 1970s providing bednight statistics for only a few tourism cities. The following case study uses the most recent development of cities in terms of arrival growth data for a time span of ten years (1984–1993), nearly comparable to the study of Choy (1992), who used 15–20 years of growth in visitor arrivals. The individual cities are regarded as products to be classified into a certain stage in the life cycle. This classification of the cities is then validated by various background variables that emerge in the literature. The background variables relate to the supposed driving forces behind the cycle, such as different patterns of management strategies and different product characteristics throughout the various stages. This validation seems highly important as the limited number of case studies in the literature has not proven the validity of the concept, neither in terms of the number of stages nor in terms of the forces driving the cycle (Getz, 1992).

One restrictive remark is in order here. In principle, the destination life cycle is a long-term theoretic concept. It was originally dedicated to the analysis of hundreds of years of development of a destination. Using only a short phase throughout this development may not correspond exactly to this theory. A diagnosis of a city's position as growth could turn out in the long run to be rejuvenation. But this restriction may not be too severe because rejuvenation can be regarded as the beginning of a new life cycle (as the product may have been changed by adding some manmade attractions like casinos), or in other words, one product life cycle may be composed of many shorter ones. As every destination develops in the course of time it may be more meaningful to analyse only short periods, avoiding the construction of one life cycle for a lot of tiny different products.

According to Haywood (1986) there are six operational decisions when using the life cycle concept which refer to the:

1. unit of analysis
2. relevant market
3. pattern and stages of the tourist area life cycle
4. identification of the area's shape in the life cycle
5. determination of the unit of measurement
6. determination of the relevant time unit.

The first stage in using the life cycle concept is the definition of the unit of analysis. In this case example the unit is the city with its political boundaries. There is no obvious advantage in limiting the analyses to certain kinds of accommodation. Moreover comparable data are available only for visitors in all kinds of accommodation. Therefore, this definition seems suitable for the analysis of urban tourism.

There has always been a discussion about the use of brands (Canon), specific models (portable electric typewriters), products (electric typewriters) and categories of products (typewriters) (Lambin, 1993, p. 216). More common names for the same things would be product class, product form and brands (Rink and Swan, 1979, p. 226). The ideal market definition for the life cycle concept is the product level, although a product can have different life cycles in different (geographic or psychographic) segments. There is an obvious problem in defining products in the field of urban tourism. Is urban tourism in one specific city one product or are there many of them? As urban tourism is grounded on a lot of different motivations it is actually misleading to speak of one product. In a typical multi-motive situation like this, it would be better to use the tourism statistics to define different products, separating the statistics for each city according to the motives. Then one could draw separate life cycles for culture tourism, business tourism and other products. Unfortunately there are no comparable motive studies available yet for cities.

The product level is not feasible with the data available. Therefore one has to go one step deeper and analyse the brand level. This means taking the cities as unit of analysis, following the idea that the life cycle approach is destination-specific. In a modern segmentation scheme each city should be separated into different segments each providing a different development. In reality, city tourism managers segment the market by country of origin. However, looking at separate life cycles for different countries of origin for many cities soon becomes too complex. It seems sufficient to divide into domestic and international tourism because differing curves are probable especially for these markets (Cooper and Jackson, 1989; Ioannides, 1992).

In fact, the problem of the definition of the unit of analysis is combined with the definition of the relevant market. Detecting meaningful submarkets of urban tourism is the core of Part III and does not lead to one unique solution. Therefore it is justified here to analyse all arrivals for all cities together, although in principle the market definition should better pre-empt the life cycle concept as it has important consequences for its validity (Brownlie, 1985).

Another important point to be determined before the analysis is the measurement approach. In the marketing literature, sales are most often taken as unit of measurement for the life cycle. It is not yet clear which measure of sales should be taken: unit volume, per capita consumption or some kind of revenue. The life cycle concept seems to be sensitive to the choice of measures (Day, 1981; Haywood, 1986). For a destination this means that arrivals, nights or some kind of revenue (perhaps including multiplier effects) can be used. It is unrealistic to expect comparable measures of revenue for different cities, so nights or arrivals have to be selected. Whereas nights are the primary concern of destination managers, as they are the common success indicator in the industry, arrivals seem more appropriate for the life cycle concept. The concept of the life cycle refers to the amount of consumers buying a certain product (visiting a city) and not the amount they buy (how long they stay). In concordance with this argument, arrivals are used in Choy (1992) and clearly favoured in Cooper (1992).

An empirical example

The destination life cycles of 43 European cities
Recommendations on how to identify the stage of a certain destination in the life cycle are sparse. One common approach is simply to plot the rate of change of visitor numbers, visitor expenditure, market shares or profitability (Cooper and Jackson, 1989) and define some rule of thumb in

terms of the amount of growth or decline for the classification. But this process can easily misclassify a city because of erratic movements or temporary developments.

For these reasons the classification of the cities into different stages should not follow a rigorous model. To classify strictly according to the percentage growth of arrivals is debatable and not empirically validated. The approach used in the following example is more straightforward. The growth data for international and domestic tourism should be regarded as variables describing the development for each year. Those cities that exhibit a similar pattern can then be grouped together. Ideally this grouping takes place on a continuum representing the different stages of the destination life cycle. This follows the notion that irrespective of the exact shape, all products have in common phases of slow, medium or high growth, constant and declining sales (Jones and Lockwood, 1990, cited in Cooper, 1992, p. 149).

The arrival data of the last ten years are transformed to nine percentage growth rates. Using the eighteen data points representing nine domestic and nine international percentage rates is not recommendable. Erratic movements even in one or a few years would strongly influence the result and mislead the interpretation. Year-to-year variations therefore seem unsuitable for the life cycle approach (Dhalla and Yuspeh, 1976), and there is a need for some kind of smoothing of the growth data. In the present case a simple three-year moving average may suffice and is available for 43 cities (see Tables 2.11 and 2.12). The moving average reduces the number of data points to seven smoothed percentage rates but warrants a better interpretability of the development.

The next step is a clustering of the cities along a continuum portraying the similarity in the development of arrival growth. The self-organizing maps (SOMs) of Kohonen are appropriate for this purpose (see the Appendix for an explanation of the method) as they result in ordered prototypes. Simply define a grid that models the stages in the life cycle and then classify each city to its winner prototype. A 6×1 grid is defined in the SOMnia program to capture the hypothesized six stages of Butler's life cycle model. This definition takes into account that the outside stages should be as different as possible (as exploration and decline certainly are), while neighbouring prototypes remain similar.

The 6×1 grid produces a reasonable solution. There is a clear differentiation between the prototypes of the six stages. While no prototypes for the beginning stages of the theoretical life cycle model emerge, the reader may verify an obvious shift of the turning point (see Figure 2.16). The lack of an introductory phase seems to be plausible in the case of urban tourism. All cities are more or less in the middle–end phase of the destination life cycle with only minor variations.

Table 2.11 Three-year moving average of arrival growth for domestic markets

Place name code	Arrival growth (%)						
	1986	1987	1988	1989	1990	1991	1992
AAH	0.5	1.3	3.5	3.5	3.5	2.3	2.2
AMS	-3.5	0.6	5.1	7.6	9.2	7.7	6.2
BAD	2.7	4.2	3.8	3.5	2.8	0.4	-2.9
BCN	4.1	-0.3	3.3	-1.4	-0.2	1.8	2.6
BER	13.8	10.3	9.3	7.7	2.9	6.4	2.5
BNJ	4.2	0.6	4.0	11.3	12.0	11.3	1.7
BRN	1.3	1.3	4.0	0.3	1.5	0.3	-0.1
BRU	2.7	0.8	7.7	3.8	0.6	1.3	2.9
BSL	3.1	-2.0	0.6	-0.5	1.1	-4.6	-4.7
BUD	-0.4	-3.8	-5.8	-11.5	9.6	-1.9	7.3
CAG	2.1	3.3	3.8	2.8	1.0	0.8	-2.7
CPH	0.9	0.1	-1.6	-1.9	-2.5	-0.1	2.1
EAS	9.9	18.2	18.9	11.0	-1.9	-4.6	-4.1
EDI	-1.5	-1.0	-4.0	-6.5	-14.2	-12.1	-7.7
FMO	15.3	10.3	8.9	4.7	1.2	-0.2	1.7
GRZ	4.3	2.3	2.2	-1.1	0.9	-1.1	-1.1
GVA	-2.2	-3.2	2.1	3.8	0.3	-1.4	-2.4
HAM	3.0	5.1	7.6	8.0	5.7	2.2	0.7
HEL	5.4	2.9	9.4	-0.8	-6.2	-6.4	-1.8
INN	-0.8	2.3	6.2	13.7	7.7	1.8	-3.9
LBC	4.7	6.3	5.4	12.4	12.7	9.9	1.1
LIS	2.7	0.6	2.0	-1.5	-0.1	-1.5	-1.8
LNZ	-0.7	1.6	2.8	4.8	5.5	2.7	1.2
MAD	4.2	6.6	5.1	1.0	-0.5	-2.4	1.4
MHG	11.6	9.0	7.4	4.4	-1.1	-2.3	0.9
MIL	14.9	8.2	8.8	-3.1	-0.8	-2.7	1.2
MUC	2.7	4.7	6.1	5.7	3.7	0.5	-3.0
OSL	3.0	1.6	-3.4	2.3	1.4	9.5	6.0
PAR	-2.4	3.3	14.6	14.7	8.2	-0.9	-6.9
PRG	0.0	0.0	3.6	4.5	5.8	-6.3	-21.3
QFB	-0.4	1.0	0.7	2.1	2.5	0.7	1.6
QGL	5.9	2.7	3.1	0.9	1.3	-2.6	-2.7
QHD	8.2	8.0	8.3	2.2	4.0	-0.9	-1.1
QKA	1.4	3.4	1.5	6.6	4.7	6.2	0.6
QWU	12.4	6.1	3.7	4.8	7.3	3.8	-0.6
REB	7.4	8.7	9.8	10.3	8.0	2.7	-1.6
ROM	-6.8	3.1	8.7	0.6	-0.7	-2.0	6.1
STO	5.0	4.0	-2.3	3.3	-3.6	-3.7	-5.1
STR	1.5	2.7	1.3	3.1	4.5	3.8	3.5
SZG	-1.2	2.1	5.1	7.0	5.0	1.3	1.1
VCE	-3.5	-1.8	2.6	3.1	2.2	-1.7	-4.4
VIE	5.1	9.0	-1.0	15.0	14.4	23.1	4.4
ZRH	-1.4	-1.1	-1.3	-1.3	-1.7	-3.1	-3.8

A method such as SOMs portrays the development of time series. The different patterns inherent in those series are extracted for subgroups with similar developments. One point should be made here. The domestic and international figures were included as separate inputs in this analysis.

Table 2.12 Three-year moving average of arrival growth for foreign markets

Place name code	Arrival growth (%)						
	1986	1987	1988	1989	1990	1991	1992
AAH	-0.1	-0.7	5.6	8.7	8.1	4.4	-0.5
AMS	-3.5	0.6	5.1	7.6	2.9	2.4	-4.6
BAD	-1.4	0.9	9.7	8.6	-0.1	-5.9	-13.5
BCN	0.9	6.0	-1.4	-4.3	-29	0.6	1.6
BER	13.8	10.3	9.3	7.7	2.9	8.5	1.7
BNJ	-0.1	-4.1	-0.5	4.4	3.1	0.1	-7.4
BRN	-2.7	-3.5	2.4	2.8	.3	-4.2	-7.6
BRU	2.5	-0.4	8.3	7.2	2.6	-0.4	-1.8
BSL	-4.2	-1.1	2.4	3.2	-1.4	-2.8	-5.2
BUD	3.5	2.3	5.6	-1.9	-2.9	-7.9	-7.7
CAG	4.1	5.9	7.0	6.2	-0.8	-2.1	-4.5
CPH	-3.2	-4.6	2.5	3.1	3.9	2.1	0.6
EAS	9.9	18.2	18.9	11.0	-1.9	-4.6	-41
EDI	6.0	1.8	6.2	0.6	3.7	7.8	6.4
FMO	1.4	7.7	8.8	7.0	6.8	2.2	-3.3
GRZ	2.5	1.6	10.8	13.9	10.7	0.9	-10.3
GVA	-2.2	-3.2	2.1	3.8	0.3	-1.4	-3.3
HAM	3.0	5.1	7.6	8.0	5.7	2.2	-1.4
HEL	3.1	3.7	9.0	4.3	-2.2	-3.9	-0.6
INN	-4.7	-4.1	7.3	6.7	1.8	-1.3	-7.4
LBC	11.5	7.1	3.5	10.2	13.7	4.3	-10.1
LIS	2.4	0.5	6.0	4.5	6.6	-0.5	-4.2
LNZ	-2.1	0.8	11.1	12.8	8.8	-0.3	-3.0
MAD	4.2	6.6	5.1	1.0	-0.5	-2.4	-3.1
MHG	-2.8	-4.3	5.5	4.5	-5.1	-1.9	-6.6
MIL	3.4	14.9	8.2	8.8	-3.1	-0.9	-2.7
MUC	3.3	0.5	8.9	10.3	4.3	-2.4	-10.6
OSL	0.2	-4.9	0.1	-1.5	3.4	8.4	5.1
PAR	-2.4	3.3	14.6	14.7	6.9	4.4	-1.7
PRG	0.0	0.0	3.6	4.5	5.8	2.5	-2.3
QFB	3.3	5.6	9.2	6.6	2.9	0.3	-6.6
QGL	5.8	0.0	3.3	4.3	6.8	-0.3	-2.9
QHD	0.4	3.0	13.4	11.0	-0.6	-3.3	-9.5
QKA	-2.8	-2.6	0.0	6.1	8.0	3.9	-1.6
QWU	2.0	-1.6	2.7	5.3	4.0	1.0	-9.7
REB	7.4	8.7	9.8	10.3	8.0	2.7	-1.6
ROM	9.8	13.1	19.0	4.2	-7.2	-6.2	-5.6
STO	1.3	-2.2	1.0	4.2	1.1	-0.6	-3.0
STR	-1.3	-0.3	4.3	6.4	5.1	-1.0	-2.6
SZG	-1.0	-0.4	9.5	10.4	5.3	-2.2	-9.0
VCE	-3.5	-1.8	2.6	3.1	-3.5	0.7	1.7
VIE	2.1	5.0	12.6	10.2	3.4	-0.6	-5.9
ZRH	-3.4	-4.6	-0.6	1.1	-0.9	-3.5	-5.1

Nevertheless, the patterns of these markets are surprisingly similar in the prototypes built by the SOMs. This means that the development of the domestic and the international market runs more or less parallel for city destinations.

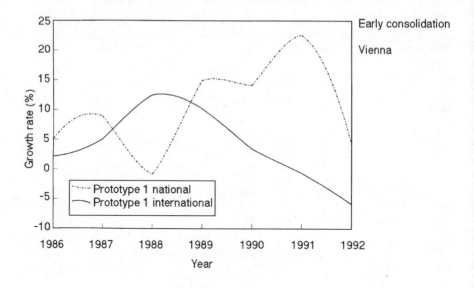

Figure 2.16a Life cycle prototypes and corresponding cities

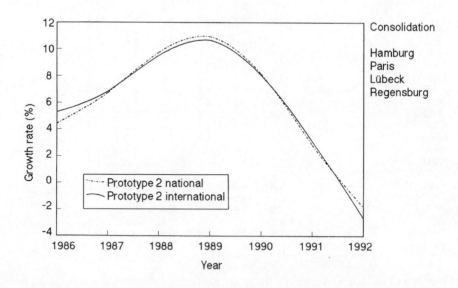

Figure 2.16b Life cycle prototypes and corresponding cities

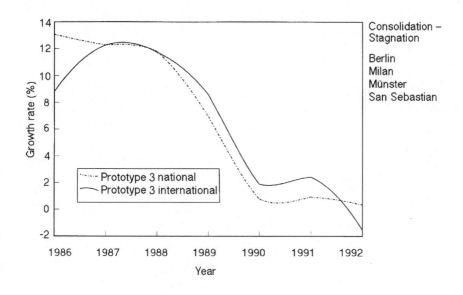

Figure 2.16c Life cycle prototypes and corresponding cities

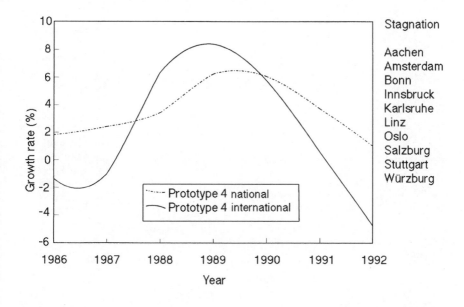

Figure 2.16d Life cycle prototypes and corresponding cities

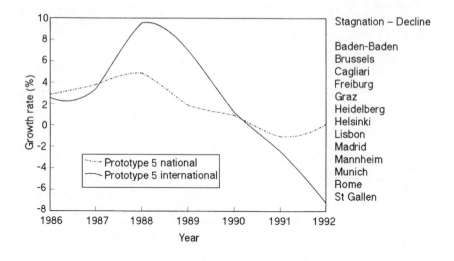

Figure 2.16e Life cycle prototypes and corresponding cities

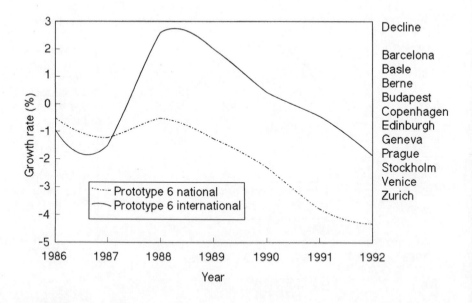

Figure 2.16f Life cycle prototypes and corresponding cities

The first prototype is the winner for only one city: Vienna. A growth in arrivals of up to 20 per cent (for the domestic market) is followed by smaller growth rates at the end of the period under consideration. This appears as the beginning of a consolidation phase. This is the only one of the six prototypes in which the development of the domestic market differs significantly from the development of the international market. The second prototype corresponds in its development very closely with the stage of consolidation: a decline of the growth rates is followed by a small decrease at the end. German cities and Paris come particularly close to this development.

The turning point in prototype three again occurs a bit earlier. The consolidation starts around 1989 and shifts to the stagnation phase in the last three years, with zero growth. A remarkable feature of prototypes two and three is the nearly perfect correspondence of the domestic and international markets. The first three prototypes include only nine out of 43 cities. It is realistic that city tourism in general has already entered the later phases of the life cycle and faces stagnation and decline as imminent threats.

Prototype four is characterized by zero growth rates at the beginning and the end of the period observed. It is a case of stagnation only interrupted by positive growth rates during the peak of European city tourism (see Grabler and Wöber, 1995). The shift from stagnation to decline is shown in prototype five. The international market in particular is likely to face a decline in arrivals. The bulk of cities (thirteen) fall into this category. The development of prototype six is even worse, with signs of the beginning of a decline in arrivals. A substantive decrease in the arrivals of the domestic market causes problems for city managers. Among the cities in this situation are most Swiss cities, Prague, Budapest and the traditional tourist destination, Venice.

Validating the empirical life cycle

Various criteria relating to different product characteristics and different management tasks and strategies can be used for the validation of the empirical city life cycle. All these criteria can be used to test the classification of the cities according to the life cycle concept, because this classification was based solely on the development of the arrivals in the cities, and no other indicator was employed.

It is common knowledge that in the early stages of the life cycle the proportion of first-time buyers is high compared to later phases (Brownlie, 1985; Cooper, 1992; Getz, 1992). Therefore, there should be a greater percentage of repeat visitors in the cities that are in their later phases. On the other hand, repeat visitors often stay for a longer period. The destination life cycle is therefore supposed to influence the length of stay of the guests (Getz, 1992).

One of the main constituent factors of the destination life cycle is competition. In the early stages of the cycle there is only one firm, an innovator, serving the market. With the progress of time the number of competitors rises, with tough competition present in the mature stages (Catry and Chevalier, 1974; Cooper, 1994). Therefore a high degree of perceived competition is expected for all cities, with a tendency for it to be stronger for the cities in later phases of the life cycle. As competition gets tougher, the price level for the tourist is likely to go down. Highest price levels should occur in the middle of the life cycle (growth and maturity).

The other marketing strategies will change in parallel with the price movement. For the growth and maturity stages the market operation will be rather undifferentiated. The mass market is the prime target group in these phases. In the introduction and decline stages a more segmented approach is prevalent (Dhalla and Yuspeh, 1976). Therefore, cities in the middle of the life cycle should reveal more target groups and a less restricted choice of target groups and distribution channels (operationalized by the countries in which the city is offered).

The longer a destination strives for tourists the broader the offer of accommodation and other services becomes. Therefore, in the late phases of the cycle a destination should suffer from overcapacity (Haywood, 1986). Because of the difficulties a city tourism manager faces with the progress in the life cycle (nights and occupancy rates diminish), new success criteria become more important. Whereas in the early phases only nights are counted, in later phases there is a shift to more sophisticated measures such as satisfaction rates.

Also on the supply side there should be differences between cities in different stages of the life cycle. Supply factors such as the combination of attractions and hotels are supposed to be one of the driving powers of the life cycle. Therefore cities in different stages should have different profiles of attractions. At the same time the responsibilities of the CTOs should vary considerably. From a normative point of view these responsibilities should vary according to the stage of the life cycle (Choy, 1993). Considering, for example, marketing, expenditure per visitor should be high in the early stages, and a shift to other tasks like research and management functions should emerge in later phases.

Data for the validation of the empirical observed destination life cycle are not available for all cities. Therefore the comparison of the new passive variables relies on a somewhat restricted sample of the cities. This is the reason why no statistical tests are applied. The results nevertheless allow for some tentative conclusions.

Table 2.13 shows the average visitor profiles for each life cycle group individually: the first-time visitor percentage, the length of stay and the Gini coefficient of the guest-mix distribution (a concentration measure) are listed. The figures in parentheses represent the number of cities on which

Table 2.13 Visitor profiles for different life cycle stages

Stage in the life cycle	First time visitor percentage	Length of stay	Guest-mix distribution
Early consolidation (1,1,1)			
Minimum	54	2.5	60
Maximum	54	2.5	60
Mean	54	2.5	60
Consolidation (0,4,4)			
Minimum	-	1.85	60
Maximum	-	2.28	88
Mean	-	2.08	79
Consolidation stagnation (2,4,4)			
Minimum	40	1.9	77
Maximum	46	3.53	93
Mean	43	2.58	84.75
Stagnation (5,10,10)			
Minimum	40	1.71	54
Maximum	70	2.72	92
Mean	57.9	2.01	76.3
Late stagnation (3,13,13)			
Minimum	25	1.63	53
Maximum	40.5	3.16	91
Mean	33.5	2.14	75.77
Decline (7,11,11)			
Minimum	25.9	1.76	61
Maximum	60	3.99	74
Mean	37.99	2.34	65.91
Grand total (24,61,61)			
Minimum	25	1.23	53
Maximum	80	6.5	93
Mean	47.38	2.32	75

the statistics are based. All figures stem from the FOTVE questionnaire (see Part I). The grand total displays the figures for all cities, including those cities for which no life cycle stage was determined because of a lack of arrivals data.

Data for the first-time repeat visitor relation is either taken from a study by the city or estimated by the managers. It indicates that the two last phases – called late stagnation and decline – relate to the lowest rates of first-time visitors to the city, which corresponds with the theory of the life cycle. No strong relationship between the length of stay, the guest-mix distribution and the destination life cycle can be detected. There is only a slightly higher length of stay for the late stagnation and decline stages, corresponding with the higher percentage of repeat visitors. The Gini coefficient for the guest mix tells about the type of city in terms of aggregated guest figures. It reveals that the decline stage contains primarily internationally oriented cities with a more even distribution of guests from different nations.

The perceived number of competitors in Table 2.14 was computed from experts' ratings of the competitive intensity between other cities and their home town (six-point scale from 1 = strong competitor to 6 = no competitor), whereby all values up to 4 were counted. The data were collected for leisure and business tourism separately. The number of competitors also corresponds with the theory of the destination life cycle. It is especially high for those cities in the decline phase (though the mean may be misleading, the minimum number of perceived competitors confirms this conclusion). This means that managers from cities facing decline in arrivals feel more pressure from competition than their colleagues from more successful cities. However, no relationship can be detected between the stage in the destination life cycle and price levels. According to a recent study (Edwards, 1993) more and less expensive cities can be found in all of the destination life cycle stages. In fact, there is too little information about the price levels to draw final conclusions about this point.

There are no systematic differences in the orientation for certain target groups for different stages (see data of Part I). Neither are specific target groups promoted nor is there a difference in the number of target groups. Looking at the data of van der Borg (1993) (Table 2.14) relating to the appearance of European cities in tour operator catalogues it is certainly not the destination life cycle that is responsible for the number of countries where a city is marketed. It rather seems to be a consequence of popularity

Table 2.14 Competition and distribution for different life cycle stages

Stage in the life cycle	No. countries city is offered	No. competitors leisure	No. competitors business
Early consolidation (1,1,1)			
Minimum	7	18	4
Maximum	7	18	4
Mean	7	18	4
Consolidation (3,1,1)			
Minimum	1	9	12
Maximum	7	9	12
Mean	3.67	9	12
Consolidation stagnation (2,0,0)			
Minimum	4	-	-
Maximum	6	-	-
Mean	5	-	-
Stagnation (8,8,6)			
Minimum	1	1	13
Maximum	7	24	27
Mean	3.25	11.5	19.17
Late stagnation (10,7,8)			
Minimum	1	3	1
Maximum	7	38	38
Mean	4.10	17.29	17.88
Decline (11,8,8)			
Minimum	2	11	9
Maximum	7	76	76
Mean	4.82	26.75	31.38
Grand total (56,37,37)			
Minimum	1	1	1
Maximum	7	76	76
Mean	3.75	17.35	17.95

and size of the city, as the lowest number is found in the stagnation stage where the (smaller) German and Austrian cities appear.

Absolutely no relationship exists with the occupancy rate. This may be due to problems with the validity of the occupancy rates (difficulties in the collection of a comparable figure for the number of beds in the cities) or to the fact that the cities are too close together in terms of the destination life cycle. The same holds true for the success factors of the CTOs. The most prominent criterion is the number of nights or arrivals with only a few unsystematic exceptions.

Amongst the most prominent drives of the destination life cycle are the supply factors. The managers rated the importance of diverse supply factors for their city marketing on a scale from 1 (highly important) to 4 (non-existent). Comparing the ratings with the empirical life cycle stages shows which offers are still appealing and which city type may revise its positioning and marketing strategies. All cities in the early stages for which arrival as well as importance rates data are available stress the culture aspect in their marketing strategies. It seems that this is still the most appealing factor in city tourism marketing resulting in growing arrivals. On the other hand there is one factor that is common amongst the cities in later phases: the business and airport importance is higher for these cities. This is especially valid for the cities in the decline stage. The supposed relation between the tasks of CTOs as presented in Part I and the destination life cycle cannot be confirmed. No systematic variations between different life cycles emerge and thus the factors mentioned in Part I remain the sole reasons for task variation.

Discussion and problems

Of the various passive variables that have been tested, only a few proved to be significant correlates of the empirical life cycle. A diminishing rate of first-time visitors is obvious for cities passing through later stages of the cycle. Correspondingly, the average length of stay of the guests rises. A regular monitoring of the guest structure could serve as a leading indicator for an imminent decline in arrivals. Competition also turned out to be a good predictor of the destination life cycle. Specifically, older tourism cities find themselves under strong competitive pressure. As more and more cities enter the market city managers have to use marketing tools more effectively. No such different marketing strategies have been detected for the cities analysed. It seems that managers have not yet reacted to their situation in terms of targeting or positioning. This may be due to the fact that profits or occupancy rates have not yet worn out. But the beginning of a decline stage means that this will happen sooner than expected.

Criticism of the life cycle concept should also be mentioned (an overtly critical but nevertheless entertaining view is offered by Dhalla and Yuspeh,

1976). A common disadvantage for the application of the life cycle concept in tourism is that unlike consumer goods a destination changes with time (Choy, 1992). This calls for the use of a new life cycle, as, for example, in the case of Atlantic City and the building of a casino. But this is actually a reaction to the life cycle and should be interpreted as an intended life cycle extension (renewal). This and other forms of life cycle extensions can be found in di Benedetto and Bojanic (1993). More strategic recommendations regarding the extension of the life cycle are given in Haywood (1986).

The life cycle is often said to be simply an outworking of management decisions and heavily dependent on external factors such as competition, shifts in consumer taste or regional policy (Cooper, 1992). Even if that were true the concept has meaning for the evaluation of the quality of city management. Therefore it is less important if it is a dependent or an independent variable. It is much more important to detect the factors that influence the cycle or are consequences of it. Irrespective of the direction of their causal relation to the life cycle, those correlates constitute important managerial information. Their empirical testing with longer and more valid time series is an area worth researching in the future.

References

Brownlie, D. (1985) Strategic marketing concepts and models. *Journal of Marketing Management* **1**, 157–94.

Butler, R. (1980) The concept of a tourist area cycle of evolution: implications for management of resources. *Canadian Geographer* **24**, 5–12.

Catry, B. and Chevalier, M. (1974) Market share strategy and the product life cycle. *Journal of Marketing* **38**, 29–34.

Choy, D.J.L. (1992) Life cycle models for Pacific island destinations. *Journal of Travel Research* **30**, 26–31.

Choy, D.J.L. (1993) Alternative roles of national tourism organizations. *Tourism Management* **14**, 357–65.

Cooper, C. (1992) The life cycle concept and tourism. In P. Johnson and B. Thomas (eds) *Choice and Demand in Tourism*. London: Mansell, 145–60.

Cooper, C. (1994) Product lifecycle. In S.F. Witt and L. Moutinho (eds) *Tourism Marketing and Management Handbook*. Englewood Cliffs: Prentice Hall, 341–5.

Cooper, C. and Jackson, S. (1989) Destination life cycle, the Isle of Man case study. *Annals of Tourism Research* **16**, 377–98.

Day, G.S. (1981) The product life cycle, analysis and application issues. *Journal of Marketing* **45**, 60–7.

Debbage, K. (1990) Oligopoly and the resort cycle in the Bahamas. *Annals of Tourism Research* **17**, 513–27.

Dhalla, N.K. and Yuspeh, S. (1976) Forget the product life cycle concept! *Harvard Business Review* **54**, 102–12.

di Benedetto, C.A. and Bojanic, D.C. (1993) Tourism area life cycle extensions. *Annals of Tourism Research* **20**, 557–70.

Edwards, A. (1993) *Price Competitiveness of Holiday Destinations. Costs for European*

Travelers, vol. 1. London: The Economist Intelligence Unit.

France, L. (1991) An application of the tourism destination area life cycle to Barbados. *Tourist Review* no. 2, 25–31.

Getz, D. (1992) Tourism planning and destination life cycle. *Annals of Tourism Research* **19**, 752–70.

Grabler, K. and Wöber, K. (1995) *Internationaler Städtebericht*. Vienna: ÖGAF, Österreichische Gesellschaft für Angewandte Fremdenverkehrswissenschaft.

Haywood, K.M. (1986) Can the tourist-area life cycle be made operational? *Tourism Management* **7**, 154–67.

Heath, E. and Wall, G. (1992) *Marketing Tourism Destinations. A Strategic Planning Approach*. New York: John Wiley & Sons.

Holloway, J.C. and Plant, R.V. (1988) *Marketing for Tourism*. London: Pitman.

Hooley, G.J. (1995) The lifecycle concept revisited: aid or albatross? *Journal of Strategic Marketing* **3**, 23–39.

Ioannides, D. (1992) Tourism development agents. The Cypriot resort cycle. *Annals of Tourism Research* **19**, 711–31.

Lambin, J.J. (1993) *Strategic Marketing. A European Perspective*. London: McGraw-Hill.

Law, Ch.M. (1993) *Urban Tourism. Attracting Visitors to Large Cities*. London: Mansell.

Lowyck, E., Van Langenhove, L. and Bollaert, L. (1992) In P. Johnson and B. Thomas (eds) *Choice and Demand in Tourism*. London: Mansell, 13–32.

Page, S. (1995) *Urban Tourism*. London: Routledge.

Rink, D.R. and Swan, J.E. (1979) Product life cycle research: literature review. *Journal of Business Research* **78**, 219–42.

Tellis, G.J. and Crawford, C.M. (1981) An evolutionary approach to product growth theory. *Journal of Marketing* **45**, 125–32.

Tse, E.C. and Elwood, C.M. (1990) Synthesis of the life cycle concept with strategy and management style: a case study in the hospitality industry. *International Journal of Hospitality Management* **9**, 223–36.

van den Berg, L., van der Borg, J. and van der Meer, J. (1993) *Upcoming Destinations of Urban Tourism*. Venice: CISET.

van der Borg, J. (1994) Demand for city tourism in Europe: tour operators' catalogues. *Tourism Management* **15**, 66–9.

Weaver, D. (1990) Grand Cayman Island and the resort cycle concept. *Journal of Travel Research* **29**, 9–15.

Part III

Analysing and monitoring demand on the disaggregate level

3.1

Satisfaction tracking for city tourists

Josef A. Mazanec

Guest satisfaction, service quality and quality management

A guest-satisfaction tracking system is a prerequisite for maintaining and improving the quality of tourist services in a destination. The principles of total quality management (Heskett *et al.*, 1990) apply to the non-profit organization of a city tourist board in much the same manner as they underlie the quality assurance practices in a private enterprise. A hotel group such as Hilton International, for example, measures customer satisfaction on a monthly basis (Vienna Hilton, 1992). National, regional and local tourist organizations fulfil marketing functions (Kaspar, 1991, p. 133). They assist the private sector in its struggle for market share and they have learned to base their tourism policy decisions on market and guest research findings. Tourist receiving countries began to introduce national guest surveys in the early 1980s. Switzerland started with its TOMAS system (Touristisches Marktforschungssystem Schweiz; Kaspar, 1990, p. 78) in 1982, but did not succeed in establishing a continuous survey. Austria conducted the first national guest survey (GBÖ – Gästebefragung Österreich) in 1983/84 and repeated the exercise in 1985/86, 1988/89, 1991/92 and 1994/95. The sample size totals 10,000 respondents with roughly two thirds of the personal interviews collected during the summer season and one third during winter (Mazanec, 1995a). Thus, the 'raw material' of customer feedback was available in various countries. The decision, however, to relate it systematically to a quality monitoring programme has not yet been taken. It is only recently that the basics of quality management have been recognized and accepted in the tourist industry (Weiermair, 1994; Witt and

Muhlemann, 1994; Witt, 1995). While the implementation in tourism management is still lagging behind the standards in other branded products and service industries, research on customer satisfaction becomes more and more sophisticated (see Hauser *et al.*, 1994, as an example).

The promise of the SERVQUAL model (Parasuraman *et al.*, 1985, 1988; Zeithaml *et al.*, 1988) to provide a general foundation for service quality and satisfaction measurement in behavioural theory cannot be maintained. SERVQUAL entailed several tentative applications in the travel, transport and hospitality sectors (Fick and Brent Ritchie, 1991; Richard and Sundaram, 1994; Ostrowski *et al.*, 1994; Martin, 1995). In a recent cross-cultural validation it even turned out to be generalizable to Australian, Japanese, Taiwanese and UK hospitality consumers (Patton *et al.*, 1994). Nevertheless, one must not overlook the critics (Buttle, 1995; Lewis, 1995). The marketing specialist who is familiar with the development of consumer research since the seminal work of Howard and Sheth (1969) may spot a number of weaknesses in the SERVQUAL concept. The need for making adjustments in the abstract service quality dimensions when dealing with different application areas such as airlines, tour operators or hotels is not surprising. But there are more serious shortcomings, such as:

- the failure to provide methodology for detecting the group-specific character of service quality perceptions;
- the reliance on just the cognitive elements in the consumers' judgement of quality, i.e. on a 'cognitive algebra' that works under a compensatory scheme of rating and combining many individual quality attributes;
- the simplicity of the measuring instruments contrasting with the techniques that have been elaborated in attitude and image research to cope with non-metric data and with emotional and connotative assessment criteria.

A similar word of caution applies to the recent tradition of service quality research (Gummeson, 1993) where the ambition to give meaning to the central construct of 'perceived service quality' leads to old ideas wrapped in new terminology. As a consequence, the research community and the managers face an irritating variety of variables such as 'attitudes', 'perceived benefits', 'service expectations and perceived performance', '(customer) satisfaction' or 'dissonance' (in its interpretation as disappointed expectations rather than 'pure' post-decisional regret). From the consumer behaviour point of view a concept like 'perceived (service) quality' is redundant and superfluous. It is rooted in a 'production-centred' way of reasoning; the attribute 'perceived' must be added to relieve the notion of quality of its commodity origin and heritage. Parsimony is one of the virtues of efficient theories. Thus one may become sympathetic to Cronin and Taylor's (1992, p. 56) assertion that 'perceived service quality is a form of attitude . . .'.

While service quality research makes little progress on the level of the language of theory, it is also slow in incorporating up-to-date methodology on the observational and measurement levels. Most authors speak of 'testing ideas, approaches and techniques' (Brookes, 1995, p. 13). The majority of the authors discussing the 'service construct' implicitly assume that consumers make a clear-cut distinction between (tangible) products and services. However, there is empirical evidence indicating 'a range of products for which both goods and services attributes are intermingled' (Murray and Schlacter, 1995, p. 522). A research focus on 'services' is no justification for ignoring the tradition of attitude measurement in consumer research. The explanatory construct of 'attitude' (a multidimensional construct made up of a list of 'attitudinal' items with 'goal-satisfying capabilities') was at the core of the Howard–Sheth model. It reflects the 'perceived quality' which the service quality researchers later on dissolved into expectations prior to service experience and performance perceived during the service production process. Measurement, therefore, may imply a 'difference approach' (service expected less service delivered) as pursued by Parasuraman *et al.* (1985, 1988) or may aim directly at the perceived degree of performance. Cronin and Taylor (1992, 1994) raise strong objections against the expectancy-disconfirmation concept. These authors argue vigorously in favour of a performance-oriented operationalization which is more in line with the mainstream of attitude theory.

Conceptual and measurement adjustments for city tourism

The impression to be gained from the quality/satisfaction issues discussed in the literature may lose its 'fuzziness' if the focus is shifted from the conceptual pseudo-problems to the 'real' measurement problems. Consider 'perceived quality' as a state of evaluation and as a dyadic concept defined on both a tourist consumer and a tourist offer. The product/service consumption process starts with 'quality expectations' and generates 'quality perceptions' through experience. 'Quality expectations' are equivalent to the attitude towards a product/service mix prior to the (next) consumption situation. From the managerial point of view 'perceived performance' is not relevant unless it relates to satisfaction gained from a consumption experience. Thus it is equivalent to attitude change through learning. Figure 3.1 shows this learning cycle for the attitude towards a bundle of services (e.g. a package tour).

'Satisfaction' may be conceived as a short-term and ephemeral state of evaluation connected with one particular service encounter. Thus it becomes transaction-specific. By contrast, 'attitudes' are then understood to be stable and long-term states of mind rendering a 'cumulative conceptualization' of 'satisfaction' (Johnson *et al.*, 1995) redundant. In tourist behaviour research one may advocate this distinction because it underlines that the time of measurement is a crucial point. Attitude formation is an intricate procedure. It depends on subjective importances

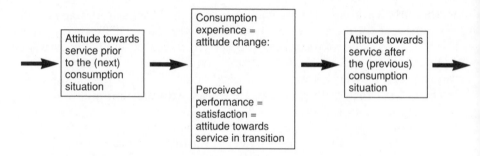

Figure 3.1 Attitude formation as a continuous process

(of the evaluative attributes) that are known to vary as time progresses. It is a popular finding among market research practitioners that evaluations measured in an 'in-resort' survey usually differ from the results collected from the same respondents three months later in their normal place of residence. To take a simple example: an attribute like 'weather' – in particular if it is not enjoyable – exerts strong influence on the tourists' well-being while in the destination. After having returned and looking back over his vacation experience the tourist modifies the relative importances of attributes. Weather – for which nobody is to blame – loses salience. Another more easily controllable attribute, say, (poor) responsiveness of the local representatives or the tour guides, is likely to increase in importance. Instead of arguing about naming an evaluative state of mind – a transient 'satisfaction' or a robust 'attitude' – proper credit should be given to the satisfaction/attitude dynamics.

An empirical example

The empirical example that follows has no ambition to contribute to the conceptual discussion about the interrelations and the viability of various explanatory variables. It assumes that the measurement of guest satisfaction indicates the perceived quality of tourist services in an urban destination. It claims, however, to offer some modest advancement in this field of study. First of all it conceives satisfaction as a multidimensional construct. The analysis commences with the hypothesis that guest satisfaction is a group-specific phenomenon. The individual satisfaction items tend to appear in a slightly different mixture for each city tourist. There may be homogeneous subgroups among the visitors to a city where each subgroup (segment) asks for specific treatment in future market operations. There may be 'lost cases', people whom there is no hope of regaining as customers. There may be partially disappointed tourists demonstrating that a city cannot equally line up to all the expectations aroused in its visitors' minds. Thus, the city tourism managers may become convinced that more than one satisfaction profile should be derived.

Guest satisfaction as a multidimensional construct

Consider guest satisfaction to be an intervening variable which stimulates word of mouth and either reinforces or dampens the intention to repeat visit. It is multidimensional, as many assessment criteria interfere in the evaluation process. Given the discussion in the literature about the weaknesses of the expectancy-disconfirmation approach (Fick and Brent Ritchie, 1991; Buttle, 1995; Ryan, 1995, pp. 88–95), a performance-based measure is preferred here. To capture the evaluative aspect the measuring instrument asks the tourist about the extent to which his or her expectations have been met. It is of minor interest whether each of these ratings is called a contribution to 'quality performance' or to 'guest satisfaction'. It is more important to understand that any result of a consumer's evaluation process – before or after gaining the experience at the service encounter – contains an element of market segmentation. Judging from more than 30 years of empirical evidence in consumer research it is a well confirmed hypothesis that evaluative constructs such as product images, attitudes, risk perceptions, dissonance, preferences or satisfaction arrive in a segment-specific set-up. It is also premature to jump to a conclusion that preferences, in general, are more meaningful segmentation criteria than benefits or attribute importance ratings (O'Connor and Sullivan, 1995). Preferences and buying intentions are immediate predecessors of purchase. Thus they are less disturbed by situational factors and tend to correlate more reliably with actual behaviour. But how to operate in a market where consumers have low brand awareness and preference formation is either still under way or very volatile? Segmentation theory must not be conceived in a narrow perspective of 'mature' and highly structured markets. In spite of these arguments many reports from travel behaviour surveys miss the opportunity to search for 'a posteriori market segments' (Mazanec, 1994a) that may hide in their database. One of the causes for the lack of interest in travel satisfaction types or segments is the difficulty of visualizing the multidimensional results in a managerially convincing and comprehensible manner.

The case example that follows exploits the subsample of city tourists in the Austrian National Guest Survey 1994/95. About 20 per cent of the master sample were visitors of the capital city of Vienna or of one of the major cities in the nine provinces. All the respondents were leisure travellers or they had extended a business trip for vacation purposes. From its early days the survey has always included a section on tourist satisfaction. The list of evaluative items was carefully gauged and kept unchanged for ten years to facilitate longitudinal analysis. According to the fashionable trend of total quality management (TQM), the 1994/95 survey included a variant of examining satisfaction by means of a performance measure ('more than met expectations', 'met expectations', 'did not meet expectations').

The SERVQUAL scales do not address prices. In tourism research this is a serious deficit, because tourists have a very incomplete knowledge about what they will be able to afford in a destination. They use 'cues' such as exchange rates or fuel prices to make generalizations about the price level and the purchasing power parity. Expectations, therefore, do not only relate to what is offered; travellers also have expectations about the level of prices. Sixteen items are needed in this study to describe the major ingredients of a leisure trip to a city:

- landscape and cityscape (abbreviated to 'landscape', 'cityscape' in the following charts)
- peace and quiet
- furnishing and pleasantness of accommodation ('accommodation')
- service in the accommodation ('service')
- cuisine and catering ('catering')
- friendliness of staff in restaurants and inns ('friendly staff')
- friendliness of the local people ('friendly locals')
- cultural life
- scope for excursions ('excursions')
- entertainment, sports and shopping facilities ('entertainment', 'sports', 'shopping')
- opening hours of shops ('opening hours')
- walking and hiking paths ('hiking')
- offers for families with children ('families').

Not all the 'ingredients' of a trip have explicit prices (e.g. landscape, picturesqueness of town, friendliness of the locals). Only seven items are indicative of how the city visitors perceive the fairness of prices and judge the value for money:

- drinks ('beverages')
- meals ('food')
- accommodation
- sports facilities ('sports')
- cultural offers, entrance fees ('culture')
- entertainment facilities ('entertainment')
- public transport ('transport').

The underlying hypothesis that tourists have segment-specific bundles of expectations that are significantly different from each other need not be tested once more. Instead, additional assumptions are analysed in this demonstration study. If confirmed they help to refine the monitoring of guest satisfaction as an 'early warning signal' and as an instrument to control service quality for fundamentally different guest segments such as 'first-time visitors' and 'repeat guests'. First, an 'outside' validation criterion is needed to decide whether a classification of guests into 'satisfaction types' is managerially meaningful or not:

- Groups of tourists, each exhibiting a significantly different mixture of travel expectations and travel experience, are called satisfaction types or segments. It is hypothesized that each segment also shows a different amount of 'overall' travel satisfaction. Hypothesis H1, therefore, relates the multidimensional performance criteria found in a specific 'satisfaction' segment to a symptomatic value of a one-dimensional satisfaction measure. One-dimensional satisfaction is measured by directly asking the tourists to what extent their city trip came up to expectations without specifying any particular attributes.

- Affiliation with a satisfaction segment should produce a behavioural effect to capture the attention of city tourism managers. A subsequent and simple bivariate hypothesis, therefore, would read: Membership in a satisfaction segment, where segments are ordered in ascending order of overall satisfaction, correlates positively with the intention to repeat visit (H2).

- But the relationship between trip satisfaction and repeat visit may not be that straightforward. Strong loyalty for a destination (i.e. a higher past frequency of visit) reduces the 'danger' of being disappointed. It renders the visitors 'immune' towards bad experience; otherwise they would suffer from dissonance. This leads to hypothesis H3: The contrast between excellently and poorly fulfilled expectations is mitigated among the loyal visitors and thus the ensuing impact on intention to repeat visit is not significant. This conjecture was confirmed for the total of travellers to Austria (Mazanec, 1996). It is imperative to examine this assumption for the subgroup of city tourists. The visitors to urban destinations exhibit a different loyalty pattern and may not obey the same cause–effect relationships.

- Other correlates of guest satisfaction are worth analysing for the purpose of quality management. A psychographic variable like guest satisfaction cannot be properly manipulated, unless it is linked to some 'objective' guest characteristics. Examples are the destination itself (which particular city), the country of origin, the usual range of demographic and sociographic personal attributes, or the observable aspects of the city trip (type of accommodation, length of stay, mode of transport). These issues are standard practice and will not be worked out here.

- Any list of satisfaction items must address the 'good value for money' question. It is of particular interest in this case study, because the Austrian tourist industry has been suffering from the hard currency policy for the Schilling for many years and criticisms about the price level have abounded in recent years. Daily expenditure may serve as a double indicator. It informs about the spending power of a visitor, and, at the same time, gives some indication about the quality of services consumed in the destination. One may, therefore, hypothesize that the average daily expenditure in a guest segment corresponds with a higher degree of satisfaction (H4). If confirmed this finding would compel managers to take priority action in the low-price-low-quality domain.

From the methodological point of view the subsequent analysis makes an attempt to visualize the guest satisfaction 'types' in a user-friendly way. The whole list of 23 satisfaction items must be processed with all its mutual dependencies; some items tend to occur in conjunction with each other, some items may prove to be incompatible. By taking into account these phenomena the manager overcomes the naive and often misleading 'inspection' of tables with one satisfaction item at a time.

The Austrian National Guest Survey measures guest satisfaction with an item battery of quality criteria such as 'landscape', 'picturesqueness of town', 'peace and quiet', 'opening hours of shops' . . . sixteen in total. The 'good value for money' issue is split up into more concrete information on particular products and services ('beverages', 'food', 'accommodation', 'sports facilities', 'cultural events', 'entertainment', 'public transport'). The guests rate each item by attributing one of three performance-oriented scale values (verbalized as expectations which are 'more than met', 'met' or 'not met'). The overall satisfaction measure relates to the whole stay consumed so far (same scale). The subsequent clustering procedure operates on the variables coded +1, 0 and -1. The search for clusters, therefore, occurs in a satisfaction dataspace with points lying in the centre or on the nodes and edges of a 23-dimensional hypercube.

A brief outline of centroid clustering, learning vector quantization and self-organizing maps

The terms 'cluster' and 'prototype' (the analyst's language), 'segment' (marketing jargon) or 'consumer type' (psychologist's language) are used interchangeably. They are indicative of the fact that today's marketing managers in all sectors of the economy have to face an increasing differentiation of benefits sought and a growing pressure to compete in highly specialized markets. In contrast with other social science disciplines (such as anthropology or sociology) the marketing researcher has no ambition to seek the one and only all-encompassing typology of consumers. The technique of market segmentation itself becomes an instrument of competitive strategy. There is an infinity of segmentation schemes for a product or service class. The marketing manager 'invents' them and tailors them according to his objectives. A service provider who makes efforts to complement the traditional segmentation variables (age, occupation, income, size of household etc.) with psychographic attributes (lifestyle, vacation style, benefits sought) will be in a better position to establish competitive advantages. He approaches his customers in a subtle and more sophisticated manner relying on a more complete profile than his competitors.

Searching for types and segments has always been a concern in the marketing applications of cluster analysis. Given the variety of clustering 'philosophies' and algorithms it may appear to be rather more 'art than science'. Hierarchical methods are unfeasible for large samples. One has to opt for a partitioning method operating on a predetermined number of clusters. The centroid method ('K means clustering') is intuitively attractive. It derives each prototype as the mean vector of a cloud of points (preferably arranged in a hyperspherical shape) in the dataspace. To evaluate a cluster solution the sum of squared distances may serve as a heterogeneity measure. The method of pairwise exchange (Späth, 1975; Ambrosi, 1978) serves as an iterative optimization procedure. It transfers cases between the clusters until the improvement in homogeneity becomes marginal. A variant of this method for an arbitrary similarity measure for binary data

(Steinhausen und Steinhausen, 1977; Formann *et al.*, 1979) will be employed in the forthcoming section on vacation styles. However, it is computationally expensive and not recommended for a sample size exceeding 2000 cases.

Centroids are built from randomly selected starting points. Each seed point 'captures' its neighbouring data points. Owing to the uneven distribution of the points in the dataspace this 'raw' centroid is a poor prototype (mean) for its data cloud. A new mean vector, therefore, will be calculated for each provisional cluster. Each of these means functions as a next generation centroid which again 'collects' the neighbouring points. This iterative procedure is bound to converge to a 'final' solution (fixed point). Neither the exchange method nor the fixed point procedure can warrant a global optimum for a predetermined number of clusters.

Learning vector quantization (LVQ) also leads to centroids. This technique originates from the communications engineering and neurocomputing disciplines (Hertz *et al.*, 1991, p. 225; Ritter *et al.*, 1992; Haykin, 1994, pp. 427–30; Rohwer *et al.*, 1994, pp. 101–3). As an 'adaptive' method it requires only local information (i.e. not more than one data vector at a time) for its iterative process called 'training'. If necessary the method works online and in real-time mode. This means that it can cope with a continuous influx of data (think of automated check-in/check-out systems or scanner data) and with samples of an unlimited size. LVQ optimizes ('trains') a predetermined number of initial data points to make them 'good' prototypes of the cases in their respective clusters. 'Competitive learning' is the underlying principle. The (provisional) prototypes compete with each other for being updated each time a data point is randomly selected to make the system learn. One of the prototypes (which resembles the data point most closely) becomes the 'winner' and is allowed to 'learn', i.e. it is pulled into the direction of the data vector. It is easy to imagine that during the training each prototype 'learns' to take responsibility for a particular type of input data thus functioning as a proxy for the cases in a homogeneous cluster. A dense region of data points attracts a prototype faster than a thinly 'populated' region in the dataspace. The resulting (local) optimum thus reflects the probability distribution of the observed data.

The centroids in the system of prototypes – as in all conventional cluster solutions – are entirely unsorted. On the other hand, they are scattered over the data space with some of them within short distance and others farther away from each other. To know more about these neighbourhood relations would be helpful in the interpretation process. It might also suggest the merger of two or more of the prototypes exhibiting an apparently similar profile. A projection of the prototypes from the high-dimensional dataspace into, say, two dimensions facilitates the interpretation significantly. This task of dimensionality reduction may be achieved by the standard method of multidimensional scaling (MDS). In this case example another technique is preferred. The satisfaction variables have values of -1, 0, and +1. An attempt to interpret the Euclidean distances in such a dataspace runs the risk of expecting too much information from the cluster solution. It is more appropriate to respect the topological structure in the data while extracting the prototypes.

The method of self-organizing maps (SOMs) serves this purpose. It tries to preserve the topologic relationships in the data as strictly as possible (Kohonen, 1982, 1984, p. 133, 1990; Pao, 1989, pp. 182–96; Freeman and Skapura, 1991, pp. 263–89; Gallant, 1993, p. 136). A modification of the LVQ learning scheme is required to respect the topology structure in the data. The principle of competitive learning is relaxed in such a way that not only the winner but also the adjacent prototypes get updated (Kohonen, 1984, p. 138; Caudill, 1993b, p. 19). This idea was inspired by findings in the brain sciences known as 'lateral interaction' (Kohonen, 1984, p. 129) or 'lateral inhibition' (Caudill, 1993a, p. 41). If the size of the neighbourhood is zero the training effect coincides with the LVQ. Then the quality of the centroids (being located in the 'real' centres of their respective clusters) is maximal, but the preservation of topology may be poor. Where it is imperative to preserve the topology structure (e.g. in applications for positioning purposes; see Mazanec, 1994b, 1995b) a small update for adjacent prototypes will be required, making them less representative of their cluster points. Thus, the analyst has to find a compromise. A projection of the prototypes into two dimensions (the 'map') alleviates this decision.

The practical work with LVQ and SOMs implies additional refinements. The size and variation of the learning rate ('cooling' or 'heating' in neuro-jargon) or the size and shape of the neighbourhood structure of the prototypes are examples. Examining the optimality of a prototype system is straightforward with the adaptive methods. By varying the learning and/or the neighbourhood parameters the analyst can probe the vicinity of the optimum found. In doing that he raises confidence in having detected a really 'good' solution to his clustering problem.

So far, the methodology of LVQ and SOMs has been presented in a sloppy and cursory outline with the intention to convey an intuitive understanding. The practical implications and usefulness will be illustrated in the next section. The reader seeking a more rigorous treatment is referred to the Appendix.

Satisfaction types among city tourists

A tailor-made C for Windows program (SOMnia 1.4.1[1]) is used to extract guest satisfaction segments. It starts with the best centroids (fixed points) out of 100 trials for randomly selected seed points. Then it tries to improve the cluster solution with LVQ and SOM methodology. Cluster heterogeneity

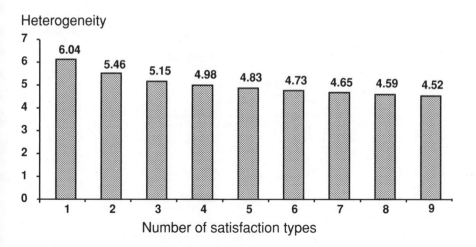

Figure 3.2 Heterogeneity of satisfaction segments

drops gradually for an increasing number of prototypes as shown in Figure 3.2. Heterogeneity is defined as the sum of squared Euclidean distances between each data vector (of satisfaction items) and the nearest prototype (centroid, cluster centre) divided by the number of cases. The formal criteria of heterogeneity reduction do not give any indication on what number of segments to choose. To illustrate the concepts of ordered prototypes and the preservation of topology two solutions are worth considering. On the lower end, four segments are the minimum requirement to differentiate between adjacent and non-adjacent prototypes (i.e. under a neighbourhood size of order 1). On the upper end, nine segments form a two-dimensional 'map' of three rows and three columns. This map promises to identify the four non-neighbouring segments #1, #3, #7 and #9 with marked differences in their profile of satisfaction ratings.

The four segments in the one-dimensional solution are ordered according to their overall similarity. There are not more than 4! = 24 different arrangements rendering an adaptive method superfluous. (The 9 cluster solution shown later allows for 9! = 362,880 different arrangements. With this number or even more segments the search for a topologically meaningful map becomes computationally intractable.) Figure 3.3 portrays the satisfaction profiles of guest segments #1 and #4 together with the average profile in the total guest sample. The guest segments with the intermediate satisfaction profiles #2 and #3 are in Figure 3.4. Table 3.1 highlights the most typical ratings out of the list of 23 satisfaction items for each of the four satisfaction types.

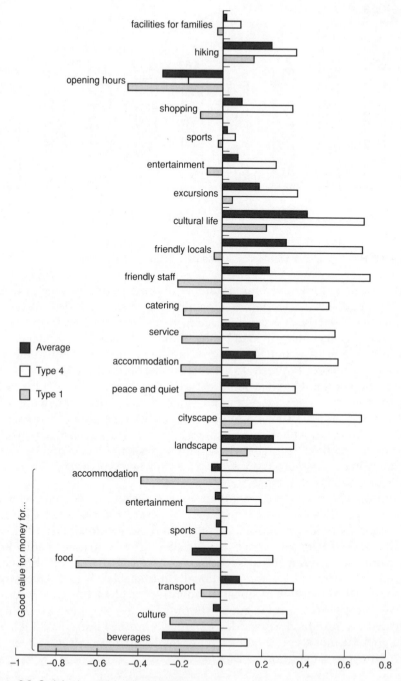

Figure 3.3 Satisfaction segments #1 and #4

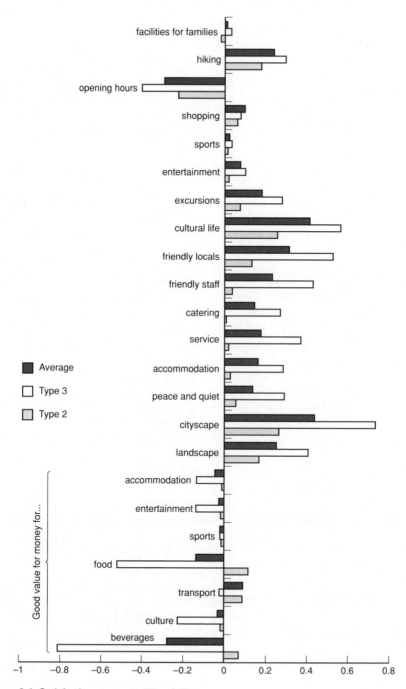

Figure 3.4 Satisfaction segments #2 and #3

Table 3.1 Summarizing results for the satisfaction segments #1 to #4

Type	Percentage	Rating
#1	16	Dissatisfied with everything except landscape and cityscape, cultural events and walking paths; extremely dissatisfied with the level of prices for beverages, meals and accommodation
#2	40	Moderately satisfied with all tourist services except opening hours of shops; no criticism for the level of prices
#3	23	Highly satisfied with all sorts of tourist services except the opening hours of shops; dissatisfaction with the price level, particularly for beverages and meals
#4	21	Highly satisfied with everything including the level of prices

The 'front-end' segments #1 and #4 are indeed extremely different in their average satisfaction ratings. Segment #1 is a small guest segment made up of the strongest critics. These city tourists were actually disappointed. Segment #2 is the majority group of guests who do not express any criticism regarding prices. Their expectations were met and this obviously includes the experience of prices. The guests in Segment #3 are characterized by a high level of satisfaction with the appearance of the city visited and its tourist services, but they cannot put up with the prices. Segment #4 contains the guests who have been positively impressed by all ingredients of their city trip, and accounts for one fifth of the total sample.

Considering now what was stated in hypothesis H1, the order of the segments according to the similarity of their satisfaction profiles should reflect the directly rated overall satisfaction with the total trip. Figure 3.5 shows a perfect, even linear relationship strongly supporting H1 ($\chi^2 = 319$; $P < 0.001$; Mantel–Haenszel test for linear association = 289, $P < 0.001$). This means that the new attribute 'satisfaction type' (i.e. affiliation with a particular satisfaction segment) may replace the direct rating in various cross-tabulations where the analyst wants to explore the joint effect of the whole profile of expectations.

The next hypothesis, H2, claims that a traveller's affiliation with a particular satisfaction type (segment) exerts an influence on the intention to repeat visit. Looking at Figure 3.6 one may find that the most extreme segments, #1 and #4, behave as expected. The intermediate trip satisfaction segments, however, do not fit into the picture. H2 must be rejected. H2 may be too naive because other moderator variables such as frequency of past visits come into play.

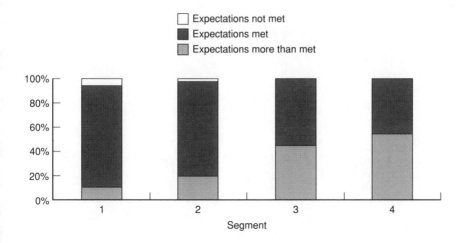

Figure 3.5 Comparing satisfaction types with an overall satisfaction rating

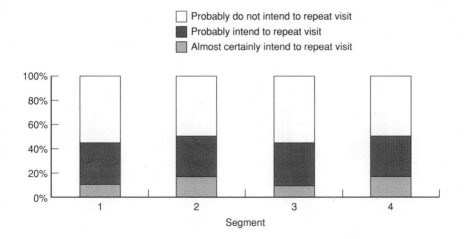

Figure 3.6 Satisfaction types and the intention to repeat visit

H3 points to an intervention effect of the number of past visits to a tourist city. The frequency or loyalty variable itself depends on several other criteria. Travel distance or the ability to afford a 'hard currency' destination (purchasing power parities, fluctuation of exchange rates) are just two examples. Figures 3.7 and 3.8 portray the relationship between the membership in a trip satisfaction segment and the intention to repeat visit when loyalty is held constant. But controlling for the past frequency of visit (i.e. first-time visitors versus loyal guests of their destination) does not

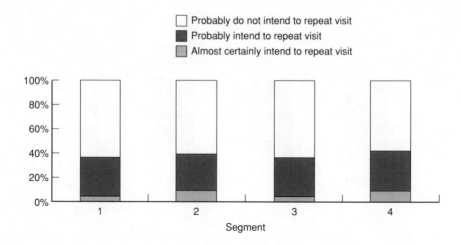

Figure 3.7 Satisfaction segment and repeat intention for the first-time visitors

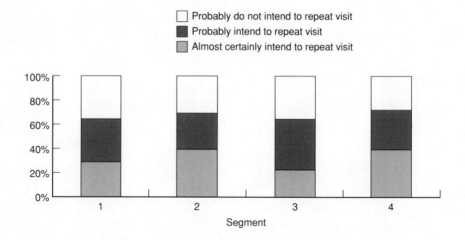

Figure 3.8 Satisfaction segment and repeat intention for the loyal visitors

purify the causal link. Neither the 'newcomers' nor the loyals produce a pattern conforming to H2 or H3.

The satisfaction–repeat visit mechanism does not seem to work for urban destinations in the same way as it governs the resort tourism for rural areas in central Europe. It is less common for an urban destination to build loyalty among its visitors. A weak intention to repeat visit need not necessarily result from dissatisfaction. Many city tourists consider a particular trip as a 'once-in-a-lifetime' experience. Thus they tend to seek variety in their choice

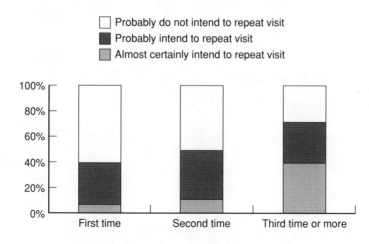

Figure 3.9 Frequency of past visits and intention to repeat visit

of a receiving city. Figure 3.9 relates the pattern of past visits directly to the intention to repeat visit to Vienna and the provincial cities in Austria. A two-thirds majority are first-time visitors and 60 per cent of them are 'probably not' inclined to return to the same place. Only one fifth are loyal visitors with more than one third of them planning to return. Other major traveller and trip attributes such as age, country of origin or spending level (highlighted in H4) also fail to differentiate between the satisfaction types. The city tourism manager must not, of course, conclude that meeting traveller expectations is irrelevant. There are still powerful consequences of a dissatisfaction experience such as word of mouth, which is well known to influence trip decisions quite strongly.

What if the segmentation into four satisfaction types was not 'fine' enough? An attempt to explore the properties of a nine-cluster solution should be made. The subsequent analysis also demonstrates how to visualize a larger number of segments and their mutual similarity. The SOM procedure implemented in the SOMnia program first lets the user define the neighbourhood relations between the prototypes he wants to extract. In this example nine types should be arranged in a lattice of three rows and three columns. The topologically sensitive SOM learning schedule then stretches and twists this 'map' to fit into the high-dimensional dataspace. To inspect the goodness of fit the prototypes are projected into two dimensions with the Sammon (1969) method. This non-linear data reduction method approximates the 23-dimensional distances between the prototypes in just two dimensions. Sammon's stress value indicates the goodness-of-fit where zero is best. The resulting 'map' appears to be 'well-behaved' if the grid of prototypes does not seriously violate the neighbourhood structure. The

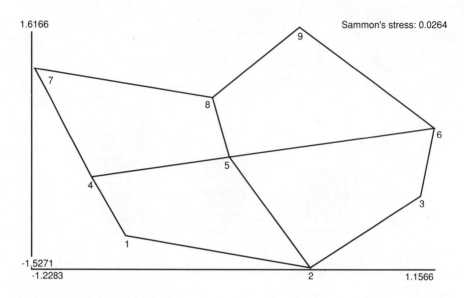

Figure 3.10 Two-dimensional map of nine satisfaction segments

preservation of topology would be rather poor if, for example, two
endpoints (#1 and #9) were less distant than 'first-order neighbours' such as
#1 and #2 or #1 and #4. Consider the screenshot from the SOMnia analysis
in Figure 3.10. Sammon's stress is acceptable and there are no topology
violations.

Table 3.2 lists the most remarkable (dis)satisfaction items for the city
travellers, sorted into nine satisfaction types. Table 3.3 adds more
information on the directly measured satisfaction rating and on the actual
and intended travel behaviour. All the associations shown are statistically
significant (P < 0.02). Types #1 and #2 are least satisfied, #2 also being
disappointed with the level of prices. Type #4 travellers found what they
expected; this type is the most experienced visitor (30 per cent loyal) and
contains an above average number of likely repeaters. Segments #7 and #9
are most enthusiastic; #7 also appreciates the level of prices, and
consequently reaches the highest value of daily expenditure among all
segments (AS2060 compared to an average of AS1655). A more thorough
examination of the two tables leads to the same observation concerning the
link between satisfaction and repeat visit. The performance perception may
exceed the expectations in terms of a multi-item or of an overall measure
(see #9 with 76 per cent perceiving a performance surplus), yet the impact
on repeat behaviour is very limited. Again, variety-seeking appears to
moderate the loyalty building process.

There is another means of portraying the differences between satisfaction
types. Take the four prototypes #1, #3, #7 and #9 in the corners of the

Table 3.2 Satisfaction segments with their outstanding items

Type	Percentage	Rating
#1	9	Very dissatisfied with standards of services in the hotels and restaurants, and with the opening hours of the shops; average satisfaction with cultural events; can put up with the level of prices
#2	11	Resembles #1 with two exceptions: satisfaction with cultural events below average, extremely dissatisfied with price level, particularly for beverages and meals
#3	10	Positively impressed by the land/cityscape, by the cultural events, and by the friendliness of staff and locals; equally critical as #2 about prices
#4	18	No dissatisfaction with anything including price levels; the (realistic) expectations were met
#5	14	Positively impressed by land/cityscape, excursions and culture; average disappointment regarding the opening hours; accepts the price level
#6	10	Highly satisfied with all trip attributes except opening hours, but very critical about prices, particularly for beverages and meals
#7	8	Extremely satisfied with everything except opening hours; highly satisfied with the level of prices
#8	11	Very satisfied with everything except opening hours; prices come up to expectations
#9	9	Even more satisfied than #7 with everything except opening hours, but critical of the prices for beverages

satisfaction map. These nodes are non-adjacent to each other and – with one node in between – represent second-order neighbours. Figures 3.11 and 3.12 show the average segment profiles of satisfaction items together with the grand mean ratings. These bar charts contain aggregate values and cannot visualize the amount of intra-segment variance.

Table 3.3 Satisfaction segments, overall trip satisfaction, past frequency of visit, and intention to repeat visit

Satisfaction and travel behaviour	Percentage for each type								
	#1	#2	#3	#4	#5	#6	#7	#8	#9
Satisfaction with trip									
better than expected	16	11	33	14	46	46	55	29	76
worse than expected	2	8	2	2	1	1	1	0	0
Intention to repeat visit									
almost certainly	16	12	9	19	12	8	13	15	15
probably not	52	55	58	45	59	57	52	53	47
Past frequency of visit									
first time	64	65	73	51	76	67	75	54	76
second or more	21	23	12	30	13	15	12	25	13

A non-metric version of principal components analysis is the appropriate method for condensing the observed list of 23 satisfaction items into a space of low dimensionality. The PRINCALS procedure (available in the SPSS Categories module) computes optimal 'quantifications' for the satisfaction items originally coded -1, 0 and +1. Simultaneously each respondent is characterized by an 'object score' on each dimension extracted from the ordinal raw data (Gifi, 1985). The object scores correspond to the positions of each individual respondent in the 'quantified' satisfaction space. The dimensions 1 and 2 account for not more than 28 per cent of variance; they are taken here to demonstrate that the satisfaction clusters are fairly homogeneous. According to the component loadings the first dimension collects the natural, man-made and social assets while the second dimension mainly depicts the (un)fairness of prices.

The satisfaction segments are not meaningful unless the segment affiliation explains a significant share of the variance observed in the respondents' object scores. Figure 3.13 demonstrates this for the four selected segments. The segment regions are well separated with some minor overlap along the borders. An analysis of variance confirms the visual result for all nine prototypes. The variance explained amounts to 67 per cent for the first axis and is slightly less for the second axis (61 per cent).

The nine-segment version replicates the major findings from the four-segment solution. It is not just travel motives, benefits sought or travel activities which arrive in symptomatic combinations. The same is true for trip satisfaction if this variable is conceived as a multidimensional construct. Many more efforts are required to disentangle the causal relationships between satisfaction and repeat visit to a tourist city. There is no simple rule and more variables will have to be included; purpose of trip, volition or dependence on other members in the travel party, habitual behaviour and variety-seeking, to name but a few, may interfere in the formation of a behavioural intention. Given the wide range of differences in the concoction of fulfilled and/or disappointed expectations, the recommendation is to

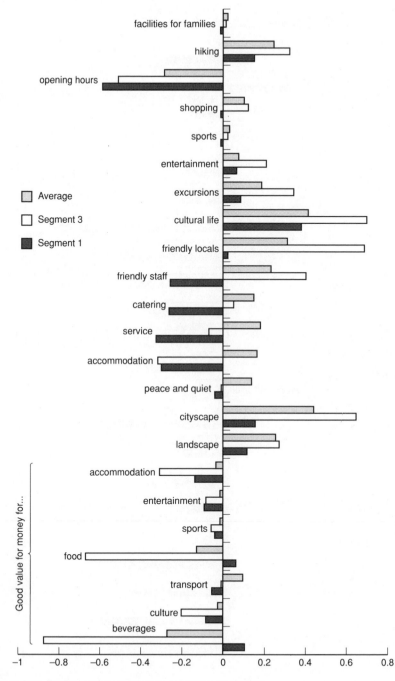

Figure 3.11 Profiles of the satisfaction segments #1 and #3

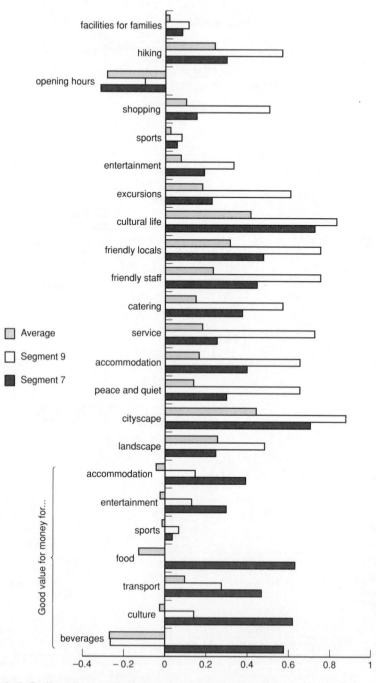

Figure 3.12 Profiles of the satisfaction segments #7 and #9

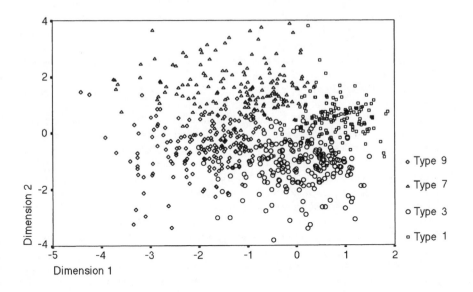

Figure 3.13 Satisfaction segments #1, #3, #7 and #9 in PRINCALS space

experiment with satisfaction types when tailoring a quality monitoring instrument. The tourist segments with their specific mixture of expectations and performance perceptions reflect a more realistic picture of guest satisfaction than a fully aggregated profile of satisfaction items. The puzzling segment structures necessitate further analyses, stimulate creativity and encourage the manager to think and act strategically.

Note

[1] The interested reader with access to the Internet may download a free copy of SOMnia 1.4.1 (DOS, Windows or Windows95 version) from the World Wide Web page http://www.wu-wien.ac.at/inst/tourism/software/of the Institute for Tourism and Leisure Studies of the Vienna University of Economics.

References

Ambrosi, K. (1978) Klassifikation und Identifikation. In O. Opitz (ed.) *Numerische Taxonomie in der Marktforschung*. Munich: Vahlen, 79–109.

Brookes, R. (1995) Customer satisfaction research. In R. Brookes (ed.) *Customer Satisfaction Research*. Amsterdam: ESOMAR, 7–18.

Buttle, F.A. (1995) What future for SERVQUAL? In *24th EMAC Conference Proceedings* vol. I. Cergy-Pontoise Cedex: ESSEC, 211–30.

Caudill, M. (1993a) *Neural Networks Primer*, 3rd edn. San Francisco: Miller Freeman, Inc.

Caudill, M. (1993b) A little knowledge is a dangerous thing. *AI Expert* **8**, 16–22.

Cronin Jr, J.J. and Taylor, S.A. (1992) Measuring service quality: a reexamination and extension. *Journal of Marketing* **56**, 55–68.

Cronin Jr, J.J. and Taylor, S.A. (1994) SERVPERF versus SERVQUAL: reconciling performance-based and perceptions-minus-expectations measurement of service quality. *Journal of Marketing* **58**, 125–31.

Fick, G.R. and Brent Ritchie, J.R. (1991) Measuring service quality in the travel and tourism industry. *Journal of Travel Research* **29**, 2–9.

Formann, A.K., Mazanec, J. and Oberhauser, O.C. (1979) *Numerische Klassifikationsprobleme in 'großen' Stichproben der demoskopischen Marktforschung: Ein empirischer Methodenvergleich von Latent Class- und Cluster-Analyse.* Arbeitspapiere der absatzwirtschaftlichen Institute der WU Wien, Vienna: Orac.

Freeman, J.A. and Skapura, D.M. (1991) *Neural Networks, Algorithms, Applications, and Programming Techniques.* Reading: Addison-Wesley.

Gallant, St. I. (1993) *Neural Network Learning and Expert Systems.* Cambridge, MA: MIT Press.

Gifi, A. (1985) *PRINCALS.* Leiden: University of Leiden, Department of Data Theory.

Gummeson, E. (1993) *Quality Management in Service Organizations.* Research report 1. New York: International Service Quality Association.

Hauser, J.A., Simester, D.I. and Wernerfelt, B. (1994) Customer satisfaction incentives. *Marketing Science* **13**, 327–50.

Haykin, S. (1994) *Neural Networks, A Comprehensive Foundation.* New York: Macmillan.

Hertz, J., Krogh, A. and Palmer, R.G. (1991) *Introduction to the Theory of Neural Computation.* Reading, MA: Addison-Wesley.

Heskett, J.W., Sasser, E.W. and Hart, C.W.L. (1990) *Service Breakthroughs.* New York: Free Press.

Howard, J.A. and Sheth, J.N. (1969) *The Theory of Buyer Behavior.* New York: Wiley.

Johnson, M.D., Anderson, E.W. and Fornell, C. (1995) Rational and adaptive performance expectations in a customer satisfaction framework. *Journal of Consumer Research* **21**, 695–707.

Kaspar, C. (1990) *Einführung in das touristische Management.* Berne: Haupt.

Kaspar, C. (1991) *Die Tourismuslehre im Grundriss,* 4th edn. Berne: Haupt.

Kohonen, T. (1982) Self-organized formation of topologically correct feature maps. *Biological Cybernetics* **43**, 59–69. Reprinted in J.A. Andersen and E. Rosenfeld (eds) (1988) *Neurocomputing: Foundations of Research.* Cambridge MA: MIT Press, 511–21.

Kohonen, T. (1984, 3rd edn 1989) *Self-Organization and Associative Memory.* New York: Springer.

Kohonen, T. (1990) The self-organizing map. *Proceedings of the IEEE* **78**, 1464–80. Reprinted in P. Mehra and B.W. Wah (eds) (1992) *Artificial Neural Networks: Concepts and Theory.* Los Alamitos: IEEE Computer Society Press, 359–75.

Lewis, B.R. (1995) Measuring customer expectation and satisfaction. In R. Brookes (ed.) *Customer Satisfaction Research.* Amsterdam: ESOMAR, 57–76.

Martin, D.W. (1995) An importance/performance analysis of service providers' perception of quality service in the hotel industry. *Journal of Hospitality and Leisure Marketing* **3**, pp. 5–17.

Mazanec, J.A. (1994a) Segmenting travel markets. In R. Teare, J.A. Mazanec, S.

Crawford-Welch and St. Calver, *Marketing in Hospitality and Tourism, A Consumer Focus*. London: Cassell, 97–164.

Mazanec, J. (1994b) Image measurement with self-organizing maps: a tentative application to Austrian tour operators. *Tourist Review* no. 3, 9–18.

Mazanec, J. (1995a) *Gästebefragung Österreich, Österreich-Bericht*. Vienna: Österreichische Gesellschaft für Angewandte Fremdenverkehrswissenschaft.

Mazanec, J.A. (1995b) Positioning analysis with self-organizing maps, an exploratory study on luxury hotels. *Cornell Hotel & Restaurant Administration Quarterly, Research Forum* **36**, 1–16.

Mazanec, J. (1996) Guest satisfaction tracking: eine Analyse am Beispiel der Sommerurlauber in Österreich. In G. Fischer and Ch. Laesser (eds) *Theorie und Praxis der Tourismus- und Verkehrswirtschaft im Wertewandel*. Berne: Haupt, 97–115.

Murray, K.B. and Schlacter, J.L. (1995) Using consumer perceptions to operationalize the service construct: exploratory research in theory extension and validation. *Psychology and Marketing* **12**, 501–30.

O'Connor, P.J. and Sullivan, G.L. (1995) Market segmentation: a comparison of benefits/attributes desired and brand preferences. *Psychology and Marketing* **12**, 613–35.

Ostrowski, P.L., O'Brien, T.V. and Gordon, G.L. (1994) Determinants of service quality in the commercial airline industry: differences between business and leisure travelers. *Journal of Travel & Tourism Marketing* **3**, 19–47.

Pao, Y.-H. (1989) *Adaptive Pattern Recognition and Neural Networks*. Reading, MA: Addison-Wesley.

Parasuraman, A., Zeithaml, V.A. and Berry, L.L. (1985) A conceptual model of service quality and its implications for future research. *Journal of Marketing* **49**, 41–50.

Parasuraman, A., Zeithaml, V.A. and Berry, L.L. (1988) SERVQUAL: a multiple item scale for measuring consumer perceptions of service quality. *Journal of Retailing* **64**, 12–40.

Patton, M., Stevens, P. and Knutson, B.J. (1994) Internationalizing LODGSERV as a measurement tool: a pilot study. *Journal of Hospitality and Leisure Marketing* **2**, 39–55.

Richard, M.D. and Sundaram, D.S. (1994) A model of lodging repeat choice intentions. *Annals of Tourism Research* **21**, 745–55.

Ritter, H., Martinetz, Th. and Schulten, K. (1992) *Neural Computation and Self-Organizing Maps, An Introduction*. Reading, MA: Addison-Wesley.

Rohwer, R., Wynne-Jones, M. and Wysotzki, F. (1994) Neural networks. In D. Michie, D.J. Spiegelhalter and C.C. Taylor (eds) *Machine Learning, Neural and Statistical Classification*. New York: Ellis Horwood, 84–106.

Ryan, Ch. (1995) *Researching Tourist Satisfaction: Issues, Concepts, Problems*. London: Routledge.

Sammon Jr, J.W. (1969) A non-linear mapping for data structure analysis. *IEEE Transactions on Computers* **C-18**, 401–9.

Späth, H. (1975) *Cluster-Analyse-Algorithmen zur Objektklassifizierung und Datenreduktion*. Munich, Vienna: Oldenbourg.

Steinhausen, D. and Steinhausen, J. (1977) Cluster-Analyse als Instrument der Zielgruppendefinition in der Marktforschung. In H. Späth (ed.) *Fallstudien Cluster-Analyse*. Munich, Vienna: Oldenbourg, 9–36.

Vienna Hilton (1992) G.S.T.S. – Guest satisfaction tracking system. *Insider Newsletter* August, 1–2.

Weiermair, K. (1994) Quality management in tourism: lessons from the service industries? In *Tourismus-Forschung: Erfolge, Fehlschläge und ungelöste Probleme.* Proceedings of the 44th AIEST Conference, St Gall: AIEST, 93–113.

Witt, Chr.A. (1995) Total quality management. In St.F. Witt and L. Moutinho (eds) *Tourism Marketing and Management Handbook* student edn. London: Prentice Hall, 229–42.

Witt, Chr.A. and Muhlemann, A.P. (1994) The implementation of total quality management in tourism: some guidelines. *Tourism Management* **15**, 416–24.

Zeithaml, V.A., Berry, L.L. and Parasuraman, A. (1988) Communication and control processes in the delivery of service quality. *Journal of Marketing* **52**, 35–48.

3.2

Perceptual mapping and positioning of tourist cities

Klaus Grabler

Introduction

Beside segmentation, positioning is one of the classic tasks of marketing management. Both the academic world and the practitioners are increasingly interested in these two managerial issues. Therefore a vast number of application studies and various techniques for positioning analysis exists in the marketing literature. Their practical usefulness is beyond doubt. Every firm has to check the positions of its products and services regularly. However, in tourism positioning is not that common. The more sophisticated techniques of positioning developed in marketing science have not yet spread into the tourist industry. Today, most applications in tourism understand positioning as simply describing strengths and weaknesses.

In this section, positioning is conceived as the visualization of consumers' perceptions. Hence, perceptual mapping is used to visualize the strengths and weaknesses of a product or service by condensing the redundant information into one pictorial representation. The core idea of positioning is the comparison of one product with its competitors. It portrays the basic cognitive dimensions the consumers use to evaluate the products and the relative positions of the products with respect to these dimensions. Normally, a position far away from the competitors is regarded as unique. Of course, positioning requires some definition of competitors in advance because one has to submit several competing offerings to the respondents. For destinations, positioning has recently gained attention (Calantone *et al.*, 1989; Gartner, 1989). However, there is no application of positioning analysis for urban tourism. This is partly due to the multifaceted character of urban tourism and the difficulties in defining the relevant competitors.

An important difference exists between perceptual and preference mapping (see Myers and Tauber, 1977, pp. 18ff.). This difference coincides with the decision process models in the behavioural sciences. In the psychological chain from the real product to product choice (the actual process of buying), behavioural scientists have found several constructs that explain some part of the choice process. In these models the perception of a product is one of the earliest steps in the process that determines the remaining products for further evaluation. It is one of the basic parts of the decision process and therefore a first hint about the success or failure of products. But it is also possible to analyse product positions in later stages. So preference mapping goes one step further and analyses positions resulting from the stated preferences of persons. Therefore, it relates closer to the final choice of a product. The following study employs perceptual mapping for six different European cities and combines this information with the preferences of the respondents. The underlying hypothesis is that the more favourable the perceptions of a particular destination, the higher the preferences for this city. This was shown to be valid for regions (Goodrich, 1978).

The classical methods used for positioning are factor and discriminant analysis, and multidimensional scaling. Another technique that is appropriate for nominal data is correspondence analysis, which belongs to the class of homogeneity analysis techniques (see Calantone *et al.*, 1989, for an application). All these techniques have advantages and disadvantages and produce perceptual and preference spaces with different meanings (Myers, 1992). There is no technique that has proved superior for all purposes. The application of a specific technique depends heavily on the data structure and the managerial aim of the exercise. The techniques often result in similar solutions. It has been shown that those generated by factor analysis are most easy to interpret (Hauser and Koppelman, 1979). With the exception of multidimensional scaling all techniques define the spaces in terms of attribute ratings by a sample of respondents.

Explanatory models in positioning analysis

Perceptual mapping requires a prior decision about the explanatory model used. Although the literature often refers to the construct 'image' it is sometimes not clear what is meant by this term. Attitude, perceived risk, image, motives and opinions are used interchangeably under the name of image measurement. The decision to use a particular concept depends on the product, the consumers and the consumption situation.

This study relies on the attitude model. It tries to detect perceptual dimensions that are controlling or are at least instrumental in the decision process. As the respondents are persons planning a city trip in the next two years a reasonable involvement should guarantee a cognitive evaluation of the cities. The attitude model corresponds closely with the construct of (the cognitive part of the) destination image. Hence it is multidimensional (Gartner, 1989) and a supposed major factor in choice decision-making (Um, 1993; Um and Crompton, 1990).

Main determinants for the perception of cities are the product familiarity (knowledge) and the origin of the respondent. This is a further indicator of product knowledge and a more general indicator of the awareness, but it includes information of different perceptions due to national differences. It is known that country or regional images may differ according to the geographical distance of the respondents. Other main variables influencing the perception of different cities are consumer characteristics such as previous travel experience, demographics or lifestyle (Manrai and Manrai, 1993). The perceptions of the cities are expected to influence subsequently the preferences, the intentions to visit a particular city and finally the decision to visit a city. Therefore, various perceptual maps are presented below for segments with differing preference structures.

Attitude positioning of six European tourist cities

The attitude model seems to fit the purpose here. Attitudes are denotative attributes that are associated more or less with a particular urban destination. Attitudes are known to be stable over time and predictors of the final choice. In this study there are no connotative image items used. Vienna, Prague, Budapest, Barcelona, Paris and Venice were chosen as a subset of supposed European competitors (see Grabler *et al.*, 1996). After a pre-test with German visitors in Vienna, twelve attributes were used as verbal stimuli. The total sample of the final study consisted of 282 respondents with Germans and British equally represented. The respondents were asked to indicate on a six-point Likert scale how much each city offers of these benefits (see Figure 3.14). However, the product knowledge was not used to filter the perceptions here. All potential city tourists were expected to evaluate all six cities, no matter now well they knew them. Hence one may argue that actually the attribute-based image (Echtner and Ritchie, 1993) of these cities is analysed in this study. The present study is a very classical kind of positioning study as it assumes that all attributes are relevant to all consumers. An alternative model is based on idiosyncratic attribute sets (Steenkamp *et al.*, 1994) or analyses the individual evoked sets of the consumers (Katahira, 1990).

A descriptive presentation of the importance of the criteria is a good starting point for the attitude maps. For the Germans the ambience of the city is the most important factor when going on a city trip, followed by the attractiveness of the price levels (see Figure 3.15). Less important are the shopping and the entertainment facilities. The needs of the British respondents are similar though not congruent. Their most important factor

Can you please indicate how much you think each city offers of the benefits listed below. Use a scale from 1 to 6, where 1 offers nothing at all and 6 very much.
It does not matter if you have not visited the cities yet or that you do not know them very well. What counts is your impression of them.
Please fill in every space!

	Vienna	Prague	Budapest	Barcelona	Paris	Venice
1. Quality and type of accommodation						
2. Entertainment facilities						
3. Ambience of the city						
4. Cultural resources						
5. Attractiveness of price levels						
6. Accessibility of tourist amenities						
7. Accessibility of the city						
8. Location of the city						
9. Originality of the city						
10. Welcoming attitude of the local population						
11. Shopping facilities						
12. Quality of food and beverages						

Figure 3.14 Attitude questionnaire used for positioning of six European city destinations

is the quality of food and beverages, followed by the ambience and the cultural resources. The shopping and entertainment facilities are least important for the British as well.

Principal components analysis of stacked data

The positioning task consists of a data reduction of a data cube (persons×products×attributes). Applications that handle three-dimensional data as such are rare (see the three-mode factor analysis of cross elasticities of Cooper, 1988, for an exception). There are two common ways of analysing such data. Frequently, the average ratings over the respondents are correlated and factors are analysed. This, however, results in an information loss of the individual differences and neglects the possibility to segment the market. Hence another way to analyse these data is to stack them, thereby receiving an elongated two-dimensional matrix. The persons and cities (objects) are stacked in order to get a matrix of persons×objects in the rows and of attributes in the columns. In the actual study this signifies a 282×6

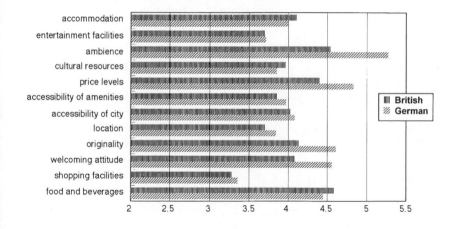

Figure 3.15 Mean importance of attributes when going on a city trip

rows and twelve attributes matrix. This modified data matrix is then analysed with a conventional principal components analysis.

Although the list of attributes was reduced after the pre-test the data are highly appropriate for principal component analysis. The eigenvalues and the scree test clearly suggest a three-factor solution explaining 62.8 per cent of the variance. The dominant first factor contains the basic facets of a city destination (Table 3.4). It therefore is called touristic infrastructure and represents the core of the urban tourism perceptions. The second factor, called image appeal, is composed of some 'soft' attributes such as the originality and the ambience of the city. The cultural resources, though not uniquely loading high, correlate significantly with this factor. The third dimension is characterized by the opposition of real friendliness versus a 'pure money-making mentality'. Attractive price levels correlate significantly with a welcoming attitude of the local population.

Perceptual mapping

Figure 3.16 shows a perceptual map of the six cities analysed. The names underlined are the average city positions of the German respondents. The others represent the average positions of the British. There are distinctly different positions for these two nations for three out of the six cities: Vienna, Prague and Budapest. This difference is probably due to the product knowledge of the Germans because of geographical nearness. The difference is especially big for the first dimension, i.e. the touristic infrastructure. All three cities are judged significantly better by the German market. Paris, Venice and Barcelona, however, have a rather stable image in

Table 3.4 Rotated factor loadings for the stacked principal component analysis

Attribute	Factor 1 (44%) touristic infrastructure	Factor 2 (10.6%) image appeal	Factor 3 (8.2%) price and attitude
Shopping facilities	0.77		
Entertainment facilities	0.73		
Accessibility of the city	0.69		
Accommodation	0.69		
Accessibility of tourist amenities	0.68		
Food and beverage	0.65		
Originality		0.84	
Ambience		0.78	
Cultural resources	0.42	0.68	
Location		0.57	
Attractive price levels			0.89
Welcoming attitude			0.73

Note: Only factor loadings of 0.40 and above reported.

these two markets. A significantly better evaluation of the Germans can be detected for the third dimension as well. Only the second factor appears to be insensitive to the country of origin. The image component therefore remains the same for different geographical distance of the respondents; the other more attitudinal components differ significantly.

In general, Vienna, Paris and Barcelona are assumed to keep a high profile of touristic infrastructure. The image appeal, however, is highest for Paris and Venice. Prague follows on this dimension. For Barcelona an image deficit is obvious while reaching acceptable values on the other dimensions. A comparative advantage for Budapest and Prague is the price – friendliness relationship. It is significantly better for these two cities. Paris has a tremendous image problem concerning this attitude facet.

Comparing cities' position on the three dimensions

A closer look at the average city positions for the total sample is essential here. The corresponding perceptual map is not presented. Instead, the ANOVA results of the factor scores for the six cities are shown. Referring to dimension one, three homogeneous disjunctive subgroups can be identified (ordered from best to worst): Paris and Vienna; Barcelona and Venice; and Prague and Budapest. For the image appeal, four such subsets can be detected: Venice, Paris and Prague; Paris, Prague and Vienna; Prague, Vienna and Budapest; and finally, Vienna, Budapest and Barcelona. The price and attitude factor distinguishes again between four subgroups: Prague and Budapest; Barcelona; Vienna and Venice; and finally, Venice and Paris. These rankings of the cities along the different perceptional criteria clearly demonstrate the strengths and weaknesses of the city destinations in

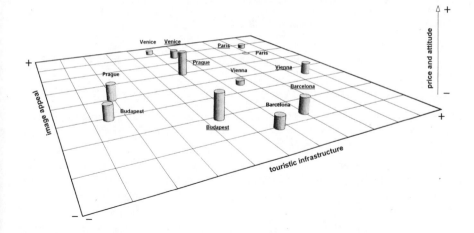

Figure 3.16 Perceptual map of six tourist cities for German and British travellers

the eyes of the consumers.

Positioning without segmenting may cause wrong conclusions. Positions aggregated over a (heterogeneous) sample cannot lead to a meaningful interpretation. Average positions may be a pure artefact of the aggregational procedure. One must always pay attention to the group-specific differences in the sample. This can be done by building a priori segments that are known to influence the perception, by constructing a posteriori segments or by simultaneous positioning and segmentation. The last idea appears in the literature from time to time, but no approach has yet reached attention and acceptance. One of the most recent ideas explores neurocomputing techniques for this purpose (demonstrated and discussed in Mazanec, 1995).

Attitude maps for preference segments

The stacked principal component analysis yielded results for both German and British respondents. As two separate analyses resulted in the same factors, the procedure of running just one analysis and subsequently taking subsamples appears justified. Principally, one could average the factor scores for any subgroup. It is a managerial problem to decide which individuals to aggregate in order to derive homogeneous segments.

The PRINCOMP analysis so far contained no information about the evaluation of the city positions. Nevertheless, attitudes are known to be linked to preferences, even in an early stage of the decision process (Um and Crompton, 1992). The individual impressions (evaluations) of each attribute are assumed to be integrated by the individuals to form preferences. Therefore, a finer segmentation step is done with respect to the

Table 3.5 Final cluster centres for short trip destination preference rankings

Cluster	Vienna	Budapest	Prague	Barcelona	Paris	Venice
1 (67)	2.4	2.7	2.7	5	3.4	4.7
2 (91)	2.5	5.2	5.3	3.3	2.3	2.4
3 (50)	5	3.9	3.1	1.9	3.3	3.8
4 (41)	4.3	4.2	3.5	5.3	1.5	2.2

city preferences of the respondents. Unidimensional preferences were collected through a ranking of the cities as short trip destinations. This ranking is used for constructing a posteriori segments that are homogeneous in terms of their city preferences. A four-cluster solution appeared to be most useful and easy to interpret (Table 3.5).

It is not the purpose here to describe exactly the segments in terms of demographic profiles. The mere interpretation of the active variables used for clustering may suffice as the aim of the exercise is the construction of perceptual maps for different preference segments. The biggest cluster, cluster two, can be called 'the classical city tourist'. The preference profile reveals a disliking of Budapest and Prague and evident affection for Paris, Venice and Vienna. Cluster one in contrast prefers Budapest and Prague while holding Vienna as favourite for a short trip. This segment thus can be called 'the Middle European enthusiast'. A complete different preference structure can be detected for cluster three. Barcelona is the clear favourite and Vienna the most unattractive city destination for this segment. The smallest cluster, cluster four, prefers Paris, followed by Venice, and is less attracted by Barcelona, Vienna and Budapest.

Before looking at different city perceptions of these segments an examination of their importance ratings is essential. Figure 3.17 contains the different importance ratings for the four segments. The different importance ratings partly explain the preferences of the four segments. The 'Middle European enthusiasts' (cluster 1) highly stress the ambience and the location of the city. The importance of the quality of accommodation and food and beverages is significantly lower for this segment. In contrast to the other segments the 'classical city tourists' (cluster 2) attach higher importance to most of the attributes. Only the ambience and the cultural resources appear to be of less significance. They strongly appreciate the personal comfort when making a city trip. The reader may draw his own conclusions for the third and fourth clusters.

An inspection of separate perceptual maps for these four segments should reveal positions that determine the preferences. For the sake of convenient interpretation the country of origin is ignored and only the preference cluster solution is considered. Figure 3.18 shows the perceptual map for cluster one, the 'Middle European enthusiasts'. Remember that Vienna, Prague and Budapest are the most preferred cities in this segment. The map appears very similar to the general one with Prague and Budapest

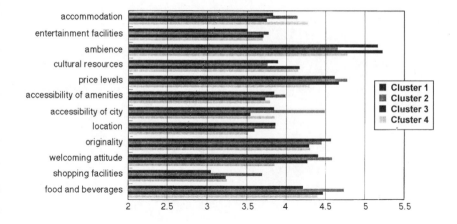

Figure 3.17 Mean importance of attributes for the four preference clusters

launching a better image appeal in this segment. The image appeal together with the low price levels are obviously the dominant criteria for the preference formation. Vienna, on the other hand, convinces with its solid infrastructure and an acceptable price/friendliness mix. There is no single dimension that influences the preferences, it rather appears that each city can draw advantages from its actual situation. For this segment a clear lower limit for the 'money-making' component and for the image appeal apparently emerges.

All segment maps are very similar with particular regard to the touristic infrastructure component that seems to be very homogeneously perceived. The 'classical city tourist' dislikes Prague and Budapest. This may be due to the less appealing image for this segment (see Figure 3.19). The price/attitude factor of these two cities is an advantage as it is for all segments. However, it is not relevant for the preferences of this segment. In fact this factor may well influence the actual behaviour without being relevant for the preferences. The image component is the main reason for the formulation of preferences here. A certain level of fulfilling basic touristic needs appears to be necessary, too.

The preferences of cluster three cannot be explained by its attitude perceptions (Figure 3.20). Barcelona as most preferred and Vienna as less liked city are located in the same corner. The only difference is the somewhat better price/friendliness relation. It does not seem enough for explaining the city preferences. It may be variety seeking or curiosity that pushes Barcelona as top preferred city in this segment. One may argue that this segment is already familiar with Vienna and seeks for another city experience. More apparent is the preference structure of cluster four (Figure 3.21).

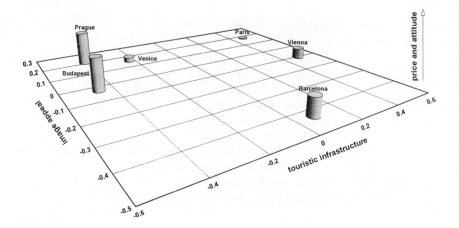

Figure 3.18 Perceptual map for the 'Middle European Enthusiasts'

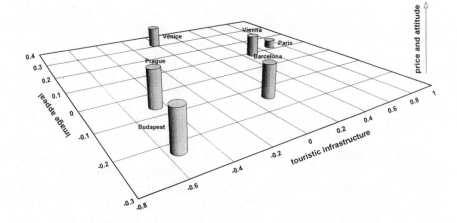

Figure 3.19 Perceptual map for the 'Classical City Tourist'

The preference rankings coincide perfectly with the positions along the image dimension.

Preference relevance of the perceptual dimensions

Summarizing the segment results one may conclude that the three dimensions influence the preference formulation with different intensity. The main explanation lies in the image appeal of the cities, whereas the touristic infrastructure appears to be more or less irrelevant for the city

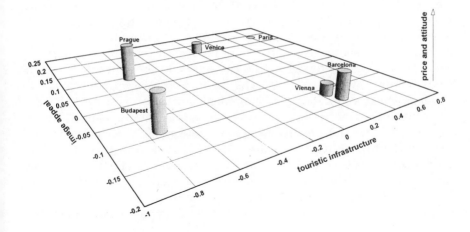

Figure 3.20 Perceptual map for the 'Barcelona Likers'

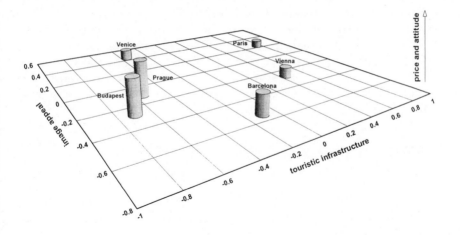

Figure 3.21 Perceptual map for the 'Middle European Dislikers'

preferences. At least it can be neutralized by the third dimension, the price/friendliness relation. The image appeal of a city seems to be the main pull factor for potential city tourists. Both price/friendliness and infrastructure can be regarded as 'hygiene factors' that must not drop below a certain limit. However, they do not heavily influence the liking of a city. Nevertheless, they strongly determine the perception of the cities. In general the importance ratings determine the preferences for particular cities more strongly than the perceptional ratings. The perceptions of the cities are relatively homogeneous. This has clear implications for the city marketing. Individual segments do not perceive the cities significantly differently. The differences in the preferences can be attributed to the needs and values of the segments. This means that the marketing manager has primarily to detect those segments for which the city offers the attributes which fit the needs of the consumers. This calls for a thorough refinement of the segmentation procedures applied in marketing urban tourism destinations.

It is the duty of the managers to compare the current destination image to the marketed place image. Preferences are more strongly determined by the needs but unintended positions may be causing failure, too. This comparison cannot be drawn in this study, as material about the intended image is not available. A study about the marketing image of the cities analysed following the recent work of Bramwell and Rawding (1996) is an area for future research to evaluate the effectiveness of the marketing strategies.

Of course, one must be aware of the set of attributes being relatively complete. The pre-test included 30 variables which were reduced to the manageable set of twelve for the actual study. Therefore it seems that the most important dimensions were covered. The high correlations of all attributes describing the touristic offer of the cities makes a finer differentiation seem unplausible. It may be a halo effect of the city's image that determines the ratings on specific attributes. It has be shown that this phenomenon actually exists in country evaluations, especially when consumers have limited familiarity with the destinations (Shimp *et al.*, 1993).

References

Bramwell, B. and Rawding, L. (1996) Tourism marketing images of industrial cities. *Annals of Tourism Research* **23**, 201–21.

Calantone, R.J., di Benedetto, I., Hakam, A. and Bojanic, B.C. (1989) Multiple multinational tourism positioning using correspondence analysis. *Journal of Travel Research* **28**, 25–32.

Cooper, L.G. (1988) Competitive maps: the structure underlying asymmetric cross elasticities. *Marketing Science* **34**, 707–23.

Echtner, Ch.M. and Ritchie, J.R.B. (1993) The measurement of destination image: an empirical assessment. *Journal of Travel Research* **31**, 3–13.

Gartner, W.C. (1989) Tourism image: attribute measurement of state tourism products using multidimensional scaling techniques. *Journal of Travel Research* **28**, 16–20.

Goodrich, J.N. (1978) The relationship between preferences for and perceptions of vacation destinations: application of a choice model. *Journal of Travel Research* **17**, 8–13.

Grabler, K., Mazanec, J. and Wöber, K. (1996) Strategic marketing for urban tourism: analysing competition among European tourist cities. In Ch.M. Law (ed.) *Tourism in Major Cities*. London: International Thompson Business Press, 23–51.

Hauser, J.R. and Koppelman, F.S. (1979) Alternative perceptual mapping techniques: relative accuracy and usefulness. *Journal of Marketing Research* **26**, 495–506.

Katahira, H. (1990) Perceptual mapping using ordered logit analysis. *Marketing Science* **9**, 1–17.

Manrai, L.A. and Manrai, A.K. (1993) Positioning European countries as brands in a perceptual map: an empirical study of determinants of consumer perceptions and preferences. *Journal of Euromarketing* **2**, 101–29.

Mazanec, J.A. (1995) Positioning analysis with self-organizing maps. An exploratory study on luxury hotels. *Cornell Hotel and Restaurant Administration Quarterly* **36**, 80–95.

Myers, J.H. (1992) Positioning products/services in attitude space. *Marketing Research, A Magazine of Management & Applications* **4**, 46–51.

Myers, J.H. and Tauber, E.M. (1977) *Market Structure Analysis*. Chicago: American Marketing Association.

Shimp, T.A., Samiee, S. and Madden, T.J. (1993) Countries and their products: a cognitive structure perspective. *Journal of the Academy of Marketing Science* **21**, 323–30.

Steenkamp, J.-B.E.M., Van Trijp, H.C.M. and Ten Berge, J.M.F. (1994) Perceptual mapping based on idiosyncratic sets of attributes. *Journal of Marketing Research* **31**, 15–27.

Um, S. (1993) Pleasure travel destination choice. In M. Khan, M. Olsen and T. Var (eds) *VNR's Encyclopedia of Hospitality and Tourism*. New York: Van Nostrand Reinhold, 811–21.

Um, S. and Crompton, J.L. (1990) Attitude determinants in tourism destination choice. *Annals of Tourism Research* **17**, 432–48.

Um, S. and Crompton, J.L. (1992) The roles of perceived inhibitors and facilitators in pleasure travel destination decisions. *Journal of Travel Research* **30**, 18–25.

3.3

Segmenting city tourists into vacation styles

Josef A. Mazanec

Tourist types as a posteriori market segments

The attempt to detect different 'vacation styles' in a population of city tourists corresponds with the concept of 'a posteriori market segmentation'. In principle, a posteriori segmentation rests on the assumption that subgroups in a consumer population may be homogeneous in terms of motives, attitudes and/or activities. This mental and behavioural homogeneity is likely to make them react to product offerings and promotional efforts in a similar manner. The earliest approach to master such a market situation is known as 'benefit segmentation', introduced by Russel Haley (1968). His argument was that consumer groups with a markedly different pattern of benefits sought should be considered to be 'natural' segments in the market. From a behavioural science point of view the notion of 'benefit' relates to the more general concept of 'attitude'. Benefits desired or expected are attitudes towards particular consumption goals (e.g. the Rosenberg (1967) model of attitude measurement). For example, a city traveller who seeks 'fun and entertainment' when choosing an urban destination attaches high salience to the quality of entertainment facilities. He holds a strong and favourable attitude towards this attribute of a destination which may become a dominant item in his overall judgement of a city trip package.

A 'vacation style' is a temporary lifestyle into which a tourist escapes from his/her everyday surroundings. It includes observable and unobservable characteristics of the tourist. A vacation style represents a cognitive and emotional state of mind as well as the accompanying behaviour. A posteriori segmentation by means of vacation styles considers more than just one type of behavioural variable. It also aims at uncovering the underlying 'motives'. This is not an easy task to solve in a standard mass survey. Motives are conceived as a state of arousal with no distinct directional effect towards a particular means of satisfaction (cf. questionnaire items such as 'to change pace', 'to realize one's creativity'). A closer examination of the commercial travel surveys reveals that many of the questions pretending to measure motives actually ask for the evaluation of some attributes of a tourist product. This, however, is the purpose of attitudinal rather than motivational items; while the motives are responsible for the arousal of behaviour, attitudes govern its direction and orientation (Kroeber-Riel, 1992). Consumers navigate through the world of products and services by constantly adjusting their personal hierarchy of attitudes. Satisfaction is an example of a transitory stage of an attitude following a particular consumption experience. Another example for a more abstract and slowly changing level of attitudes is 'value systems' (Kamakura and Novak, 1992) which have attracted attention in travel segmentation theory and practice more recently. Motivational and attitudinal variables related to various domains of everyday life are combined to yield lifestyle types. If 'everyday life' gets replaced by 'leisure travel' the output is called 'vacation styles'.

Travel and vacation 'activities' are also useful raw material for constructing a posteriori segments (Hsieh *et al.*, 1992). Questions about the tourist's activities are customary in travel or guest surveys. The concept of 'tourist roles' as suggested by Yiannakis and Gibson (1992) is also closely linked to travel activities. Tourist activities easily lend themselves for segmentation purposes. The objective is to overcome the trivial single-item classification (sightseeing tourist, culture-seeker, museum visitor) and to replace it with a multivariate activity pattern. In contemporary activity segmentation it is the 'activity bundle' which characterizes an activity segment. In a vacation style the activities are also regarded to come up in symptomatic combinations.

The concept of a posteriori segmentation via vacation styles should be intriguing to tourism managers. It draws a more 'real-life' picture of their customers, who are more than just 'cases' of a certain age in a particular income bracket and with more or less travel experience. The vacation type becomes a more complete entity by exhibiting more 'human-like' contours. Vacation styles, like lifestyles, are more stimulating to the creative designers of trip packages or media advertisements. The manager interested in vacation and traveller typologies needs an intuitive understanding of cluster analysis. The reader may remember what was previously stated about market segmentation strategies. It is not the aim to detect the 'true' and 'one and only' segment structure in the market. But it may pay off to elaborate a new and different typology which inspires the specialization strategy required to operate – albeit temporarily – in a 'quasi-monopoly'.

The forthcoming application example utilizes the guest database of leisure travellers to Vienna and the major Austrian provincial cities during summer 1994. The analytical tools do not get an in-depth treatment in this demonstration study. The reader interested in a more rigorous outline of the clustering procedures used is referred to the Appendix.

Reconstructing the vacation styles for city tourists

The local tourism managers in the city tourist boards of Vienna, Graz, Linz, Salzburg, Innsbruck or Klagenfurt – to name the major urban destinations in Austria – want to evaluate the current 'guest mix' in terms of vacation styles. Knowing these results they can figure out their cities' strengths and weaknesses and may then decide on the type of visitors they should continue to attract. A motivational segmentation approach is chosen to explore the 'driving forces' underlying the guest expectations. If the interrelationships among the travel motives turn out to be symptomatically group-specific a second analytical step will be taken. A 'motive segment' lacks commercial value unless it manifests itself to the outside world. Various personal descriptors, therefore, will have to be examined. The travel activities are paramount for this subsequent processing step. A number of identifiable and significantly differentiated subgroups among the city travellers will warrant the term 'vacation styles'. Looking into these styles, the managers may discover to what degree their respective destination with its local tourist services matches each of the motivational/behavioural profiles.

The database of the Austrian National Guest Survey (summer 1994) contains a sufficiently large number of approximately 2000 cases who declare themselves to be 'city tourists'. This survey measures the travel motives with an instrument developed by the Europäisches Tourismus Institut GmbH at the University of Trier, Germany. The motives are operationalized by means of four-point scale ratings for personal statements on travel-related desires, likings and consumption goals. The instrument applies to all tourists in the summer season. The visitors to Vienna were not exposed to the statements which are clearly irrelevant for 'exclusive' city tourists ('water and sun', 'unspoilt nature and natural landscape'). The respondent's reactions are prompted by the phrase: 'What is important to you during your present holiday? Please tell me for every one of the following statements, if it applies to you totally, mostly, a bit, or not at all.' There are 23 statements. The abbreviations which will later be used in the figures and tables are added in parentheses:

- When I am on holiday I want to rest and relax (relax).
- On holiday I am looking for comfort and want to be spoilt (comfort).
- On holiday I want to exert myself physically and I play sports (sports).
- This holiday means excitement, a challenge and special experiences for me (excite).

- On holiday I want to realize my creativity (creative).
- When choosing a holiday destination I put much emphasis on cultural offers and sights (culture).
- On holiday I am looking for a variety of fun and entertainment (fun).
- On this holiday good company and getting to know people is important to me (people).
- When choosing a holiday destination I pay attention to unspoilt nature and natural landscape (nature).
- I use my holiday for the health and beauty of my body (body).
- I go on holiday for a change to my usual surroundings (change).
- On this holiday I put much emphasis on free-and-easy-going (easy).
- I like to spend my holidays where there are sufficient entertainment facilities (entertain).
- On holiday a sensual atmosphere plays a major role for me (atmosphere).
- When choosing a holiday destination I put much emphasis on a romantic and nostalgic atmosphere (romantic).
- On holiday I am interested in the lifestyle of the local people (locals).
- The special thing about my holiday is an intense experience of water and sun (sun).
- On holiday I look for cosiness and a familiar atmosphere (cosy).
- On holiday it is important that everything is organized and I do not have to care about anything (organized).
- When choosing a holiday destination it is important to me that there are offers and care for the children (children).
- On holiday the efforts to maintain unspoilt surroundings play a major role for me (surround).
- When choosing a holiday destination it is important to me that I can feel safe (safe).
- On holiday good food and beverages are important to me (f&b).

One has to admit that some of these statements are fairly specific but the majority may be considered as indicative of abstract travel motives. It is hypothesized that the city tourists, though being on vacation in the same region and urban destination, are still heterogeneous in terms of motivation.

Deriving the motivational segments

This case example employs the BINCLUS partitioning (non-hierarchical) clustering procedure (Formann *et al.*, 1979; Mazanec, 1980, 1984) already mentioned in the previous section on tourist satisfaction. To capture the most significant travel motives the four-point scale is translated into more elementary zero–one data. Only the motives reported to apply totally are coded with 1 and all the weaker grades of agreement are coded with 0. Another decision that must be taken prior to clustering the respondents refers to the similarity measure. A simplistic way of establishing similarity for each pair of respondents is the counting of 1 and 0 matches. However, the information residing in the 1 and 0 answers is not symmetric. Knowing that two tourists are 'totally' driven by a particular travel motive tells more about their respective state of mind than knowing about the absence (or low

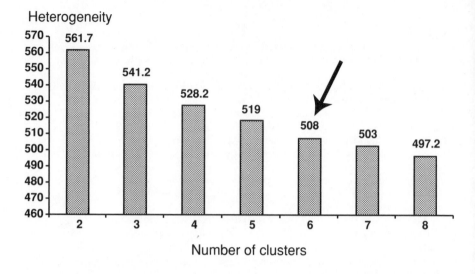

Figure 3.22 Heterogeneity decrease with growing number of motive clusters

priority) of such a motive for both respondents. Therefore, the asymmetric similarity measure called the Tanimoto coefficient is preferred in this context. In the Tanimoto measure the zero matches are neutralized. Two city travellers do not become more similar by not exhibiting the same motives. Tourists cannot be attributed to the same motive segment unless they share a reasonable number of 1 matches, i.e. motives that apply to them 'totally'.

The analyst is facing still another decision concerning the appropriate number of clusters (segments). The assistance to be gained from a formal measure of heterogeneity is limited. The heterogeneity of a cluster solution is bound to decrease with a growing number of clusters, an expected 'elbow' kink occurs very rarely and, even more disillusionary, a range of astonishingly different cluster solutions may show an almost identical level of heterogeneity. The interpretative aspects of the solution, therefore, play a significant role. (The reader is reminded of the strategic function of market segmentation. A formally excellent solution does not necessarily deliver a viable specialization concept.) Heterogeneity in the travel motive clusters is based on the sum of Tanimoto distances observed within each cluster. According to the bar chart in Figure 3.22 the heterogeneity value drops from 561.7 for a bisected sample to 497.2 for eight clusters.

The slope gives a hint as to the 'right' number of segments. The decrease in heterogeneity amounts to 9.2 and 11.0 from four to five and from five to six clusters; then the decrease drops to 5.0 between six and seven clusters. The face validity of the mixture of travel motives also speaks in favour of the six clusters solution. Each of the six clusters accommodating between

182 (9 per cent) and 443 (22 per cent) self-declared 'city tourists' shows a very typical profile of travel motives. In Figure 3.23 types 1 and 4 are compared to the average motive profile. Type 1 is highly motivated by comfort and relaxation while type 4 seeks cosiness most of all and also exposure to the locals and to nature with intact surroundings.

Types 2 and 3 in Figure 3.24 are excellent examples of the versatile and demanding tourist, who strives for a broad range of need fulfilment, and of the modest traveller with a rather low motivational level. Type 5, according to Figure 3.25, resembles type 4 with the marked exception of the cosiness motive. Fun, excitement, change and entertainment are extremely motivating for type 6.

The following analytical step evaluates the contribution of each of the motive variables to establishing the motive segments. Multiple discriminant analysis (MDA) is applied to verify the clustering results and to draw statistical inferences. The MDA examines the predictive power of the tourist motives regarding their affiliation with a motive cluster. It tells the analyst about the chances to correctly classify a city tourist into the appropriate motive cluster given his/her motive profile. Prior to clustering all variables have already been recoded into dichotomous data. To avoid a predictive bias an MDA should exclude one part of the sample for later validation. In this case the sample is divided into two halves randomly. As there is no particular order in the sample it is convenient to divide into odd- and even-numbered respondents. One subsample serves the estimation, the other half (the split-half, hold-out or validation sample) is preserved for testing purposes.

The MDA on 1017 respondents extracts five (i.e. the number of groups less one) statistically significant discriminant functions. Three of them are relevant with eigenvalues of 0.58, 0.45 and 0.28, with canonical correlations of 0.61, 0.56 and 0.47, and with a Wilk's Lambda of 0.28, 0.44 and 0.64. In total the three-dimensional discriminant space accounts for 87 per cent of the variance in the observed motive variables. The observed motives also correlate with the discriminant axes in a way leading to very plausible contextual interpretations according to the highest loaded variables:

- Axis 1 is an emotional 'atmospherics' dimension: cosiness and a familiar atmosphere (0.56), sensual atmosphere (0.44), romantic and nostalgic atmosphere (0.37).
- Axis 2 is a 'fun and activity' dimension: rest and relax (-0.47), fun and entertainment (0.42), sufficient entertainment facilities (0.39), excitement and challenge (0.35).
- Axis 3 is a 'nature and locals' dimension: unspoilt surroundings (0.49), lifestyle of the locals (0.40), comfort (-0.36). It gives credit to the fact that roughly half the sample are visitors to provincial cities and not exclusively interested in an urban environment.

Figure 3.26 portrays the group means for the six motive segments in the dimensions 1 to 3 of the discriminant space.

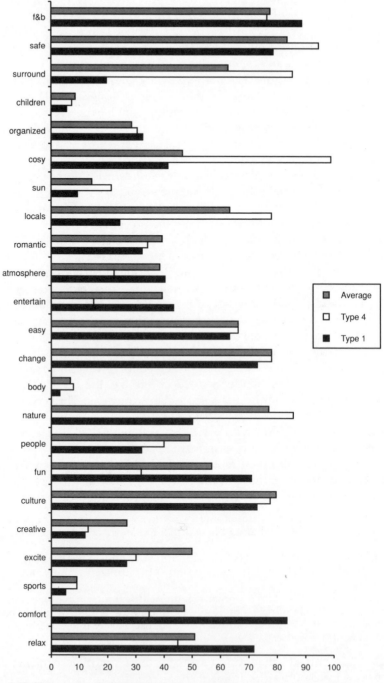

Figure 3.23 Motives as active variables for types 1 and 4

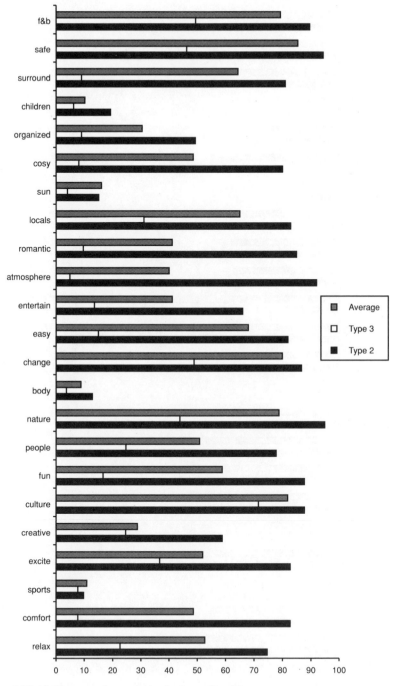

Figure 3.24 Motives as active variables for types 2 and 3

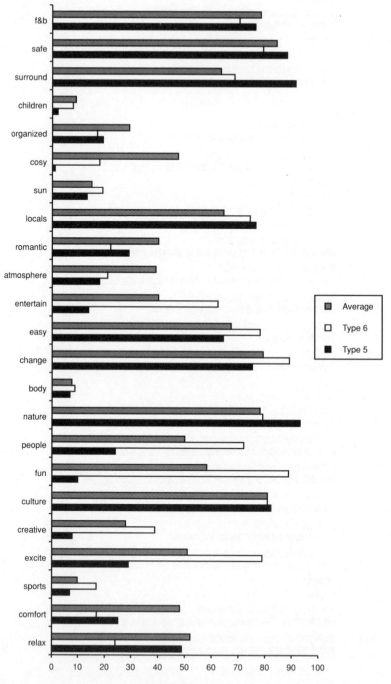

Figure 3.25 Motives as active variables for types 5 and 6

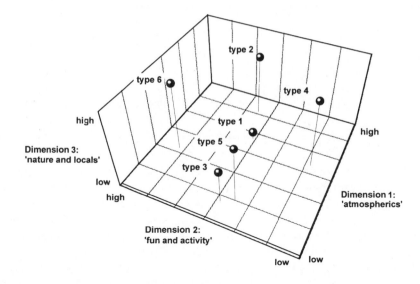

Figure 3.26 Six motive segments in the discriminant space

The test which is most convincing for managers requires the construction of a classification matrix for the hitherto unused cases. The percentage of the cases correctly classified (%CC) into a motive cluster is a practical and intuitively convincing measure for the amount of information extracted from the motive variables. To compare the %CC with random classifications the proportional and the maximal chance criteria Cpro and Cmax (Morrison, 1969, p. 323) are calculated. Segment 2 (226 new cases) is the largest. If all of the 1016 hold-out tourists were attributed to segment 2, 22 per cent would be correct just by coincidence and thus the Cmax value would be 0.22. This value, however, neglects all the remaining groups. The Cpro value instead assumes that 20 per cent of the cases are randomly selected and assigned to segment 1, 22 per cent are randomly selected and allocated to segment 2, etc. The %CC value resulting from this random allocation describes the probability of actually being a segment 1 member multiplied by the probability of being allotted to segment 1 plus the analogous products for segments 2 to 6. Hence, if '**2' denotes raising to the second power, Cpro = 0.20**2 + 0.22**2 + 0.08**2 + 0.16**2 + 0.15**2 + 0.20**2 = 0.18. This means that 18 per cent of all tourists are expected to be correctly classified into one of the six motive segments by pure chance. An MDA run which exploits the information residing in the motive variables yields a %CC of 49.9. Thus, knowing about a respondent's motives almost triples the ability to produce a correct classification of 'new' cases (Table 3.6).

Table 3.6 Motive segment classification matrix for the hold-out sample

% Actual	% Predicted to belong to segment						Absolute no.
segment	1	2	3	4	5	6	(=100%)
1	42	12	6	17	9	14	201
2	15	43	8	13	7	14	226
3	6	2	55	9	22	6	82
4	13	9	7	54	13	5	164
5	12	6	17	1	61	2	144
6	5	11	11	10	12	52	199

Motive segment 5 is most easily recognized (61 per cent), segment affiliations 1 and 2 are harder to predict (42–43 per cent). The MDA does not provide new exciting insights aside from testing the formal meaningfulness of the clustering solution. So far there are fairly differentiated motive profiles. But if vacation styles are considered to be temporary lifestyles they ought to include many more AIO-activities-interests-opinions variables (Wells and Tigert, 1971; Wells, 1974; Darden and Darden, 1976; Cathelat, 1985; Bernard, 1987; Veal, 1989; Kramer, 1991; Kreutzer, 1991; Mazanec and Zins, 1992, 1993). More 'flesh' on the motivational 'bones' is required to arrive at the complexity expected from 'vacation styles'.

Enrichment with travel activities

Table 3.7 looks into the activities the leisure travellers reported to do 'often' during the particular holiday. The relevant part of the list of activities for urban destinations comprises:

- go for walks
- participate in organized excursions
- make excursions into the near surroundings (not organized)
- relax/do nothing
- go out in the evenings
- shopping
- go to concerts
- visit sights
- visit museums
- visit exhibitions
- go to the theatre, musical, opera.

An activity is mentioned only for the most conspicuous traveller types ranking highest with a statistically significant difference from the sample average. Plus and minus signs denote a less remarkable but still symptomatically high or low frequency level.

For type #1 a strong preference for eating out and evening entertainment is added to the list of motives. Type #2 seems to indulge in 'spectator' activities; #3 does not take part in any of the frequent activities. Type #4 has an inclination for outdoor activities; #5 ranks highest in 'sightseeing' occupations and #6 uses a cultural minority offer such as exhibitions most frequently. The #2 and #3 activity patterns nicely reflect the contrasting motivational states of these types. The vacation styles are gaining shape.

Table 3.7 Frequent travel activities

Motivational type					
#1	#2	#3	#4	#5	#6
-		-	Go for a walk	+	+
	Participate in organized excursions	-			
		-	Make (not organized) excursions		
-	Relax/do nothing			-	
Go out in the evenings	+				+
	Shopping Go to concerts	-			
		-		Visit sights Visit museums	+
	-				Visit exhibitions

More passive variables for managerial meaningfulness

A managerial evaluation of the motives/activities types is of limited use, unless the segments' profiles also differ in additional geographic, demographic, socio-economic, satisfaction and behavioural intention criteria. Cross-tabulating the vacation styles with various demographic, socio-economic and trip-related criteria reveals substantial correlations. Characteristics where some styles are significantly over-represented are itemized in Table 3.8. Fifty-five per cent of type 2 tourists are to be found in Vienna, 45 per cent in other provincial cities, and vice versa for the other types. The association of type 2 with the origin country Japan is startling; 37 per cent of these tourists are Japanese compared to 13 per cent of the total sample. The other types except #1 also originate from their particular generating countries which contribute 50 per cent up to 120 per cent more to the guest mix than their fair share would justify. Type #2 and #6 tourists are much younger than the type #5 tourists. Types #2 and #3 are most extreme in terms of daily expenditure and types #1 and #6 contain the most different mixture of first-time and repeat visitors.

The information processed up to this point completes the picture of the city vacation styles. A 'hedonistic vacation style' like #2 corresponds to an extremely attractive market segment. As far as daily expenditure is

Table 3.8 Personal and trip-related attributes

	Motivational types				
#1	#2	#3	#4	#5	#6
Provincial cities	Destination Vienna	Provincial cities		Provincial cities	
	From Japan	From Italy	From Germany	From France or the UK	From the USA
30–49 years	< 29 years Highest daily expenditure AS 2300	Lowest daily expenditure AS 1300		50+ years	< 29 years
Many repeat visitors					Many first-time visitors
	Highly satisfied	Found what they expected			
High intention to repeat visit			High intention to repeat visit	Low intention to repeat visit	

concerned, the gap between type #2 and #3 is enormous. Type #3 denotes a 'modest style' with a low motivational level and ensuing spending pattern. With a strong need for social contact with the locals, for nature and for outdoor events vacation style #4 appears to be least typical for city tourists. Types #5 and #6 are the busy types of city tourists who adapt their motives and activities patterns to their respective age groups. To sum up, the style extraction experiment leads to one important conclusion. Even a seemingly homogeneous population of city tourists visiting the same receiving country may be dissociated into fairly distinct motivational and behavioural subgroups:

- the relaxation-and-comfort-seeker style
- the atmospherics-seeker/demand-and-afford style
- the modest-and-low-profile style
- the emotionally attracted place-and-people style
- the emotionally detached place-and-people style
- the fun-and-excitement-seeker style.

Vacation styles – like lifestyles in general – stimulate the product/service design of travel packages and imaginative communication strategies. They tell the manager about the commonalities and the diversities in the real-life traveller segments. In this analysis for a central-European country, the vacation style ingredients such as a strong cultural motivation, the need for safety, or a favour for good food and beverages do not differentiate between segments of city tourists. The atmospheric attributes of a city trip are much more varied. They may be exploited to build uniqueness and identity for tailor-made travel products in a city travellers' submarket.

Condensing multivariable classifications into 'styles' also reduces the danger of misinterpretation. Motive items like 'fun' and activity items like 'going out in the evenings' convey a different meaning when they become either strongly or weakly associated with 'excitement', or when they relate to different age groups. There are other pitfalls in understanding psychographic data collected in a mass survey. An aye-saying tendency (type #2) or a lack in cooperation and responsiveness (type #3) may disturb the personal profiles. Taking #2 as an example, the fact that 37 per cent of the type #2 vacationers are Japanese partly accounts for the consistently high motive/activity frequencies and satisfaction ratings. But the bias is mitigated by including more comprehensive information. The high spending level lends credibility to the high-flying expectations encountered in this vacation style. It must be considered together with the purchasing power advantage for the Japanese visitors which suppresses the 'value-for-money' criticism. Therefore, it is plausible that the above-average satisfaction level for type #2 cannot entirely be accredited to a culture-specific trait of avoiding open criticism. And, by the way, there are fifteen other countries of origin represented among the remaining 63 per cent of type #2 vacationers.

References

Bernard, M. (1987) Leisure-rich and leisure-poor: leisure lifestyles among young adults. *Leisure Sciences* **10**, 131–49.

Cathelat, B. (1985) *Styles de vie* vols 1 & 2. Paris: Editions d'organisation.

Darden, W. and Darden, D. (1976) A study of vacation life styles. *Travel & Tourism Research Association, Proceedings of the 7th Annual Conference*. Salt Lake City: TTRA, 231–6.

Formann, A.K., Mazanec, J.A. and Oberhauser, O.C. (1979) *Numerische Klassifikationsprobleme in 'großen' Datensätzen der demoskopischen Marktforschung: Ein numerischer Methodenvergleich von Latent Class- und Cluster-Analyse*. Arbeitspapiere der absatzwirtschaftlichen Institute der Wirtschaftsuniversität Wien, Vienna: Orac.

Haley, R.J. (1968) Benefit segmentation: a decision-oriented research tool. *Journal of Marketing* **32**, 30–5.

Hsieh, Sh., O'Leary, J.T. and Morrison, A.M. (1992) Segmenting the international travel market by activity. *Tourism Management* **13**, 209–23.

Kamakura, W.A. and Novak, Th.P. (1992) Value-system segmentation: exploring the meaning of LOV. *Journal of Consumer Research* **19**, 119–32.

Kramer, S. (1991) *Europäische Life-Style-Analysen zur Verhaltensprognose von Konsumenten*. Hamburg: Dr. Kovac.

Kreutzer, R. (1991) Länderübergreifende Segmentierungskonzepte – Antwort auf die Globalisierung der Märkte. *Jahrbuch der Absatz- und Verbrauchsforschung* **37**, 4–27.

Kroeber-Riel, W. (1992) *Konsumentenverhalten*, 5th edn. Munich: Vahlen.

Mazanec, J. (1980) Deterministische und probabilistische Klassifikation in der Konsumverhaltensforschung: Ein empirischer Anwendungsversuch der Quervalidierung clusteranalytischer Verfahren für qualitative Daten mit der Latent Class Analyse. In G. Fandel (ed.) *Operations Research Proceedings 1980*. Berlin, Heidelberg, New York: Springer, 296–305.

Mazanec, J.A. (1984) How to detect travel market segments: a clustering approach. *Journal of Travel Research* **23**, 17–21.

Mazanec, J.A. and Zins, A. (1992) EUROSTYLES and SOCIO TARGETS as guest segments: selected findings, a brief outline of the EUROSTYLES typology. *Revue de Tourisme* no. 2, 5–8.

Mazanec, J.A. and Zins, A. (1993) Tourist behavior and the new European lifestyle typology: exploring the managerial relevance for tourism marketing. In W. Theobald (ed.) *Global Tourism: The Next Decade*. Oxford: Butterworth-Heinemann, 199–216.

Morrison, D.G. (1969) On the interpretation of discriminant analysis. *Journal of Marketing Research* **6**, 156–63.

Rosenberg, M.J. (1967) Cognitive structure and attitudinal effect. In M. Fishbein (ed.) *Readings in Attitude Theory and Measurement*. New York: Wiley.

Veal, A. J. (1989) Leisure, lifestyles and status. *Leisure Studies* **8**, 141–53.

Wells, W.D. (1974) *Life Style and Psychographics*. Chicago: AMA.

Wells, W.D. and Tigert, D.J. (1971) Activities, interests and opinions. *Journal of Advertising Research* **11**, 27–35.

Yiannakis, A. and Gibson, H. (1992) Roles tourists play. *Annals of Tourism Research* **19**, 287–303.

Part IV

Urban destinations under competitive pressure

4.1

A guest mix approach

Josef A. Mazanec

The underlying hypothesis

The following case study is about capital cities in Europe. It regards these cities as providers of tourist services. A supply-oriented approach to identifying competitors using macro data would compare the overall structure of tourist services available in each of the cities. A very similar profile of the number and standards of attractions would imply a strong likelihood of substitution and thus of competitive threat. A demand-driven approach to define the 'relevant market' is preferred here. It neither relies on aggregate market response figures such as cross elasticities (see Cooper, 1988, for a three-mode factoring of repeated measurements of price elasticities), nor does it require disaggregate data on the perceptions and evaluations (Urban and Hauser, 1993; Roberts and Lilien, 1993, pp. 43–50) or destination switching behaviour collected from individual consumers. Instead, it involves macro data which are easily accessible.

The analysis is based on the simplified assumption that the European cities base their marketing effort on a geographical segmentation approach. Actually, this is not a severe restriction as it corresponds to strategy guidelines followed by many tourist organizations. They choose to allocate their budgets according to the attractiveness of the major countries of origin. Therefore, it is the underlying hypothesis that two destinations are expected to compete with each other more fiercely the more similar they are in terms of their guest mix.

Definition of guest mix and the database

The study is restricted to the largest metropolitan city in each of sixteen European countries. With few exceptions (the Netherlands, Switzerland) each of these cities is (or, as in Germany, is becoming) the governmental and

Cities only
Budapest
Lisbon
Prague
Zagreb

Cities and generating countries	
Amsterdam	Netherlands
Berlin	Germany
Brussels	Belgium
Helsinki	Finland
London	United Kingdom
Madrid	Spain
Oslo	Norway
Paris	France
Rome	Italy
Stockholm	Sweden
Vienna	Austria
Zurich	Switzerland

Generating countries only
Australia / New Zealand
Canada
Greece
Japan
USA

Figure 4.1 Cities and generating countries in the database

administrative centre of its respective country. Unlike an earlier analysis of 26 cities (Mazanec, 1995) the group of cities selected for this demonstration study is comparable in size and centrality functions. The guest mix is defined as the relative frequency distribution of the bednight figures for the eighteen leading tourism-generating nations which dominate the international travel market. The same range of nations in the guest mix applies to each city; the eighteen nations add up to the 100 per cent guest total for each destination. Therefore, domestic tourism is included for those countries which figure among the world's leading generators. Figure 4.1 lists the metropolitan cities, the tourism generating countries, and the overlap of nationality. Budapest, Lisbon, Prague and Zagreb are the cities 'deprived' of their domestic markets; the shares of the nationals are not considered as Hungarians, Portuguese, Czechs and Croats are not among the eighteen largest guest nations. This curtailment somewhat disturbs the comparison of the degree of 'internationality' which is subject to a slight upward bias for these cities.

An experienced travel manager may question the basic assumption. Two or more cities may exhibit a similar guest mix merely because they are frequently tied together in the same travel package by tour operators. The same effect occurs if individual travellers symptomatically visit these cities on a round trip. Though the cities included in round trips (e.g. by Americans touring through Europe) and the guest nations preferring this type of travel are well known, this effect cannot be separated. An even greater weakness of the database is the failure to differentiate between business and leisure trips. Taking these caveats into account a look into the guest structures is a useful initial step to uncover the competitive relationships.

The data originate from the TourMIS system described in Part II. In most cases statistics from official sources are collected and checked for plausibility. The whole process lasts about two years. There is always a lack of conformity of data compiled by the municipal statistical offices. The data prepared for this study also suffer from non-compliance in a uniform definition of urban tourism. One has to examine the forms of accommodation (non-commercial included or excluded) and the breakdown by tourism-generating countries. Political transition, changing methods or databases, or the unknown percentage of visits to friends and relatives affect the reliability of trip, arrival and bednight figures. All the data were subject to careful screening and harmonization. This database covers sixteen European cities and the eighteen largest guest nations for a time period of eighteen years between 1975 and 1992. From both the marketing researcher's and the practitioner's point of view avoiding spurious results and artefacts is a major concern. Two different analytical methods will be employed to corroborate each other.

The guest mix analysis of eighteen successive years

Any method of analysis which is chosen should exploit the available data as fully as possible. It should recognize the fact that there are eighteen years of the history of guest mix development. Most tourism market researchers would expect the guest mix structures to be fairly stable in the short run. Given two decades, however, there may be long-term shifts owing to new guest nations entering the travel markets. Other nations may approach their saturation levels of travel demand. Still others may decline or oscillate in cycles of several years. Such trends change the competitive relationships and the managers must be aware of the winners and losers in the market. It is of particular importance to check whether a destination reflects the overall shifts in demand or deviates from this pattern.

The guest mix data are not very convenient to look at in their three-way format of cities × nations × years. Some condensation will be required to extract the message in these eighteen data matrices. A data reduction method transforming the cities' guest profiles into a spatial representation is appropriate. Standard principal components analysis or factoring processes two-way data. The first idea that comes to mind is to have the data aggregated over the whole time span. But the aggregation destroys the time-dependent information. Another alternative – not very elegant, but effective – is to analyse each year separately. Afterwards, however, one may find that the annual results are difficult to compare. Quite frequently a three-way profile data matrix is rearranged by stacking the submatrices into an elongated two-dimensional array. In the case of the tourist cities the new two-mode matrix has 288 (i.e. sixteen cities by eighteen years) rows and eighteen columns (each for one guest nation). According to Dillon *et al.* (1985) it would be beneficial to standardize across the cities for each separate year to suppress spurious results caused by confounding two sources of variance (guest mix percentages over cities with city variation within each year). The cities' positions in the reduced, low-dimensional space then are derived by averaging the component scores over the years (Roberts and Lilien, 1993, p. 48).

Some advanced three-mode component and factor models according to Tucker (1964) or less general derivates such as CANDECOMP (Carroll and Chang, 1970) and PARAFAC (Harshman and Lundy, 1984) may also be employed to generate component/factor loadings for all three sources of variation (cities, nations, years; Snyder *et al.*, 1984; Kroonenberg, 1984; Kiers, 1991). To quote a related example, Cooper (1988) demonstrates how three-mode factoring can be adapted to analyse the competitive patterns hidden in 52 weekly measurements of (asymmetric) cross-elasticities.

Neither an intricate three-mode factor analysis nor the stacking of the annual matrices for subsequent factoring are recommended here. One of the standard multidimensional scaling models is well suited to visualize the competitive relationships between the cities.

The time series of eighteen years represents a sequence of repeated measurements of the shares of guest nations. The INDSCAL model (Carroll and Chang, 1970; Young, 1987) is adopted here to account for the eighteen replications of data matrices available for the entire period 1975–92. Individual differences scaling has been firmly established as a method for perceptual mapping in the consumer research toolkit for a long time (Mazanec, 1978, pp. 231–5, 430–3). Originally, it was introduced to allow for individual or group-specific perceptual variations within a sample of respondents. In INDSCAL the consumers share a common perceptual space of brand positions, but with individual dimension weights. This means that the relative positions of brands and ideal products in a market – though rated on a common basis of evaluation criteria – are subject to more flexibility in the preference and brand choice implications of these criteria.

For the tourist cities the similarity information rests in a sixteen by eighteen matrix of profile data constructed for each of eighteen successive years. The time periods are considered in just the same way as individual respondents would be modelled in a consumer application – as replicated measurements containing something worth knowing about individual cases (such as time periods). The weights of the dimensions of the similarity/guest mix space are allowed to vary over time indicating that some origin countries are gaining importance in determining the competitive pressure between cities, while other countries are losing salience.

Deriving an INDSCAL space for competing cities

The guest mix profiles are first translated into Euclidean distances for each pair of tourist cities in each year. The subsequent INDSCAL run (with the metric individual differences option of ALSCAL in SPSS for OS/2) condenses the resulting matrices of proximities into a configuration of low dimensionality. The distances in this space approximate the original dissimilarities as closely as possible. Given the goodness-of-fit (Young's stress = 0.27, Kruskal's stress = 0.20, average squared correlation = 0.86), a three-dimensional solution is preferred over two dimensions (with stress values of 0.37 and 0.29, averaged RSQ = 0.74). The goodness-of-fit is satisfactory for this bulk of data where the INDSCAL model estimates not more than 102 parameters (3×16 coordinates = 48 plus 3 dimension weights$\times 18$ years = 54) out of 2160 data restrictions ($16 \times (16-1)/2$ dissimilarities for each of 18 years).

Take a look at the development of the importance weights for the city space dimensions during 1975 to 1992. INDSCAL assigns each year its individual set of dimension weights. In doing that it squeezes or stretches the space to accommodate the city profiles and the inter-city similarities in each period. The weights show an interesting pattern. They are of roughly equal size and remain in a small interval (0.46, 0.60) in the first half of the time period. From 1983 on, all of a sudden, the first dimension rises in importance while the second dimension keeps its importance level and the third dimension drops in weight from 0.58 to 0.32. The trends are reflected in the time plot of Figure 4.2. The conclusion is that those guest nations which are strongly linked to the first axis have gained some weight in locating the cities in the competitive space; those connected with the third dimension have considerably lost importance. The search for 'conspicuous' nations follows after examining the city positions.

The INDSCAL guest mix space for tourist cities in Figure 4.3 represents the average situation within the entire period 1975–92. The German metropolitan city of Berlin lies out in the western corner. The northern European capitals Oslo and Stockholm tend to the north. (Note that there is no geographical meaning in these locations. The direction of each axis can be inverted without altering the conclusions about competitive relations.) Madrid gets separated in the east. Rome is highest up the third dimension.

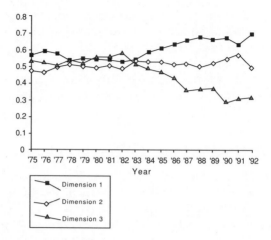

Figure 4.2 Temporal change of the city space dimension weights

The majority of central and western European capital cities are accumulated in the centre of the city space. Budapest, Vienna, Prague and Zagreb are most similar in their guest mix profiles. Zurich resides next to this group.

A contextual interpretation of the points' positions along the axes is tempting but it is not strictly necessary for the purpose of competitor detection. Geographical distances are obviously not implied. Two other aspects should be examined. One relates to the correspondence between the underlying guest nations and the axes. Another deals with the variety of the guest nations in a city's profile; the guest distribution may be fairly diversified or it may be rather imbalanced.

More substantial help can be gained from correlating the series of coordinates along each axis with the observed percentages of the guest nations. Correlations are computed for the most recent time period of 1992. It reveals that the strongest positive association of a city's position along the first axis are with guest shares for Swedes ($r = 0.65$, $P < 0.01$) and Norwegians ($r = 0.53$, $P < 0.05$) and the strongest negative correlation is with Germans ($r = -0.71$, $P < 0.01$). The largest contribution to separating the cities along the second axis stems from the shares of Germans ($r = 0.54$, $P < 0.05$) and Spaniards ($r = -0.84$, $P < 0.01$). A prominent position along the third dimension coincides with high share of Italians ($r = 0.69$, $P < 0.01$), and, to much lesser extent, with American and Japanese travellers ($r = 0.45/0.47$, $P < 0.08/0.07$). The apparent reason is that the nationalities who tend to patronize their domestic cities more than others account for exceptionally large shares in the guest mix. These cities are dragged out of the space centre into the peripheral regions. The cities in the gravity centre are most dependent on international travellers. There they are exposed to tough competition from other internationally diversified destinations.

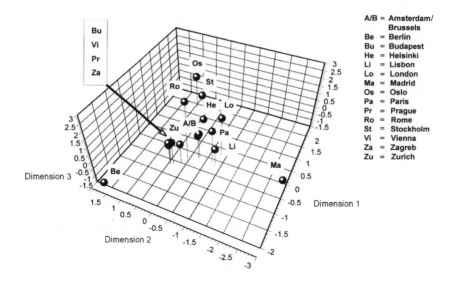

Figure 4.3 The competitive space for tourist cities

Returning to the comment on a well-balanced or ill-balanced guest mix, the same year of 1992 may serve as the reference period. The standard deviation of the guest mix percentages observed in a city profile (together with min/max values and kurtosis) is regarded as a simple indicator of concentration. Table 4.1 lists the cities in ascending order of variability (i.e. in descending order of guest mix concentration). Berlin and Madrid are heavily biased toward domestic tourism. Brussels on the other extreme is by far the most diversified internationally. These cities together with London as an intermediate sample are portrayed in Figures 4.4 to 4.7.

Table 4.1 Variability or concentration in the cities' guest distributions

City	Guest mix (standard deviation of % values)	Minimum (%)	Maximum (%)
Berlin	17.86	0.21	76.98
Madrid	15.42	0.15	66.64
Stockholm	14.66	0.30	63.84
Oslo	12.89	0.22	56.40
Helsinki	10.79	0.31	47.41
Rome	10.76	0.35	46.67
Prague	7.88	0.32	34.36
Paris	7.48	0.35	31.85
London	7.43	0.47	30.60
Vienna	6.91	0.43	26.94
Zurich	6.58	0.63	23.02
Lisbon	6.50	0.05	24.33
Budapest	6.48	0.66	26.26
Amsterdam	5.36	0.65	20.58
Zagreb	4.85	0.34	15.74
Brussels	4.69	0.66	14.97

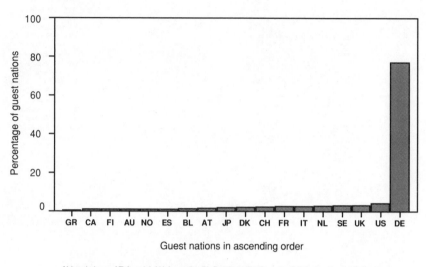

Figure 4.4 Berlin with a dominant share of German visitors

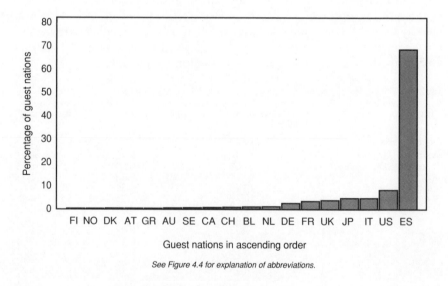

See Figure 4.4 for explanation of abbreviations.

Figure 4.5 Madrid with a dominant share of Spanish visitors

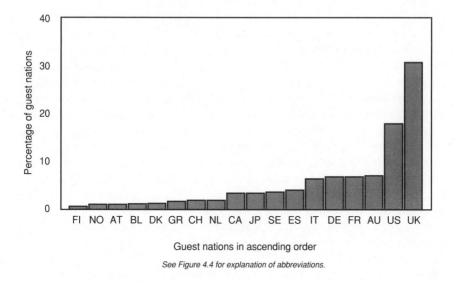

Guest nations in ascending order

See Figure 4.4 for explanation of abbreviations.

Figure 4.6 London as a fairly diversified destination

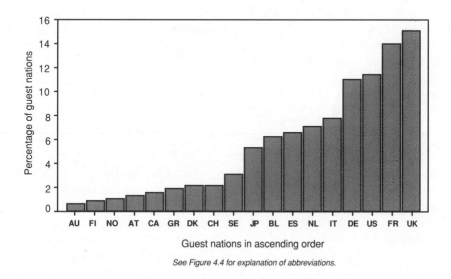

Guest nations in ascending order

See Figure 4.4 for explanation of abbreviations.

Figure 4.7 Brussels with an extremely diversified guest mix

Judging from the results presented so far there are two groups of cities recruiting very similar portions of their visitors from the same countries of origin. The central European cities of Budapest, Prague, Vienna and Zagreb form one competitive group. The western European cities of Amsterdam and Brussels constitute the second of these groups which are easily verified in Figure 4.3. To complete the analysis with traditional methodology a clustering procedure will be applied to the original data of Euclidean distances between the city profiles. Only the data for 1992 are selected to assess the competitive relationships at the end of the monitoring period. The clustering procedure is tailored to assist in competitor detection. Like any product brand a tourist city may compete in more than just one competitive cluster. Hence a non-disjunctive cluster analysis is preferred. It does not attribute the cities into mutually exclusive competitive groups by enforcing rigorous cluster boundaries. The CLIP clustering model and program (Peay, 1975; Mazanec, 1976) performs this type of analysis in a hierarchical manner. The reader interested in more details will find a comprehensive treatment of the graph-theoretic principles underlying the CLIP routine in the Appendix.

Consider the initial stages of the hierarchical grouping in Table 4.2. Budapest and Vienna are most similar in terms of their guest mix. This first city cluster results if the distance limit is set to 9.19. On the next distance level of 10.65 Amsterdam and Brussels enter a second cluster. On level 11.50 Budapest also starts rivalling Prague. Then a triple-city cluster appears at distance 14.17. A Euclidean distance of 14.15 brings Amsterdam and London into perspective, a pair of cities which are not closest neighbours in the visual output of Figure 4.3. But the spatial representation captures the average situation in the 1970s and 1980s while Table 4.2 exploits the 1992 guest mix data. Another attempt to uncover the competitive relationships between the cities relies on the neurocomputing technique of self-organizing maps (SOM) that has already been instrumental in constructing satisfaction segments.

Competing cities in a self-organizing map

The second analysis with the SOM methodology introduced in Part III should not benefit from what is already known from the INDSCAL solution. Assume that the analyst starts from scratch. The raw data again are the guest mix profiles for sixteen cities repeatedly measured over eighteen years and stacked in a (16318)318 supermatrix. First the analyst has to decide on the number of city prototypes to be expected from this database. The prototypes will be represented by the nodes in a two-dimensional grid or 'map'. As there are eighteen replicated measurements for each city the guest mix profiles vary over the cities as well as over time.

Table 4.2 Non-disjunctive city clusters of extreme homogeneity

Distance	Hierarchical, non-disjunctive city clusters emerging with increasing distance												
95.80													
. . .													
16.36	. . .												
14.17	Be	Ma	Os	St	He	Am, Lo	Ro	Bu, Pr, Vi	Pa	Li	Zu	Am, Br	
14.15	Be	Ma	Os	St	He	Am, Lo	Ro	Bu, Pr	Pa	Li	Zu	Am, Br	Bu, Vi
11.50	Be	Ma	Os	St	He	Lo	Ro	Bu, Pr	Pa	Li	Zu	Am, Br	Bu, Vi
10.65	Be	Ma	Os	St	He	Lo	Ro	Pr	Pa	Li	Zu	Am, Br	Bu, Vi
9.19	Be	Ma	Os	St	He	Lo	Ro	Pr	Pa	Li	Zu	Am	Bu, Vi

Am = Amsterdam; Be = Berlin; Br = Brussels; Bu = Budapest; He = Helsinki; Li = Lisbon;
Lo = London; Ma = Madrid; Os = Oslo; Pa = Paris; Pr = Prague; Ro = Rome; St = Stockholm;
Vi = Vienna; Zu = Zurich.

If a destination changes its guest mix dramatically within the time period of eighteen years it may face a different set of competitors in different years. This information will be recovered to show the dynamics and structural changes of inter-city competition. It is reasonable to consider the number of sixteen cities as an upper limit for the number of prototypes to be extracted. The objective, however, is to condense further the city profiles into a smaller set to visualize the inter-city similarities.

The data need not be rescaled for the SOM processing. Each individual city comes along with its series of eighteen guest mix profiles. The data are bound to the value range between 0 and 100 per cent; 16×18 cases = 288 data vectors are available for the network training. Three maps of different size are examined. The largest has four rows and four columns, the others are sized 4×3 and 4×2. The training always starts with 'good' centroids (i.e. the best seed points out of 300 trials and after convergence according to the fixed point procedure outlined in Section 2.2 and the Appendix). The SOM learning process with randomly selected input vectors then tries to improve the centroids' positions in the eighteen-dimensional dataspace while observing the neighbourhood restrictions imposed by the grid. The SOM training itself indicates if there are more nodes in the map than prototypes required. It may be that some of the prototypes become 'inactive'. In this case they never win in the learning contest and therefore do not get updated. This happens for two nodes in the 4×4 and for one node in the 4×3 map; all nodes 'learn' in the 4×2 map which is presented here. After 90,000 training iterations with a decreasing learning rate (0.01–0.0001) and a

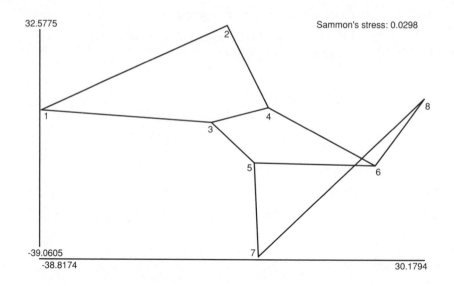

Figure 4.8 Sammon projection of the 4×2 map of city prototypes

neighbourhood update factor of 0.1 the 4×2 SOM settles to a final pattern of 'weights' that cannot be further improved. The weights correspond to the guest mix values of the prototypes. The resulting prototypes are representative of their city profiles (which is reflected in the 'heterogeneity' measure, i.e. the sum of squared Euclidean distances of all city points in the dataspace to their centroid divided by the number of data vectors). At the same time the two-dimensional map preserves the topology of the observed data fairly well. A non-linear projection algorithm (Sammon, 1969) is used to illustrate this point. Figure 4.8 shows the projection of the 4×2 lattice from the eight-dimensional dataspace into two dimensions. Except for prototype 8 the grid observes the imposed structure of neighbourhood relationships.

With the training finished the guest mix profiles can now be arranged in the 4×2 format. This step is called a 'recall' run where no more learning takes place. But for each input pattern (i.e. one city in one year) that is fed into the network, one SOM prototype will be the winner and take care of this particular guest mix profile. Thus the network classifies cities and years simultaneously. As each city/year can have its individual guest mix the positions of a city may be scattered over the map. A more stable guest mix will lead to more concentrated locations of a city on a few SOM units. The competitive map of all sixteen cities in Figure 4.9 shows that the city profiles in terms of guest mix are very stable as twelve cities stick to their prototype by activating a single SOM unit during the whole period from 1975 to 1992. Four destinations change their guest mix sufficiently to change positions. In

1 **Oslo** (75–92)*	2 **Helsinki** (75–92) **Stockholm** (75–92)	3 **Amsterdam** (75–92) **Brussels** (75–78, 80–90) **Lisbon** (75–79, 87–90, 92) **London** (75–92) **Prague** (75–83)	4 Brussels (79) **Rome** (75–92)
5 **Berlin** (75–92) **Prague** (86–91) (75–92) Zagreb (86)	6 **Budapest** (75–92) Prague (84, 85, 92) Prague (84, 85, 92) **Vienna** (75–92) **Zagreb** (75–85, 87–91) **Zurich** (75–92)	7 Brussels (91, 92) **Paris** (75–92) Zagreb (92)	8 Lisbon (80, 86, 91) **Madrid** (75–92)

*Figures in parentheses are the years between 1975 and 1992 when a city is represented by this prototype.

Figure 4.9 The competitive map of 16 European cities

total, the guest mix profiles do not fluctuate significantly. The major positions occupied for several years are indicated in bold face. The temporary changes (in small print in Figure 4.9) are limited to neighbouring units.

The guest mix information may easily be brought into perspective. Each of the eight city prototypes carries its unique pattern of guest mix percentages (its 'weights' in neurojargon). The 4×2 map in Figure 4.10 is filled with the guest nations carrying the most conspicuous weight values. It is apparent that a small number of 'prototypical' nation variables accounts for a city's affiliation with a competitive prototype. Italy, Spain, Germany and the Nordic countries are responsible for dragging their 'own' cities into the corners of the competitive map. The cities represented by prototypes #3 and #6 are subject to tough international competition. A guest nation like the USA does not make a distinction in any special region of the map. Americans are important for most urban destinations in Europe; they are the typical tourists on a round trip visiting more than one capital. Generating by far the largest market volume in Europe the German travellers are to be found in several destinations while not being the typical city tourists.

The competitive 'map' of Figure 4.9 differs from the usual geometrical display (cf. Figure 4.3). It conveys discrete information rather than variations along a continuum (dimensions in factor or MDS spaces). Nevertheless SOM networks prove to be capable of condensing multidimensional information into a 'space' of very small dimensionality

1 **Norway (33%)** Germany (15%) USA (10%) Sweden (9%)	2 **Sweden (25%)** Finland (17%) USA(10%)	3 **UK (18%)** USA (15%) Germany (10%)	4 **Italy (40%)** USA (12%)
5 **Germany (53%)**	6 **Germany (24%)** USA (13%) Italy (10%)	7 **France (18%)** USA (12%) Germany 911%) Italy (10%) UK (9%)	8 **Spain (45%)** USA (11%) Italy (9%)

Figure 4.10 The dominant guest nations

quite effectively. But a direct comparison of the SOM and INDSCAL spaces also reveals that there is a trade-off. The spacing of the SOM units in a neighbourhood grid is arbitrary. It has ordinal meaning and must not be interpreted in terms of distances. For the purpose of competitor detection the method performs reasonably well. The tourist destinations subject to the toughest competition because of a similar guest mix and segmentation concept are not just neighbours. They are even captured by the same prototypes which improves the visualization of competitive relationships.

Conclusions about the competitive relationships between European metropolitan cities

The findings for the group of European metropolitan cities confirm the results of two earlier studies. In principle, the picture does not change if more than one urban destination within a tourist-receiving country enters the database (Mazanec, 1995). The exclusion of domestic tourism for all cities also does not alter the competitive situation for Budapest, Prague and Zagreb (Grabler *et al.*, 1996). For Prague, for example, the proportion of domestic tourism in 1994 accounted for 688,000 out of 3.5 million bednights (i.e. 20 per cent). Budapest sold 793,000 bednights to domestic visitors in 1993 compared to a bednight total of 4.3 million (i.e. 19 per cent; no data are available for Zagreb). Together with Vienna and Zurich these central European cities are rivalling in a 'truly international league'. The temporal changes in the prototypes for the central-eastern European destinations (Figure 4.9) do not coincide with the removal of the Iron Curtain in 1989/90. This event produced a volume impact rather than a sales mix effect. The competitive pressure in the central European city cluster did not remain hidden to the major tourist companies. Viennese hoteliers, for example, have begun to expand into Budapest and Prague. Austrian travel agencies specializing in inbound tourism have reacted quickly in incorporating two or three cities in their packages particularly offered to overseas visitors. This is an instructive example of how a competitive threat due to a similar appeal to several tourist nationalities may influence the strategy of new product planning. Destination packages assist in 'neutralizing' the rivals to some extent. They cannot eliminate competition entirely because the city travellers tend to reduce the average length of stay in the destinations visited during their (round) trip. The typically short duration of city trips rather declines for 'destination-collectors' such as Americans or Japanese. The Budapest-Vienna-Prague-Zagreb-Zurich city cluster is symptomatic and appears in the INDSCAL and in the SOM results with equal precision.

Amsterdam and Brussels seem to strive for the same mixture of target segments. London and, to some extent, Lisbon and Paris interfere with these guest mix profiles. Again this view is confirmed in both analytical approaches. Berlin and the northern and southern European capitals are largely dependent on their own nationals and stay in prototypes of their own. The INDSCAL and the SOM results clearly support these conclusions on the consequences of a large home market such as Germany, Spain or Italy. However, the Italian and Spanish capitals are joining the domain of tough international competition once the share of domestic travel has been removed (Grabler *et al.*, 1996).

It is a serious weakness of the guest mix approach that leisure and business trips cannot be distinguished in the overall bednight figures. The information collected from official sources is incomplete and insufficient. On a European scale it appears that the quality of data obtainable from the national bureaus of statistics is deteriorating in spite of the harmonization efforts of the EU and the WTO. On the other hand the commercial surveys still suffer from an inadequate sample size in many generating countries. Tourism managers may hope that some day the European Travel Monitor will evolve to replace the official bednight statistics. A separate analysis for leisure and business travel, or even more diversified market segments, would increase the information output from competition studies significantly.

References

Carroll, J.D. and Chang, J.J. (1970) Analysis of individual differences in multidimensional scaling via an N-way generalization of 'Eckart–Young' decomposition. *Psychometrika* **35**, 283–319.

Cooper, L.G. (1988) Competitive maps: the structure underlying asymmetric cross elasticities. *Management Science* **34**, 707–23.

Dillon, W.R., Frederick, D.G. and Tangpanichdee, V. (1985) Decision issues in building perceptual product spaces with multi-attribute rating data. *Journal of Consumer Research* **12**, 47–63.

Grabler, K., Mazanec, J. and Wöber, K. (1996) Strategic marketing for urban tourism: analysing competition among European tourist cities. In Ch.M. Law (ed.) *Tourism in Major Cities*. London: International Thomson Business Press, 23–51.

Harshman, R.A. and Lundy, M.E. (1984) The PARAFAC model for three-way factor analyis and multidimensional scaling. In H.G. Law, C.W. Snyder Jr, J.A. Hattie and R.P. McDonald (eds) *Research Methods for Multimode Data Analysis*. New York: Praeger, 122–215.

Kiers, H.A.L. (1991) Hierarchical relations among three-way methods. *Psychometrika* **56**, 449–70.

Kroonenberg, P.M. (1984) Three-mode principal component analysis: illustrated with an example from attachment theory. In H.G. Law, C.W. Snyder Jr, J.A. Hattie, and R.P. McDonald (eds) *Research Methods for Multimode Data Analysis*. New York: Praeger, 64–103.

Mazanec, J. (1976) *BMDIC – ein demoskopischer Indikator zur Messung der Intensität der Substitutionskonkurrenz zwischen Produktmarken*. Working Paper #5, Institute for Advertising and Market Research: Vienna University of Economics and Business Administration.

Mazanec, J. (1978) *Strukturmodelle des Konsumverhaltens*. Vienna: Orac.

Mazanec, J. (1995) Competition among European tourist cities: a comparative analysis with multidimensional scaling and self-organizing maps. *Tourism Economics* **1**, 283–302.

Peay, E.R. (1975) Nonmetric grouping: clusters and cliques. *Psychometrika* **40**, 297–313.

Roberts, J.H. and Lilien, G.L. (1993) Explanatory and predictive models of consumer behavior. In J. Eliashberg and G.L. Lilien (eds) *Marketing*. Amsterdam: North-Holland, 27–82.

Sammon Jr, J.W. (1969) A non-linear mapping for data structure analysis. *IEEE Transactions on Computers* **C-18**, 401–9.

Snyder Jr, C.W., Law, H.G. and Hattie, J.A. (1984) Overview of multimode analytic models. In H.G. Law, C.W. Snyder Jr, J.A. Hattie and R.P. McDonald (eds) *Research Methods for Multimode Data Analysis*. New York: Praeger, 2–35.

Tucker, L.R. (1964) The extension of factor analysis to three-dimensional matrices. In N. Frederiksen and H. Gulliksen (eds) *Contributions to Mathematical Psychology*. New York: Holt, Rinehart & Winston.

Urban, G.L. and Hauser, J.R. (1993) *Design and Marketing of New Products*, 2nd edn. Englewood Cliffs, NJ: Prentice-Hall.

Young, F.W. (1987) Theory. In F.W. Young and R.M. Hamer (eds) *Multidimensional Scaling: History, Theory, and Applications*. Hillsdale: Lawrence Erlbaum, 42–158.

4.2

The managerial perspective

Klaus Grabler

Introduction

This section focuses on understanding the competitive situation in European city tourism as seen by managers working in this field. The data as well as the method used are exploratory. The purpose is to examine the competitive perceptions of experts in the city tourism market and to detect the underlying criteria. The basic hypothesis is that managers have some intuition about competition that guides their strategic thinking. It is assumed that there are different manager types who rely on different criteria in their marketing behaviour. Therefore, it is expected that the solution will not compare fully with the foregoing guest mix approach or with the consumer approach below. Nevertheless, the assessments of the managers determine their actual competitive position to some degree. Their marketing strategies influence the image transferred and the pricing or distribution decisions. These factors have a strong impact on the competition between cities. It is a similar image or a similar price level that provokes competition. Thus, even if their view cannot be supported conclusively by the hard data available, it is an important determinant that has to be considered. Initially, the target market segments as well as the competitors are abstractions. They are then given meaning by the selective perceptions and simplification processes of the managers working in this field (Day and Nedungadi, 1994). Hence the expert approach is a 'quasi supply-oriented' approach. Determinants of competition rather than its outcomes (such as the other two demand-oriented approaches discussed in this section) are presented here.

Interestingly enough, managers are often expected to judge specific economic criteria relating to competitors more reliably than the competitive intensity itself. Managerial judgements are commonly applied to defining a relevant market prior to determining the competitive market structure (DeSarbo *et al.*, 1993). However, if managers are really able to broadly structure the market they should also be able to evaluate the competitive intensity in this restricted market. Actually, it is not obvious that these are indeed two different tasks. The following approach thus tries to combine the two tasks into one. The actual difference is a matter of degree. The information has nominal character in the first task where managers judge whether a brand belongs to the relevant market or not. This task appears to be rather fuzzy in city tourism because it is difficult to draw clear boundaries for the 'relevant' market. A finer distinction may be desirable for urban tourism.[1] Moreover, it is a priori inappropriate to claim that managers see a relevant set of cities in urban tourism differing from all European cities.

Expert opinions

As factual information is often unavailable or costly to collect it is a common procedure to replace such data by expert judgements, either for the construction of expert systems (e.g. Mazanec, 1986; Rita and Moutinho, 1994a) or for comparison with other hard data (for example the life cycle approach in Getz, 1992). One may argue that managers make use of marketing criteria to evaluate their competitive position as they usually have more confidence in hard data (see Rita and Moutinho, 1994b). On the other hand expert judgements are often applied because they indirectly represent the opinions of the consumers (Gearing *et al.*, 1974). Given this assumption it is worthwhile to compare the 'expert judgement' solution to the guest mix approach and to the (direct) consumer point of view.

Recently, Moutinho and Brownlie (1994) introduced an expert system to determine the competitive position of products. In contrast to the approach pursued in this section they do not collect expert judgements on the competitive intensity perceived. Rather, they replace hard data like market shares or ROS or R&D intensity (those attributes that dominate most multifactor portfolio analyses) by expert opinions. However, this information, together with the available facts, is afterwards processed by established techniques such as factor analysis, multidimensional scaling and hierarchical cluster analysis to derive the cities' competitive positions.

Data characteristics

Who can evaluate the competitive situation of a city more competently than the managers working in the local tourist offices? A questionnaire directed to the managers of nearly 80 European CTOs was used for the data harmonization process described in Part I. It included one question about the managers' understanding of the competitive situation. A list of potential competitors containing 77 European cities was presented to the experts. Each city manager indicated the degree each other city competes with his home city in the leisure and business markets on a scale ranging from 1 (strong competitor) to 6 (no competitive relationship)[2] (see Figure 4.11). These individual perceptions of the competitive situation have to be aggregated to allow for a managerially meaningful conclusion. Out of the 77 cities 40 cities responded to this question. Considering the two tasks (relevant market, competitive intensity) inherent in this procedure all cities that receive a rating of at least 5 constitute the relevant set of competitors for a particular city. The '6' ratings for no competitive relationship nevertheless remain in the analysis.

Before commenting on the techniques to cope with such data it is essential to take a closer look into the properties of the data. First, the data matrix is not symmetric. If one city manager considers another city as a '1' competitor this does not mean that the same judgement is made by the opposite manager. This asymmetry of competition is quite realistic. The measure most frequently used for competition, viz. brand switching, is also an asymmetric measure. A recent study of the competitive effects in decision-making similarly revealed an asymmetric nature of the competitive effects (Laroche *et al.*, 1994). The asymmetry of the matrix inhibits the proper use of hierarchical clustering as one has to make decisions on which half of the matrix to analyse (DeSarbo and De Soete, 1984). Of course, the two upper and lower halves of the matrix contain different information. Hence the analysis of these data is not straightforward. Moreover, the distribution of the data is very skew with only a few 1s meaning 'strong competitor' and a lot of 6s meaning 'no competitor'. Immediate use of an MDS algorithm or one of the other common procedures mentioned above is not justified. It may be too simplistic to regard the raw data as an asymmetric distance matrix.

The 40 city managers judging the bulk of 77 cities result in a rectangular data matrix of 40 rows (city managers judging) and 77 columns (cities that are judged). The properties of the data do not suggest a conventional analysis based on distance measures. In principle, the purpose of the analysis is equivalent to detecting the structure in a multiway contingency table. Actually the data are not a contingency table but the competitive intensity on the rating scale may be interpreted in the same manner. The data resemble six experts judging the competition among the cities on a nominal scale. Turning the scale around and setting the minimum to zero, a rating of 5 then means that all managers classified the particular city as competitor. Regarding it this way one has to search for differences between the observed and expected frequencies in such a table to reveal the inherent structure (van der Heijden and Worsley, 1988). A technique that decomposes the variations from the average frequencies seems appropriate.

Questions concerning <u>the competitive situation</u> of your city
1. Please mark the following European cities **according to your opinion** about the **competitive situation they have to your city**. As this competitive situation will be different for leisure and business tourism, please indicate by writing '**L**' for leisure and '**B**' for business tourism; if it is the same write 'L' and 'B' in one box.

For example:

	B		L			Aachen
		BL				Aachen

or

Strong competitor — No competitor

Strong competitor — No competitor

						Aachen
						Aix-en-Provence
						Amsterdam
						Andorra
						Augsburg
						Athens
						Avignon
						Baden-Baden
						Barcelona
						Basle
						Berlin
						Berne
						Bonn
						Bordeaux
						Bremen
						Budapest
						Bratislava
						Brussels
						Cagliari
						Cardiff
						Copenhagen
						Dijon
						Dublin
						Edinburgh
						Frankfurt
						Fribourg
						Geneva
						Glasgow
						Graz
						Hamburg
						Heidelberg
						Helsinki
						Innsbruck
						Istanbul
						Karlsruhe
						Lausanne
						Linz
						Lisbon
						London

						Lübeck
						Lucerne
						Luxembourg
						Lyon
						Madrid
						Milan
						Malta
						Manchester
						Mannheim
						Marseilles
						Monaco
						Munich
						Münster
						Nantes
						Nice
						Oslo
						Paris
						Potsdam
						Prague
						Regensburg
						Rome
						Rostock
						Salzburg
						San Sebastian
						Saragossa
						St Etienne
						St Gallen
						Stockholm
						Stuttgart
						Tarragona
						Toulon
						Trier
						Venice
						Vicenza
						Vienna
						Würzburg
						Zagreb
						Zurich

Figure 4.11 Competitive part of the FOTVE questionnaire

Methodology

Without a preceding data reduction the simple plotting or the well known chi-square methodology (for the bivariate case) are useless. One way of dealing with such tables is to use log-linear models which search for interactions between the variables. However, with a higher number of variables and/or categories it becomes very cumbersome to calculate and interpret the large number of parameters. Moreover a log-linear analysis results in mere numeric figures in the form of interaction parameters. This output is difficult for managers to interpret. An important improvement for marketing purposes is the graphical representation of such data. Multidimensional scaling, discriminant analysis, canonical correlation analysis, factor and principal components analysis are popular techniques to serve this purpose, but they have limited applicability for categorical data (Hoffman and Franke, 1986).

Correspondence analysis

Another way to solve the dilemma caused by the data properties is to portray the rows and columns separately in a tree or a map (DeSarbo *et al.*, 1993). The decision has to be based on the importance of the row and column scores from a managerial point of view. Correspondence analysis is an appropriate method as it achieves the mapping of both datasets. It belongs to the family of dual scaling algorithms. The underlying principles of this method can be found in many multivariate techniques differing by just imposing various forms of restrictions on the parameters (van der Burg and De Leeuw, 1988). One special kind of restriction that determines quantifications for the categories of one or more variables, depending on single or multiple analysis, characterizes correspondence analysis. The simple idea behind this is that objects in the same category get the same quantification (van der Burg and De Leeuw, 1988). Correspondence analysis is claimed to be the appropriate technique for condensing nominal data in the aggregated form of frequency data (DeSarbo and Hoffman, 1987; see an example for purchase frequencies in Elrod and Keane, 1995). Hoffman and Franke (1986), Greenacre (1984, 1993) and Nishisato (1994) offer introductions to this method.

Applications

Applications of correspondence analysis are sparse in tourism research.[3] Although the use of nominal scales is widespread the author is aware of just one application (Calantone *et al.*, 1989). This study deals with positioning and employs correspondence analysis to produce maps for a complex data matrix with nominal variables describing the multinational origin, the multinational destination and multiattribute criteria. Though the most prominent application field is product positioning it is not the only marketing usage domain of correspondence analysis. By quantifying qualitative data, market segmentation is facilitated. Forced classification as an application of dual scaling with a modified data matrix (for paired comparison or rank-order data) also serves as a segmentation tool (Nishisato, 1988, 1994). Correspondence analysis as a technique for analysing choice data similarly to conjoint analysis is demonstrated by Kaciak and Louviere (1990).

Data input

Data input for correspondence analysis is in the form of a rectangular data matrix with non-negative entries. The scale format reaches from contingency/frequency data, multiple choice data, paired comparisons, ratings, ranking or sorting data to multiway data (Nishisato, 1994; van der Kloot and van Herk, 1991; Nishisato and Gaul, 1988). There are no assumptions about the distribution of the data or the sample size (Backhaus and Meyer, 1988). Various options to handle missing data exist in correspondence analysis. The same holds true for structural zeros, when the diagonal cells are not defined or not of interest (e.g. impossible combinations that often emerge; De Leeuw and Van der Heijden, 1988). Correspondence analysis is often used as a complementary procedure for further processing the residuals in log-linear models that do not fit the data well.

The basic idea of correspondence analysis

In contrast to an MDS solution correspondence analysis places overlay points in the spaces for columns and rows and thus constructs a joint map. In MDS the original data are used to calculate some kind of distance or similarity measure or, as in the present study, are direct input as (a)symmetric similarity measures. In correspondence analysis the data are also used directly but not as direct distance measure. The methodology guarantees optimal scaling of column and row profiles. Although this does not happen simultaneously there is one optimal solution for both datasets. The basis for this is the similarity of the profiles (Sawatzke, 1991) with negligence of the absolute levels. Deviations from the average profile are the key concept in correspondence analysis. In the spatial solution objects located at the origin are very similar to the average profile whereas objects positioned off the centre are different. The profiles represent the relative frequencies of the variables that may be interpreted as conditional probabilities as well. Correspondence analysis performs a 'singular value decomposition' that is also used in principal components or canonical correlation analysis (Backhaus and Meyer, 1988) and spectral decomposition (Grover and Dillon, 1988).

The idea of the profiles is important for the following study. There is no need to compare the absolute levels of competition of different cities as judged by the managers. The individual differences in using the scale render the calculation of Euclidean distances rather meaningless. It is the profile of the cities that is of interest.[4] Profiles representing the relative frequencies can be computed for both rows and columns. In the present study the column profiles are of main interest because of two assumptions:

1. The classification of two other cities as being competitors by one city manager implies competition between all three.
2. Because of the individual differences it is not so much the individual profile that has to be compared but the aggregation of different managers classifying a particular city.

Consider a fictitious example for the illustration of the column and row profile idea. Suppose that the three managers from Rome, Paris and Vienna gave the following ratings:

	Rome	Paris	Vienna
Rome	1	2	2
Paris	3	1	2
Vienna	6	6	1

Looking at the ratings from the manager from Rome one obviously concludes that Paris and Vienna are judged as competitors. This also implies that Paris and Vienna experience competition as is meant by the first assumption given above. The competitive relationship is displayed in similar column profiles. Now consider the outlier judgements from Vienna. Regarding the row profiles Vienna would receive a very different position from the other two cities. This strong influence of one particular manager is weakened by the focus on the columns. The columns contain information from three as opposed to one manager in the rows. Whereas the column profiles of Paris and Vienna, for example, are relatively similar the difference of the two row profiles is enormous. The consideration of the opinions of 40 managers therefore is supposed to be more valid for a general picture of the competitive relationships between the European cities.

Masses and inertia

A central concept of correspondence analysis is the masses, which are the row and column sums. They are used for weighting each profile point in proportion to its frequency (Hoffman and Franke, 1986). As a result the centroid is closer to objects (variables) that have a higher frequency. The masses also determine the scales of the dimensions. Small masses stretch the dimensions and vice versa. This means that (small) distances on attributes with low frequencies appear larger in the map.

The total inertia is the weighted sum of the squared (Euclidean) distances of the original data points from their respective centroids. In correspondence analysis there are different weights in the form of the masses that stretch or shrink each axis. The ordinary Euclidean distances where all dimensions have the same weight[5] are modified by a certain weight factor. This factor is equivalent to the inverse element of the average profile (thereby stretching distances with low frequencies) which is equivalent to calculated chi-square distances (Greenacre, 1993, p. 27). The procedure of weighting facilitates the interpretation of the map that can now be read in terms of ordinary Euclidean distances. The total inertia is a sum of the deviations that is weighted twice: first by the weighting of the dimensions (factor 1/expected or average profile) and second by the mass of each point. A high inertia stands for very different profiles whereas a small inertia means that there are only slight differences. Hence the total inertia is a measure for the association between the columns and rows.

The total inertia can be decomposed into different solutions that are characterized by their eigenvalue. In fact these solutions are principal axes found by the method of singular value decomposition. It is guaranteed that the first axis explains the highest amount of the total inertia and so forth. These dimensions define the coordinate axes for the perceptual map.

Column normalization

Most texts on correspondence analysis discuss the joint normalization of columns and rows. However, for most applications either the rows or the columns are of prime interest. Therefore, the ANACOR procedure in SPSS lets the analyst choose a normalization option. The normalization does not affect the solution geometrically, but because of the joint space formulation it does affect the interpretability (Hoffman and De Leeuw, 1992). The same procedure can be applied for the analysis of the row or the column profiles which is important for the connection of the two datasets. The joint normalization makes between-set interpretation of the points impossible and the chi-square distance for within-set interpretation irrelevant. Hence it is very difficult to interpret at all. For runs that use either row or column normalization it is the centroid interpretation that is valid for the between-set interpretation.[6]

In the present case the information sought apparently lies in the columns. The individual differences in the rows are disturbing a meaningful generalization of the results. Hence, a column normalization was chosen. In the asymmetric plot applied the masses of the row profiles represent the average profile ('principe barycentrique') of the columns and vice versa.

This has two important implications:

1. The row points tend toward the column points with high profile elements (Greenacre, 1989).
2. The total inertias are the same for columns and rows and this is also true for the principal inertias (Backhaus and Meyer, 1988).

Interpretation of a correspondence analysis map

Although it is possible to construct a joint map of row and column profiles it is not recommended to interpret distances between individual points of different datasets (Hoffman and Franke, 1986). But it is legitimate to compare the position of one point to all points of the other set. This means that one set may help to interpret the dimensions of the reduced space and this 'space definition' guides the interpretation of the points of the other set (Greenacre, 1993, pp. 70ff.). Therefore, one may take the variables to attach meaning to the derived space and then position the objects in this meaningful space.[7] This 'factor-analytic' interpretation is valid for all scalings, irrespective of whether classical correspondence, multiple correspondence analysis or the Carroll–Green–Schaffer Scaling is applied. In an asymmetric plot, where one dataset is depicted in standard coordinates that represent the vertex points, a formally clearer relationship is given by the barycentric interpretation (Greenacre, 1989). Carroll *et al.* (1986) introduced various routines to handle the comparability of columns and rows by redefining the representation metric. However, there is no universally accepted solution to this problem and their approach is criticized as well (Greenacre, 1989). Hence the asymmetric plot with the barycentric interpretation appears to be optimal. The column normalization results in such an asymmetric map.

Competition in the leisure market

Number of dimensions

The principal axes found through correspondence analysis assist in structuring the market in a similar way to the nodes in hierarchical cluster analysis. In cases where the data occupy a region along a continuum correspondence analysis is superior to hierarchical cluster analysis (Greenacre, 1984, p. 200). The determination of the number of dimensions raises the same problems in correspondence analysis as in other multivariate methods. It depends on a compromise between parsimony and interpretability. The principal inertias of the single dimensions provide a measure to be inspected for this purpose.

As expected, the inertia in this study is spread over many dimensions. It is therefore misleading to present a spatial solution in two or three dimensions as these capture not more than 32 per cent or 41 per cent of the inertia (see Table 4.3). Although there is one relatively dominant dimension

Table 4.3 High contributions of city points for five dimensions

Dimension 1 (23.4%)	Dimension 2 (8.8%)	Dimension 3 (8.4%)	Dimension 4 (6.6%)	Dimension 5 (5.4%)
		Negative weights		
Freiburg	Monaco	Dijon	Lausanne	Munich
Würzburg	Nice	Lyon	Geneva	Avignon
Trier	Malta	Andorra	Lucerne	Brussels
Heidelberg	Salzburg	Aix-en-Provence	Berne	Frankfurt
Karlsruhe		Bordeaux	Zurich	Zurich
Augsburg		San Sebastian	Graz	Bonn
Regensburg		Avignon		Berlin
				Vienna
		Positive weights		
London	Berlin	Prague	Trier	Glasgow
Paris	Edinburgh	Rome	Madrid	Cardiff
Barcelona	Dublin	Venice	Augsburg	Linz
Madrid	Glasgow	Budapest	Athens	Bordeaux
Venice	Frankfurt	Vienna	Potsdam	Berne
Vienna	Manchester	Amsterdam		
Amsterdam	London			
Rome				

explaining 23 per cent of the inertia, ten dimensions explain 72 per cent and it takes twenty dimensions to explain 91 per cent. In absolute terms the total inertia is expectedly small. The association between the experts judging and the cities evaluated in terms of competitive intensity therefore appears to be weak. This finding is underlined by the eigenvalue of 0.31 for the first dimension which may be interpreted analogous to a Pearson's correlation coefficient (SPSS Inc., 1990, p. B-37). However, this is also a sign for the small differences in the frequencies due to the scale compared to real contingency tables and should not be considered indicative of the goodness of fit.

Interpretation of dimensions

An important part of the information hides in the meaning of the axes. A dimension acquires its meaning through the points that contribute much to it. In principle, a point contributes much if it has either a large mass or a long distance from the centroid (Hoffman and Franke, 1986). A large mass relates to the row or column sums and, therefore, to the absolute levels of frequencies (cities which are often regarded as strong competitors). Remoteness from the centroid indicates uniqueness. For each point the contribution to the inertia of each axis can be computed: it is the mass of the point multiplied by the squared distance of the point from the centroid (Greenacre, 1984, p. 67). The principal axes tend more towards the points with high masses. In the cities' case these points characterize a region of strong competitive intensity. Hence the interpretation is similar to factor loadings in interpreting principal components. The counterparts of the communalities in standard principal component analysis are the relative contributions: they are a measure for the loss of information by reducing dimensionality (Calantone *et al.*, 1989).

The first dimension carries an unambiguous meaning (Table 4.3). It exactly separates the smaller German cities from the most popular tourist cities. The main indicator for competition in the eyes of the experts is obviously the type of league a city competes in. This can be a small geographical area on the one hand or the international league on the other. The dominant first axis reflects a significant amount of competition among the tourism intensive cities. The ranking of the big tourist cities nearly coincides with the number of bednights they sell. The second dimension has large positive and negative contributions for cities attracting a high number of tourists. Both ends are associated with cities reaching the same number of bednights as the popular tourist cities in dimension 1. The tourism concentration is obviously not the only component for competition. The difference to the first dimension may be the size of the city itself. The cities loading high on the second dimension are not too big and may not be equally appealing as the classical city destinations. They represent the second league of urban tourism. The exact criteria dividing the two groups is hard to illustrate. There is a geographic component as well as a component in the offer of the cities. The cities with high negative weights primarily consist of modern and relaxing cities, whereas the positive weights are typical for traditional and highly industrialized cities.

The third dimension again appears to rest on a geographical popularity scheme. The negative weights represent French cities with the exception of coastal cities and Paris. They all are characterized by their strong dependence on the home market (Grabler and Wöber, 1995). The positive weights build a cluster that has partly emerged in the guest mix structure discussed previously: cities like Prague, Rome, Vienna and Budapest, Venice and Amsterdam have an internationally diversified guest mix. Dimensions 4 and 5 are more difficult to interpret. In total ten dimensions explain between 23 and 93 per cent of the inertia of the column points. This means that not all the cities can be reconstructed adequately in ten dimensions. Linz and Innsbruck, in particular, display low 'communalities'. All other cities are reproduced in an acceptable manner.[8]

Clustering the city scores

The dimensions describe the competitive relationships along different criteria. A map of the column scores would yield a summarizing picture that is easy to grasp. As the information in the present study is spread over so many dimensions such a map bears too little information. Hierarchical clustering is recommended to receive a managerially useful solution by fully exploiting the information. The coordinates (row and column) of the cities are derived quantifications with metric properties. These coordinates are submitted to a hierarchical clustering using one of the clustering procedures in the SPSS package. Note that an immediate clustering of the original data is not meaningful because of the properties of the rating data mentioned above. By using correspondence analysis prior to a clustering routine one can derive metric data for which the usual Euclidean distance measures are easily calculated. That is the reason why it is sometimes recommended to run a correspondence analysis prior to cluster analysis in the case of categorical data (Green *et al.*, 1988).

Ward's algorithm was applied to the column scores of the first ten dimensions containing 72 per cent of the information. The resulting dendrogram is presented in Figure 4.12. The elbow in the fusion coefficients would suggest four clusters. The competitor group at the top of the dendrogram is very heterogeneous. This is primarily due to the missing responses from some of these city managers. Although the judgements of the other experts convey information about these cities as well, the missing judgements bias the results. In general, all the cities appear as competitors rather infrequently. This leads to a cluster of cities that are extremely rarely evaluated as competitors and thus explains why the positions of Oslo and Helsinki are far away from the other capitals. Nevertheless, this first cluster is dominated by smaller southern cities.

The British cities, with the exception of London, form a subcluster distinctly different from the other cities. In the centre of the dendrogram the prime tourist cities aggregate and confirm the interpretation of the dimensions outlined above. A separate cluster is formed by smaller German cities which have no tradition of tourism. Their guest mix is highly dependent on the home market (Grabler and Wöber, 1995). The other (bigger) German cities form the last cluster together with the Swiss cities. Brussels, too, belongs to this cluster and faces tough competition from Munich and Zurich. Besides the non-response cities of Oslo, Helsinki and Zagreb, only few capitals are not in the middle cluster. This may be due to the importance of business trips to these cities. The appeal for leisure tourists is not comparable to the other capitals. This explains one important difference from the conclusions of the previous guest mix analysis where separate data for business and leisure travel were not available.

The size of the city (in terms of number of inhabitants and tourists) is a dominant feature in this solution. It is not yet clear if this is just due to the population size, the number of bednights or to the cities' history as 'classic city destinations' as there are parallels to the classic destinations found by van der Borg (1994) in his analysis of tour operator catalogues. Controlling for the size effect may lead to further insights. To make the

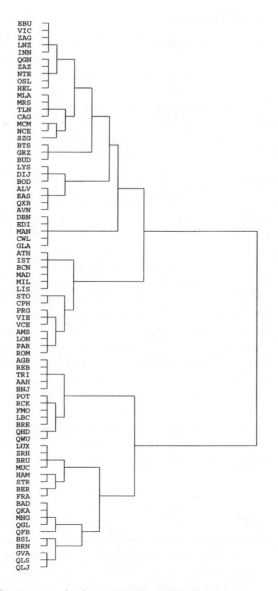

Note: See list of place name codes for explanation of abbreviations.

Figure 4.12 Competitive relationships in leisure tourism between 77 European cities

results fully comparable with the guest mix analysis in section 4.1 a second analysis also limited to the capital cities is run. It may yield finer dimensions of the expert opinions and help to evaluate the actual use of such hard data by the experts.

Analysis of European capitals

The quasi-contingency table to be analysed for the metropolitan cities is a 40 managers (rows)×16 cities (columns) matrix. The information inherent in this data table spreads out into fewer dimensions. The first dimension is not as dominant as in the former analysis. A singular value of 0.17 explains 28.4 per cent of the total inertia. Although there is again an enormous information loss in the low-dimensional solution a three-dimensional map carrying 56 per cent of the inertia (see Figure 4.13) can be constructed.

Competitive map of European capitals

The interpretation of the map is straightforward. Cities that are close together have similar profiles. Cities with low marginal frequencies are positioned at the edges of the map whereas cities with high marginal frequencies are plotted at the centre (Hoffman and De Leeuw, 1992). Hence cities that are judged uniquely will be plotted at the edges of the map. The centre is only thinly populated which means that all capitals are subject to a rather unique competitive evaluation. The map confirms the results of the general analysis. There is strong competition between the tourism intensive cities like London, Paris, Vienna, Rome, Amsterdam and Prague. Unique positions for Budapest and Madrid can be detected among the capitals. Helsinki and Oslo join Zagreb, Berlin and Stockholm. A comparison with the guest mix results reveals big differences: the position of Lisbon, for example, does not coincide with the guest mix results. The experts regard Madrid and Zurich as Lisbon's main competitors. However, some competitors detected by the guest mix approach (Amsterdam, London) are perceived as less similar. In general, only a few cities are located in a similar competitive position in both analyses. Among them is the cluster of Helsinki, Stockholm and Oslo.

Interpretation of dimensions

The position of the outliers has to be considered with caution. The first three dimensions only contribute about 29 per cent of the inertia of Lisbon to take one example. As the explained proportion of the total inertia sums up to not more than 56 per cent for the first three dimensions there are some other points not well represented in the map: Amsterdam (41 per cent), Berlin (38 per cent), Madrid (36 per cent) and Stockholm (23 per cent). Hence a closer examination of the dimensions seems advisable. The contribution of the column points to the inertia of the dimensions coincides with the positions in the map. The first dimension is characterized by the opposite locations of Paris, London and Vienna (on the positive side) and Zagreb (on the negative). An index for tourism bednights would result in a similar ranking.

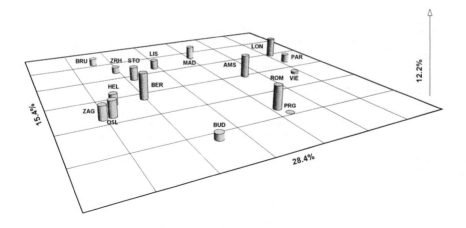

Figure 4.13 Competitive map of European capitals

Contributions to the second dimension are highest from Budapest, Prague and Rome as opposed to Brussels and Madrid. An interpretation in terms of modernity seems obvious.

Berlin, Amsterdam and Rome are in front of Prague and Vienna on the third dimension which is difficult to interpret. In general, the four cities depicted unsatisfactorily (Amsterdam, Berlin, Madrid and Stockholm) do not fit well into this evaluation scheme. It appears that they combine some elements of the criteria underlying the dimensions and cannot be described solely as tourist cities with either a modern or a traditional appeal.

Clustering city scores

Because of the information loss it is advisable to check the validity of the map by running a cluster analysis over ten dimensions. These ten dimensions contain 96 per cent of the inertia thus exploiting nearly all the information. Using Ward's criterion and squared Euclidean distances results in the dendrogram in Figure 4.14. The visual interpretation of the three-dimensional map is confirmed with a few exceptions. Berlin is more uniquely represented in the cluster solution, whereas the detached positions of Budapest and Lisbon cannot be confirmed. It appears that Budapest in general competes strongly with Prague, like Lisbon with Madrid. Hence geographical vicinity is a stronger determinant in the solution over ten dimensions. This means that geographical vicinity is a component

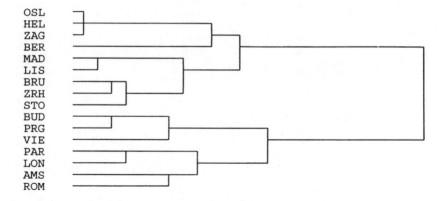

Note: See list of place name codes for explanation of abbreviations.

Figure 4.14 Competition in the leisure market among 16 European capitals

influencing many dimensions and dominating the cluster solution. It may be a good indicator for competition in general but there are still other criteria that define competitors. The interpretation of competition along these different criteria is more to be recommended as it reveals the competitive structure in different segments. It depends on the managerial task which of the dimensions should be investigated. In sum, the results obtained from managerial judgements only partially prove the validity of the guest mix concept for urban tourism (see Grabler *et al.*, 1996; Mazanec, 1995; and the preceding section).

Discussion and suggestions for further research

One important problem in the expert approach is the incomplete response from some city managers. Though partly compensated by emphasizing the aggregated column profiles it results in a clustering of the 'poor response cities'. This is due to the fact that few managers regarded several cities as competitors. It is an option to exclude these cities from the analysis. However, with the 40 managers evaluating all cities it was possible to infer adequately positions for cities that had not responded. The information value of a larger number of city positions was appreciated more than the bias involved.

Correspondence analysis is an appropriate technique to analyse the type of data presented. However, there is one important disadvantage of this procedure: it is impossible to determine the adequacy of the technique in terms of statistical fitness criteria. The total inertia is just an index for the association of the columns and rows. It permits only some tentative conclusions on the strength of this association together with the eigenvalues. The absolute amount of the total inertia, however, depends heavily on the data.

This disadvantage aside, correspondence analysis offers some outstanding possibilities for further analyses. The solutions described above are based on equal importance of all city managers' opinions. This means that the solution is equally influenced by cities with small or large market shares. Although the focus on the columns partly compensates this effect by taking an aggregate view, the results may be misleading. It depends on the underlying theory and the aim of the analysis whether the neutralization of city size is unintended or not. In any case correspondence analysis offers a way to deal with this problem. The masses of each city could be determined a priori according to the bednights in the cities. Through the higher masses the cities with a large number of bednights dominate the final solution. Thus a higher weighting of the judgements about the dominating cities will be achieved.

The problem of defining the criteria behind the dimensions may be solved by simply introducing cases (fictitious persons) that evaluate the competitive intensity accurately according to specific criteria such as geographic distance, budget or bednights. By examining the positions of these cases one can easily detect the managers relying on this information. By multiplying these data vectors this evaluation aspect is enforced to dominate the solution. The procedure is known as forced classification (Nishisato, 1988; Nishisato and Gaul, 1988). By examining the individual positions of the managers in such a solution their evaluation criteria may be inferred. Forced classification may thus be used to segment the respondents according to their managerial judgement style.

Notes

[1] These boundaries are much clearer in the case of products. Contrary to services there are some product features that may be used for the determination of the relevant market.

[2] A pre-test showed that a separate collection for the leisure and business markets was necessary because managers take different criteria into consideration in evaluating these markets. For a better comparison with the consumer data in the following section, the leisure market is chosen for presentation here.

[3] In fact applications in the marketing literature are sparse, too. Papers dealing with applications are in the minority compared to papers dealing with the method itself, just using an application for illustration purposes. This may be due to the difficulties in the interpretation of the joint maps (of columns and rows) that are often stressed. It is indeed a paradox that the advantage of a combined output must not be read the way it apparently seems. This and the complex matrix algebra underlying correspondence analysis let the number of applications stay small

although the nature of the data is often highly appropriate. This lack of application studies is aggravated by the technical nature of most articles dealing with correspondence analysis (Kaciak and Louviere, 1990).

[4] Similar to correlation coefficients this neutralizes the effect of the absolute level.

[5] Equal weighting is a concept implicit in many of the simple statistics that are often used. Calculating proportions of persons who indicate a certain attribute or calculating the mean means to weight all subjects and person equally.

[6] This means that points from one set are the weighted averages of the other set. In the actual example this signifies that using columns normalization the position of a particular city is exactly a weighted average of the judgements of all managers resulting in closer relationship to its perceived competitors. This close relationship is true for all scalings but not that formally clear in joint normalization.

[7] This is at least true for the classical simple correspondence analysis with the joint normalization of objects and variable categories which results in a symmetric (or French) plot (Greenacre, 1989) that actually overlays two incongruously defined spaces. Nevertheless, within-set distances are approximately chi-squared (Carroll *et al.*, 1989). Hoffman and De Leeuw (1992) present a geometrical interpretation of multiple correspondence analysis that follows the centroid principle instead of the traditional chi-square interpretation.

[8] Actually these 'communalities' or contributions of dimensions to the inertia of the city points could be used to explain the predominant criteria for competition of each city individually. High contributions of a certain dimension equal an importance of this dimension for the competitive situation of a particular city. Having interpreted dimensions this conveys the important managerial information of the significance of certain criteria for a particular city. The results correspond closely to the 'loadings' and are not presented here.

References

Backhaus, K. and Meyer, M. (1988) Korrespondenzanalyse. Ein vernachlässigtes Analyseverfahren nicht metrischer Daten in der Marketingforschung. *Marketing ZFP 10. Jg* **4**, 295–307.

Calantone, R.J., di Benedetto, I., Hakam, A. and Bojanic, B.C. (1989) Multiple multinational tourism positioning using correspondence analysis. *Journal of Travel Research* **28**, 25–32.

Carroll, J.D., Green, P.E. and Schaffer, C.M. (1986) Interpoint distance comparisons in correspondence analysis. *Journal of Marketing Research* **23**, 271–80.

Carroll, J.D., Green, P.E. and Schaffer, C.M. (1989) Reply to Greenacre's commentary on the Carroll–Green–Schaffer Scaling of two-way correspondence analysis solutions. *Journal of Marketing Research* **26**, 366–8.

Day, G.S. and Nedungadi, P. (1994) Managerial representations of competitive advantage. *Journal of Marketing* **58**, 31–44.

De Leeuw, J. and Van der Heijden, P.G.M. (1988) Correspondence analysis of incomplete contingency tables. *Psychometrika* **53**, 223–33.

DeSarbo, W.S. and De Soete, G. (1984) On the use of hierarchical clustering for the analysis of nonsymmetric proximities. *Journal of Consumer Research* **11**, 601–10.

DeSarbo, W.S. and Hoffman, D.L. (1987) Constructing MDS joint spaces from binary choice data: a multidimensional unfolding threshold model for marketing research. *Journal of Marketing Research* **24**, 40–54.

DeSarbo, W.S., Manrai, A.K. and Manrai, L.A. (1993) Non-spatial tree models for the assessment of competitive market structure: an integrated review of the marketing and psychometric literature. In J. Eliashberg and G.L. Lilien (eds) *Handbooks in Operations Research & Management Science* vol. 5 (Marketing) Amsterdam: Elsevier, 193–257.

Elrod, T. and Keane, M.P. (1995) A factor-analytic probit model for representing the market structure in panel data. *Journal of Marketing Research* **32**, 1–16.

Gearing, C.E., Swart, W.W. and Var, T. (1974) Establishing a measure of touristic attractiveness. *Journal of Travel Research* **12**, 1–8.

Getz, D. (1992) Tourism planning and destination life cycle. *Annals of Tourism Research* **19**, 752–70.

Grabler, K., Mazanec, J. and Wöber, K. (1996) Strategic marketing for urban tourism: analysing competition among European tourist cities. In Ch.M. Law (ed.) *Tourism in Major Cities*. London: International Thomson Business Press, 23–51.

Grabler, K. and Wöber, K.W. (1995) *City Tourism in Europe, Results of the 1995 FOTVE/FECTO Survey*. Unpublished research report, Institute for Tourism and Leisure Studies: Vienna University of Economics and Business Administration.

Green, P.E., Schaffer, C.M. and Patterson, K.M. (1988) A reduced-space approach to the clustering of categorical data in market segmentation. *Journal of the Market Research Society* **30**, 267–88.

Greenacre, M.J. (1984) *Theory and Applications of Correspondence Analysis*. London: Academic Press.

Greenacre, M.J. (1989) The Carroll–Green–Schaffer Scaling in correspondence analysis: a theoretical and empirical appraisal. *Journal of Marketing Research* **26**, 358–65.

Greenacre, M.J. (1993) *Correspondence Analysis in Practice*. London: Academic Press.

Grover, R. and Dillon, R. (1988) Understanding market characteristics from aggregated brand switching data by the method of spectral decomposition. *International Journal of Research in Marketing* **5**, 77–89.

Hoffman, D.L. and De Leeuw, J. (1992) Interpreting multiple correspondence analysis as a multidimensional scaling method. *Marketing Letters* **3**, 259–72.

Hoffman, D.L. and Franke, G.R. (1986) Correspondence analysis: graphical representation of categorical data in marketing research. *Journal of Marketing Research* **23**, 213–27.

Kaciak, E. and Louviere, J. (1990) Multiple correspondence analysis of multiple choice experiment data. *Journal of Marketing Research* **27**, 455–65.

Laroche, M., Hui, M. and Zhou, L. (1994) A test of the effects of competition on consumer brand selection processes. *Journal of Business Research* **31**, 171–81.

Mazanec, J.A. (1986) Allocating an advertising budget to international travel markets. *Annals of Tourism Research* **13**, 609–34.

Mazanec, J.A. (1995) Competition among European tourist cities: a comparative analysis with multidimensional scaling and self-organizing maps. *Tourism Economics* **1**, 283–302.

Moutinho, L. and Brownlie, D. (1994) The stratlogic approach to the analysis of competitive position. *Marketing Intelligence & Planning* **12**, 15–21.

Nishisato, S. (1988) Market segmentation by dual scaling through generalized forced classification. In W. Gaul and M. Schader (eds) *Data, Expert Knowledge and Decisions*. Berlin: Springer, 268–78.

Nishisato, S. (1994) *Elements of Dual Scaling. An Introduction to Practical Data Analysis*. Hillsdale, NJ: Lawrence Erlbaum.

Nishisato, S. and Gaul, W. (1988) Marketing data analysis by dual scaling. *International Journal of Research in Marketing* **5**, 151–70.

Rita, P. and Moutinho, L. (1994a) Promotion budget allocation for national tourist offices using an expert system. In St.F. Witt and L. Moutinho (eds) *Tourism Marketing and Management Handbook*, 2nd edn. New York: Prentice Hall, 377–81.

Rita, P. and Moutinho, L. (1994b) An expert system for promotion budget allocation to international markets. In M. Uysal (ed.) *Global Tourist Behavior*. New York: International Business Press, 101–21.

Sawatzke, F. (1991) MDS, Correspondence Analysis und Biplot: drei Verfahren zur räumlichen Darstellung von Kreuztabellen. *Planung und Analyse* **3/91**, 89–92.

SPSS Inc. (1990) *SPSS Categories*. Chicago, IL: SPSS.

van der Borg, J. (1994) Demand for city tourism in Europe: tour operators' catalogues. *Tourism Management* **15**, 66–9.

van der Burg, E. and De Leeuw, J. (1988) Homogeneity analysis with k sets of variables: an alternating least squares method with optimal scaling features. *Psychometrika* **53**, 177–97.

van der Heijden, P.G.M. and Worsley, K.J. (1988) Comment on 'Correspondence Analysis Used Complementary to Loglinear Analysis'. *Psychometrika* **53**, 287–91.

van der Kloot, W.A. and van Herk, H. (1991) Multidimensional scaling of sorting data: a comparison of three procedures. *Mutlivariate Behavioral Research* **26**, 563–81.

4.3

The city travellers' view

Klaus Grabler

Demand side approaches for measuring competitive market structure

This section discusses the competitive situation in the urban tourism market from a demand side view. It is the necessary complement to the supply-oriented view of the experts and the supply–demand combined view of the guest mix approach. Only the use of multiple techniques to seek contradictions and consistencies in the solutions can lead to the cross validation that is necessary for such a fuzzy task as defining competitors, where the boundaries are never clear-cut (Day *et al.*, 1979). Therefore a perceptual technique is used as a complement in this last approach of defining competitors (Fraser and Bradford, 1984). As a perceptual measure the results are expected to reveal a broad definition of competitive groups. This is the reason why it is sometimes argued that perceptual approaches should pre-empt behavioural approaches as they provide a finite and bounded set of potential competitors (Fraser and Bradford, 1984). These competitors can be analysed more accurately in a second step using behavioural approaches such as brand switching. Note that brand switching or cross-price elasticity require some definition of the market in advance.

A perceptual approach is known to be appropriate to measure potential competitors through the use of soft data (Fraser and Bradford, 1983). Consumers' perceptions of similarities rather than behavioural data such as brand switching (see, for example, Zahorik, 1994) or cross elasticities (e.g. Cooper, 1988) inform about the competitors of a particular city by detecting substitutes that may emerge in the near future. Moreover, the validity of destination switching for the analysis of competition in urban tourism has yet to be proven. It can be argued that destination switching occurs because of variety seeking and hence two cities represent 'temporal complements' rather than competitors (Zahorik, 1994) with distinct features rather than common attributes.[1] It is known that consumers may have distinctly different destinations in their short list of vacation destinations (Woodside and Carr, 1988). Beside the data collection this is probably the main reason why there is no tourism study analysing destination switching. Recently Uysal *et al.* (1995) applied a Markov chain model for the trip type switching. However, their study concerned product categories (trip type) not brands and was not designed to measure competition but to identify current trends.[2] The perceptual study below is not affected by this variety-seeking phenomenon and therefore suits the concept of strategic long-run marketing. It complements perfectly the guest mix approach that uses actual data. The time point of the data collection is another important determinant of the scope of the results. The study below is a pre-travel approach which emphasizes the strategic character of the study.

However, demand-oriented perceptual approaches suffer from the problems of sampling errors or the aggregation over different consumer segments. They are more unstable than the guest mix approach because consumer tastes and preferences change more rapidly, which has immediate consequences for the analyses on the individual level (and is blurred by aggregated analyses like guest mix approaches). It is more costly and difficult to apply a demand side approach. Knowledge about data collection methods and especially about data analysis techniques is necessary and therefore their use is less common.

One of the most established and widely used definitions for competition is substitutability (Coltman, 1989). It is the classical definition of competition and means that consumers' perceptions of substitutable products are collected. Srivastava *et al.* (1984, p. 32) correspondingly define a market as 'the set of products judged to be *substitutes* within those usage situations in which similar patterns of benefits are sought by groups of consumers'. If somebody regards two products as very similar (substitutable) he chooses one of them mainly by chance and situational influences. Hence, the evaluation of two competing products proved to be a better predictor of buying intentions than one product alone (Laroche *et al.*, 1994). This means that two similar products both influence the final decision and are therefore in tough competition. They define the set from which the choice follows. The idea of substitutability is also the core of every positioning analysis. Strategic marketing recommendations always seek a unique position far away from the rivals.

All strategic analyses of consumer perceptions or behaviour suffer from a common problem: the person–situation–product interdependency. This interdependency is burdensome for positioning, segmentation or the demand approach of competitor identification. The occasions and the interaction between persons and usage situation are predominant for the analysis of competitive relationships (Srivastava *et al.*, 1984; Shocker *et al.*, 1984). Not only have different persons different perceptions, but also one person may seek different benefits on different occasions which is especially valid in tourism. One product may be used in various usage situations from persons with different attitudes. Therefore the managerial objectives of the task have to be specified exactly in advance.

Competition in the leisure segment

Tourism in general consists of a diversity of products and product usages which is even more valid for urban tourism because of its fragmented offer. One has to decide which of these products to analyse. It can be assumed, for example, that two cities compete within the congress business but are not competitors in the culture market. It is also important whether one is searching for preferences or similarities (Lefkoff-Hagius and Mason, 1993). In positioning theory this is known as perceptual or preference mapping and repeatedly leads to divergent results. The following study analyses the situation in the leisure market only, with a focus on short holidays. Competition is in segments (Bordas, 1994) and although the short holiday market is a restriction to just one of many segments of international urban tourism, it is one of the main target segments. Moreover it seems easier to identify competitors for the business market as there are unique prerequisites that determine the set of possible destinations (e.g. congress centres, airport distance). The dimensions that are responsible for competition, therefore, are more easily identified in the business segment.

In the leisure market, however, it is not yet clear which criteria determine the market structure. There is a lack of material about the perceptions of different cities, or about the dimensions of satisfaction or the criteria used in the decision process.[3] Haywood and Muller (1988) report sixteen attributes that influence satisfaction in urban tourism, far too many to really determine perceptions or the decision process finally. There has to be some simplification in the perceptions of the consumers that makes their decision process more manageable. Due to this uncertainty it seems appropriate to use a data collection method without using any kind of attributes as stimuli. This guarantees that the dimensions found in the study below are composed of criteria that are readily accessible in the minds of the consumers. It can be argued that these dimensions are important determinants or moderators for the attitude–behaviour relationship (Shimp *et al.*, 1993). It is the cognitive structure in the minds of the consumers that governs the behaviour. This may be particularly true in the case of low city knowledge and familiarity. The following example therefore seeks not only to explore the competitive intensity of European cities in terms of perceived similarities but also to understand the underlying dimensions on which the competition is based. It can be argued that these dimensions differ from the guest mix hypothesized in the preceding sections.

Sample characteristics

The field study took place on the ferry from Germany to Great Britain and consists of about one half British and one half German respondents. The convenience sample includes only persons planning a city trip within the next two years in order to guarantee a certain level of involvement in the study theme. The sample consists of approximately 50 per cent men and 50 per cent women. There is a small over-representation of younger people which seems acceptable as the younger age groups tend to be more interested in city tourism (Woodside *et al.*, 1989). The total sample consists of 272 persons. Data were collected for 30 cities, including the most prominent capitals of Europe in terms of tourism nights as well as certain destinations like Bruges, Cologne or The Hague which were included because of their specificity (see Table 4.4 for the list of cities). This means that the cities analysed are those that the respondents are familiar with to a certain degree either because of their (tourism) popularity or because of their geographical vicinity to the respondents.

Sorting data

The data collection method for the present task fulfils two basic requirements: it has to measure similarity without attributes and it has to collect similarities for a large number of cities. For this purpose a sorting approach is one of the most practicable forms of data collection. Pairwise comparisons or anchor point techniques are not suitable for ten objects or more. To let the respondents group stimuli according to their feeling of substitutability is a relatively easy task. It seems to be an appropriate way to deal with as many as 30 objects. Cards containing the names of the cities were handed out and each person was allowed to create as many piles as (s)he wished, with each pile containing a free number of cities. It is one of the least-biasing instructions and shifts the problems from the respondent to the researcher who has to preprocess the nominal data collected.

The rationale of this data collection method and the consequent analysis

Table 4.4 The 30 cities analysed

Amsterdam	Frankfurt	Oslo
Athens	Geneva	Paris
Barcelona	Hamburg	Prague
Berlin	Helsinki	Rome
Bruges	Istanbul	Salzburg
Brussels	Lisbon	Stockholm
Budapest	London	The Hague
Cologne	Madrid	Venice
Dublin	Milan	Vienna
Edinburgh	Munich	Zurich

is that the sorting results should correspond to the map in the minds of the consumers. It should portray the dimensions of the evaluation process as well as the positions of the objects (cities) in this perceptual space. Of course, different consumers have different criteria of sorting in their minds. This becomes a problem if there is too much heterogeneity in the sample. Then, aggregating results becomes meaningless. The heterogeneity may be due to different levels of product knowledge, different value and attitude structures or simply to different social classes or cultures.

There are several ways of analysing sorting data. The original data matrix consists of 272 rows (persons) and 30 columns (cities) with as many nominal code values as groups have been built (see the upper part of Table 4.5). In this case an open sorting task was formulated, so the number of groups and code numbers differ among the respondents.[4] Usually a symmetric stimulus×stimulus (30×30) matrix is generated for each respondent (middle part of Table 4.5). The cells of the matrix contain either a 1 or 0. This binary code just means that two cities are similar (in the same group) or not in the eyes of the particular respondent. Hence, 272 individual square data matrices serve as raw data input.

Table 4.5 Schematic presentation of the data structure and preprocessing

Original data matrix

Respondent number	Amsterdam	Athens	Barcelona	Vienna	Zurich
1	2	4	1	4	7
2	1	1	1	4	3
⋮					
272	2	4	2	2	3

Individual binary similarity matrix
272 × (respondents) = input for SOM analysis

Respondent 1	Amsterdam	Athens	Barcelona	Vienna	Zurich
Amsterdam	1	0	0	0	0
Athens	0	1	0	1	0
Barcelona	0	0	1	0	0
⋮					
Vienna	0	1	0	1	0
Zurich	0	0	0	0	1

Aggregated squared similarity matrix (frequencies)
272 – frequency = input for MDS analysis (distance matrix)

	Amsterdam	Athens	Barcelona	Vienna	Zurich
Amsterdam	272	67	125	89	90
Athens	67	272	145	189	100
Barcelona	125	145	272	200	77
⋮					
Vienna	89	189	200	272	179
Zurich	90	100	77	179	272

MDS analysis of sorting data

Traditional ways of analysing such data require some aggregation over the subjects first. The usual aggregation is done by summing up the frequencies of similarities over all respondents (lower part of Table 4.5). This yields a symmetric matrix containing figures from 0 to 272 which may be interpreted as overall similarity measures. These measures can be refined using some correction rule like the size of a group one builds ('height of partition'), following the idea that cities in larger groups are facing lower competitive intensity compared to groups with only two or three cities. In this manner the similarity measure is refined with a factor representing the size of the group resulting in a refined distance measure.[5] The same idea of converting empirically observed similarity measures into distance measures used as input for multidimensional scaling underlies the distance-density model of Krumhansl (see for example DeSarbo *et al.*, 1990; DeSarbo and Manrai, 1992). The assumption in this model is that the distance of two objects depends, besides the perceived similarity, on the density of the region where it is located. This means that a pair of objects differing by an equivalent amount in terms of Euclidean distance in a dense region would be subject to less intensive competition than objects in a thinly populated region of the stimulus space.

After transforming the (original or refined) similarity matrix into an aggregate distance matrix one can easily apply multidimensional scaling or cluster analysis or a mixture of both (the common procedure of using hierarchical cluster analysis and multidimensional scaling on the same data set is heavily criticized by Glazer and Nakamoto, 1991). For the actual data this traditional way does not lead to a meaningful solution. Because of the loss of the individual differences there is hardly any structure left in the dataset. The result is a solution with high stress values and low R-Square (for five dimensions stress = 0.22 and RSQ = 0.18). The traditional way clearly fails to analyse the actual data that seem to be highly heterogeneous.[6]

Heterogeneity and unfamiliarity

The heterogeneity is just one of the specific problems of the empirical data. Another problem is the number of cities that have not been grouped, but have been ignored because of sparse product knowledge. Although the cities analysed are those that the respondents should be familiar with, it is unrealistic that all people know all cities. Unfamiliarity with products has always been a burden for constructing perceptual maps. Data collection methods using attributes to derive similarities between objects implicitly assume that all people are familiar with all products and that all need the same attributes to evaluate these products. Therefore techniques to cope with this problem have been derived, such as the sorting data or the pick-any data procedure (Holbrook *et al.*, 1982). In most cases they are combined with specific techniques for their analysis (e.g. LOGMAP-M by Katahira, 1990). These procedures take the idiosyncratic nature of the evoked sets into account leaving out those products the respondent is unfamiliar with. The same holds true for the use of idiosyncratic attributes as they too represent a source of bias (Steenkamp *et al.*, 1994). Although it was stressed that the personal impression is important no matter if the city is really known, some respondents ignored about ten to fifteen cities because they were unfamiliar with them. This has to be borne in mind when analysing the data as the information in these groups does not have the same meaning as that in the other groups. The common attribute of the cities in these groups is simply that they are unknown. It is not sufficient to handle such data as missing, nor is it advisable to regard it as comparable information.

New methodology for analysing sorting data

As mentioned, the traditional way of processing sorting data is to aggregate the individual sortings and use the aggregated data matrix for cluster analysis or multidimensional scaling with all the problems of 'noisy data' because of different frames of references, different criteria for grouping or different attitude structures (Day *et al.*, 1979). Newer ways of coping with these data are correspondence analysis or some other kind of optimal scaling procedures (Nishisato, 1994). These procedures do not necessarily need an aggregation step prior to the analysis (van der Kloot and van Herk, 1991). Tabu search (see Coates *et al.*, 1994) or simulated annealing are two of the other new computer intensive methods that are slowly being adapted by marketers (Coates *et al.*, 1994). These are techniques to solve the combinatorial problems inherent in the ordering task. Although originally created to avoid local optima it was shown that traditional pairwise interchange strategies are not markedly inferior (De Soete *et al.*, 1988).

In the following example the neurocomputing technique of Kohonen's self-organizing feature maps (SOMs) is used. The SOM technique has already been used successfully to analyse the competitive relationships with guest mix data (Mazanec, 1995a, and section 4.1). Hence, the competitive learning of the algorithm proved to work out in the case of metric data. In this section it is demonstrated that the technique works with nominal data, too. It serves as a new methodology for analysing sorting data that has the potential of solving the aggregation and segmentation problems.

SOMs versus cluster analysis

The SOMs are able to process the data individually. The complete analysis is done on an individual level; it is the final classification run and the subsequent interpretation that reduces the data in order to detect the market structure of European city tourism. What are being searched for are the patterns inherent in the individual data. It is similar to clustering data into similar groups. The technique behind the SOM is called unsupervised learning, a fundamental concept of neurocomputing techniques. Of course, a simple clustering technique like k-means clustering does not fulfil the requirements of market structuring. A mere clustering does not reveal competitive relationships. The SOM is not only a clustering technique but it attempts to find the topological structure hidden in the data (Pal *et al.*, 1993).[7] This structure reflects the competitive intensity between the European tourist cities. The result of a SOM analysis does not yield continuous dimensions (like in map-generating techniques) nor simple discrete clusters (as in traditional tree solutions like hierarchical clustering).[8]

The SOM technique considers that certain cities are more often in one group than others and therefore competitors. Of course, one should not aggregate first because there are always segments that have different structures which the aggregation destroys. The SOMs, however, segment and position the cities, at the same time guaranteeing that different market structures are portrayed for homogeneous subgroups. This is similar to the idea of overlapping rather than disjunctive clustering which is promoted by several authors for analysing market structure (Moore, 1990). Beside the heterogeneity the SOM technique also solves the problem of unfamiliarity. It is expected to separate the data vectors representing the groups which are left out by the individual consumers, hence leaving an interpretation free to the researcher without distorting the analysis (Mazanec, 1995a).

A reasonable map size for the present task is a 3×3 grid. Nine prototypes seem to be fine enough to portray 30 cities.[9] A one-dimensional solution would not be enough to portray the complex competitive relationships between cities. Some cities only compete in one league (for example, smaller cities) whereas others are hypothesized to compete with regional neighbours as well as with other cities in the same league (compare leagues in Ashworth and Voogd, 1990, pp. 4ff.). Therefore a quadratic grid meets with the requirements of the task. An SOM grid follows the idea of substitutability not as a pure classificational approach because it is also a measure of degree. Cities within one prototype are the toughest competitors and this intensity weakens with growing distance between the prototypes. Competitive relationships are not a question of being competitors or not but should be differentiated at least on an ordinal level.

Prototypes in Euclidean space

Before the prototypes are described in detail the quality of the results is examined by traditional methods. The SOM solution asserts that neighbours are more similar than prototypes further away. To show this topological structure of the prototypes an MDS was run with the coordinates of the nine

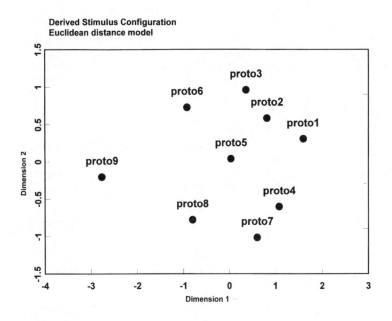

**Derived Stimulus Configuration
Euclidean distance model**

Figure 4.15 MDS solution of prototypes

prototypes (Figure 4.15). The underlying similarity matrix is derived from the 30 weights corresponding to the cities used as variables in the analysis. The two-dimensional solution is acceptable. As the reader may verify the neighbour relationships (and therefore the assumed degree of competition between prototypes) in terms of actual Euclidean distances correspond to the ordinal structure and define a reasonable quadratic grid. An outlier is prototype nine. It is the representative of those cities which were left ungrouped in the sorting task. Due to the large number of such cities the weights are all near 1, because all those cases defined by the ungrouped cities consist of many 1s. Hence it is not similar to any of the subgroups defined by the other prototypes. However, the SOM analysis reduced the 30 dimensions in a satisfying manner.

SOM weights as competition indicators

To analyse competitive relationships the cities belonging to each prototype have to be determined. Figure 4.16 shows the highest weights for all prototypes. Note that each prototype actually is the typical profile of a certain subset of the data. It therefore represents certain cities (as seen by one respondent) in terms of similarity. In fact, a prototype can be responsible for either different cities perceived as similar by one respondent or one city as seen by different respondents. Each prototype can be regarded

❶	❷	❸
The Hague: 0.33 Amsterdam: 0.33 Edinburgh: 0.29 Bruges: 0.25 Stockholm: 0.24 Dublin: 0.23 Helsinki: 0.23 Brussels: 0.23 Paris: 0.22 Zurich: 0.22	London: 0.62 Berlin: 0.56 Paris: 0.52 Stockholm: 0.42 Vienna: 0.36 Amsterdam: 0.36 Rome: 0.34 The Hague: 0.34	Salzburg: 0.67 Venice: 0.65 Budapest: 0.61 Prague: 0.52 Vienna: 0.51 Lisbon: 0.43
❹	❺	❻
Rome: 0.58 Milan: 0.52 Barcelona: 0.45 Istanbul: 0.42 Madrid: 0.38 Prague: 0.33 Athens: 0.32 Lisbon: 0.32	Oslo: 0.54 Helsinki: 0.52 Stockholm: 0.51 Dublin: 0.45 Edinburgh: 0.45 Lisbon: 0.43 Bruges: 0.42 The Hague: 0.41	Zurich: 0.70 Geneva: 0.67 Venice: 0.66 Salzburg: 0.63 Brussels: 0.62 The Hague: 0.61 Stockholm: 0.59 Budapest: 0.58 Cologne: 0.58
❼	❽	❾
Cologne: 0.74 Frankfurt: 0.65 Munich: 0.64 Hamburg: 0.61	Frankfurt: 0.70 Milan: 0.68 Barcelona: 0.67 Istanbul: 0.66 Rome: 0.62 Munich: 0.60 Geneva: 0.57 Prague: 0.57	Istanbul: 0.85 Cologne: 0.85 Geneva: 0.84 Milan: 0.84 Helsinki: 0.83 Athens: 0.83 Budapest: 0.83 Munich: 0.81

Figure 4.16 Highest prototype weights for the 3×3 SOM grid

as a subset of the market and the information of similarity between submarkets (and therefore degrees of competition) is added. The weights of the prototypes depict the degree of similarity a particular prototype has with each individual city. Similar weights on a prototype mean that those cities are competitors because they evidently emerged frequently in the same group. A weight of one for two cities would mean that those cities are perfectly represented by the prototype and are tough competitors. As the results are aggregated all values are below one. The topological structure of the map guarantees similar prototypes as neighbours.

The prototypes 1 and 9 represent the two extremes. The absolute level of similarity is consistently low in prototype 1 and high in prototype 9.[10] The first prototype therefore represents those cases where a city's position was regarded as unique. The competitive relationships within these prototypes are weak compared to the rest. Geographical vicinity is an obvious reason that formed this class of competitors. On the other hand there is a cluster with high weights for all cities (9). This is a result of the individual differences and the often undifferentiated big groups due to unfamiliarity. These data vectors build one group as expected. Still this means that there is a certain degree of competition between all cities. As has been explained, perceptual approaches are appropriate for detecting potential competitors. Hence, all European cities can be regarded as potential competitors to some degree. This does not sound very absurd and shows that there are potential substitutes for all cities or 'to some degree, in some circumstances, almost everything can be a partial substitute for almost everything else. A (fifteen-cent) stamp substitutes to some extent for an airline ticket' (Moran, 1973, cited in Day *et al.*, 1979, p. 9).

Competition is strongest inside of a prototype and neighbours constitute competition of lower intensity. Hence, prototype 2 includes some cities that also appear in the first one (Stockholm, Amsterdam, The Hague) but is composed of the most popular tourist cities.[11] A possible interpretation is that consumers perceive partial substitutability between nearby regional cities and the appealing popular tourist cities. Prototype 4 contains further competitors: Rome, Milan, Barcelona, Istanbul and Madrid with the highest weights and Athens, Lisbon and Prague then define a clear cluster of southern cities that are seen as similar holiday destinations. It is interesting that some of these cities appear again in prototype 8 together with German ones. It may be argued that the southern cities represent substitutes for the short-haul destinations for both Germans and British. It seems that the criteria used are dominated by geographical aspects. Primarily the vicinity of the home cities makes them substitutable. Another prime aspect is the popularity as a tourist destination. A third aspect may be verified to be a trade-off between cities that are close and those that are more attractive but further away. In the language of decision research the forces behind the groupings may be called acceptability and accessibility (Sambandam and Lord, 1995). Accessible in mind are those that are geographically near or popular and the acceptability coincides with the trade-off mentioned. Hence, a city can have different competitors based on different criteria. It is the managerial task to define the relevant criteria as this depends solely on the aim of the analysis.

Dimensional interpretation

The SOM solution cannot be interpreted geometrically in terms of spatial dimensions. Spatial models have always been more comfortable and easier to interpret. Their popularity lies in the easy-to-grasp meaning of the results. It is still possible to use a spatial model (a classical MDS) in a second step. The weights derived through the SOM can be used as input for an MDS. It makes sense to use the column profiles (representing the aggregated city profiles for nine prototypes of Figure 4.16) to compute similarities between the 30 cities. The resulting similarity matrix serves as

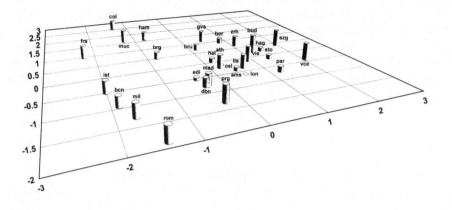

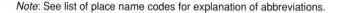

Note: See list of place name codes for explanation of abbreviations.

Figure 4.17 MDS solution for prototype weights

input for an MDS. Figure 4.17 shows the resulting map. A three-dimensional solution has satisfactory goodness-of-fit criteria (stress = 0.14; RSQ = 0.89). It is obviously possible to reduce the dimensionality of the dataset by Kohonen's competitive learning scheme. Although the original SOM solution is interpretable only on an ordinal level and does not permit any dimensional interpretation, the MDS solution can be inspected for dimensions underlying the solution. But there is not necessarily any meaning in the dimensions. The dimensional interpretation is allowed but not required (Torgerson, 1986).

The MDS map confirms the partially geographical interpretation of the SOM grid. The German cluster in particular appears in the MDS solution, too. But geography cannot explain one of the axes in general. It rather seems that there is no meaningful dimensional interpretation. Nothing can be added to the ordinal information from the SOM. It is even more difficult to define the dimensions behind the MDS solution. It may be discrete features rather than continuous dimensions that determine the market structure on the demand side. This coincides with the fact that brands as opposed to categories are usually evaluated on the basis of dichotomous attributes (Johnson *et al.*, 1992). The supposed popularity of a city in terms of tourism nights does not dominate a single dimension. Of course, the competitive relationships need not necessarily be determined by city attributes. It is possible that travel motives or occasions define the submarkets described. This means that the respondents had different frames of reference in mind when sorting the cities.

Comparison with other studies

Mayerhofer (1994) recently studied the image of Vienna and its alleged competitors Prague, Budapest, Rome and Munich among the Viennese inhabitants. He used verbal and non-verbal image attributes and found that Vienna has a unique image (this may be typical for a self-image). In his study Prague and Budapest are perceived as very similar and are the only immediate competitors throughout these five cities. Though not designed for tourism purposes the results partly coincide with the tourism substitutability results here. The main difference lies in the close substitutability of Prague and Budapest that is perceived by city travellers for Vienna. The reason for this difference is probably the self-image effect of Mayerhofer's study.

Typologies of cities offer another interesting comparison (see Page, 1995, pp. 16–17). Page's typology, which represents an unsystematic approach, makes use of a lot of different criteria to build the various groups. The groups range from capitals (political criteria) to cultural/art cities or industrial cities (historical/economic). One can see from this classification that there is no sole grouping criterion and this holds true for the consumer point of view, too. This multicriteria situation can be explained by looking at the determinants of tourism demand. Among them are motivations, destination features and contingency factors relating to traveller's choice (Pearce, 1993, cited in Page, 1995, pp. 27–8). All these factors or some combination may influence the substitutability perceptions. Of course, this multicriteria situation is strongly aggravated by the use of a free sorting task as individual differences are revealed.

Segmenting the market

Interpreting the weights of the prototypes is not the only way to attach meaning to the results. The usual way that is used for segmentation purposes is to run a classification. This means that all individual cases are classified according to their nearest prototype. The result is a clustering of the cases which leads to simultaneous segmentation and positioning (Mazanec, 1995b). Marketers have been striving for that since the work of Grover and Srinivasan (1987). In the present study cities frequently seen as similar should often emerge in one particular prototype. But because of the large individual differences there is no reasonable classification result. The individual cities are classified as seen by one consumer, so the distribution of the cities over the prototypes is even (see for example Brussels, Prague and Rome in Figure 4.18). The classification is strongly determined by the size of the groups built in the sorting exercise. As most cities are in relatively small groups, the bulk of cases is classified to the first prototype because of its low weights. The distance computed between a particular

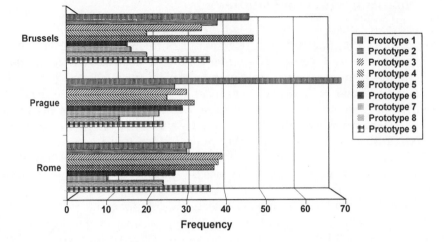

Figure 4.18 Cities' distribution over prototypes

prototype and one data vector is equally influenced by all 30 similarity codes. The 'zero-vector' similar prototype produced by the small groups therefore has the shortest distance in most cases because of the large number of zero codes in the individual cases. Thus it dominates the subsequent classification.

There are principally two simple ways to cope with this problem. A first idea modifies the data for the final classification run. As the zeros and ones in the dataset obviously have different meanings, one could just use these ones for the computation of the distance to the prototypes. This is similar to the idea of different weights of nominal codes in the computation of matching coefficients such as in the Tanimoto coefficient. The disadvantage in this solution is that many cities are classified to the 'one-vector' presented in prototype 9 because of its high weights. It is also questionable if it is meaningful to neglect completely the information of unsimilarity (the zeros) in the classification exercise.

A better solution preprocesses the input data matrix. The present problem manifests in the strong influence of the zeros for the distance computations. Therefore there has to be a weight factor for the few ones that compensates for the high frequency of the zeros. A simple idea is to fix a constant amount of similarity points that each person hypothetically distributes for each city. Assume that 30 similarity points constitute the constant sum scale. An extreme respondent who groups all cities as substitutes hence results in a vector containing only ones (the 30 points divided by the number of cities in each group). A small group including three cities gets assigned ten similarity points for each of these three cities. This simple weighting scheme guarantees a stronger influence of the information in the particular groups regarding small groups as more competition-intensive. The final prototype weights then are not restricted between one and zero and hence the distance of the real substitutes has a stronger influence on the classification results. By this preprocessing the dominance of the group size in the classification could be eliminated.

Such data modifications improve the possibility of the classification as a starting point for the task of segmentation. With the modified data matrix the classification not only clusters together cases with a comparable amount of city similarity codes, but also persons seeing the same cities as competitors. These groups apparently build a homogeneous subgroup of consumers. Then one could fuse the results with demographic or other personal variables to analyse the consumer market. This could yield hints for the forces behind the differing perceptions of European tourism cities. The segmentation possibility methodologically exists for the actual data as well. However, because of the heterogeneous groupings segmentation is not managerially meaningful without the described data modifications.

For the present results the weights (Figure 4.16) nevertheless represent a useful solution that can serve as a broad frame for the competitive relationships in European city tourism from the consumer point of view. From a non-formal point of view a narrower definition of a usage context (e.g. shopping or honeymoon trips) in the wording of the sorting task may result in more homogeneous judgements and more concrete findings about the competitive structure. However, a restriction to just one of these motives at the expense of generalization was not the aim of this section.

Notes

[1] A test for the existence of the variety-seeking phenomenon in brand switching is given in Kannan and Sanchez (1994).

[2] Their US data showed that apart from outdoor vacationers, city tourists are the most loyal segments in terms of the trip type. About one third of the city tourists plan their next trip to be a city trip again. Switches to a city trip can be expected primarily from touring vacationers and visitors to theme parks, exhibitions and special events. It appears that city tourism appeals to more active vacationers.

[3] Today the author is not aware of any study about a posteriori derived perceptional dimensions or decision-making in urban tourism.

[4] The information of open sorting task tends to distribute widely over many dimensions (Nishisato, 1994, p. 173) and therefore is sometimes hard to interpret. Nevertheless, it fits the purpose by not forcing respondents to build the same number of groups.

[5] Implicitly this is a weighting of the respondents according to their product knowledge. Those who know the market well will create more and smaller groups which results in a stronger influence on the final distance measure. For details see the Appendix.

[6] To define some segments a priori and run an INDSCAL model could improve the

results but no perfect solution can be expected. Deterministic models such as these MDS techniues confound variation (e.g. because of hetrogeneous perceptions) and distance (Mackay and Zinnes, 1986).

[7] As there is a methodological appendix at the end of the book a short non-formal explanation of the differences between k-means clustering and Kohonen's SOMs will suffice here (compare Gallant, 1993, pp. 134–9). The differences are twofold:

1. k-means clustering always uses all data, calculates all differences from data points to the actual cluster centres (prototypes), classifies and calculates the new barycentres. In the SOM there is always one data point drawn by chance that changes the prototype.
2. k-means clustering always changes the barycentres individually (independently) whereas the SOM technique always changes prototypes and neighbours in the same direction.

[8] It is not yet clear for which kind of data the SOM technique is appropriate. The decision between spatial or non-spatial models should be directed by the concreteness of the product and the data collection method (attribute ratings versus direct similarity ratings; Ghose, 1994) as well as psychological considerations regarding the existence of dimensions or features guiding consumer evaluations (Glazer and Nakamoto, 1991). As the SOM technique combines some characteristics of both, recommendations in terms of data and object interdependencies are an area for future research.

[9] The number of prototypes is arbitrary as in cluster analysis. It has to be chosen by the researcher with the help of homogeneity and topology-fitness indices. The present solution was the best available.

[10] One remark is in order here. Strictly one can only interpret neighbours as being similar. Two objects need not necessarily be dissimilar if they are not represented by neighbours (Mazanec, 1995a). This makes an important difference in the interpretation compared to classical MDS procedures where the dissimilarity is the main source of interpretation.

[11] Prototypes 1 and 2 are the most similar in terms of Euclidean distance followed by 1 and 4, 2 and 3, 5 and 8. The least similar neighbours constitute prototype 9 with both its neighbours.

References

Ashworth, G.J. and Voogd, H. (1990) *Selling the City: Marketing Approaches in Public Sector Urban Planning*. London: Belhaven.

Bordas, E. (1994) *Competitiveness of Tourist Destinations in Long Distance Markets*. Paper presented at the TRC-Congress, 13–16 May 1994, Swansea.

Coates, D., Doherty, N. and French, A. (1994) The new multivariate jungle: computer intensive methods in database marketing. In G.J. Hooley and M.K. Hussey (eds) *Quantitative Methods in Marketing*. London: Academic Press, 207–20.

Coltman, M.M. (1989) *Tourism Marketing*. New York: Van Nostrand Reinhold.

Cooper, L.G. (1988) Competitive maps: the structure underlying asymmetric cross elasticities. *Management Science* **34**, 707–23.

Day, G.S., Shocker, A.D. and Srivastava, R. (1979) Customer-oriented approaches to identifying product-markets. *Journal of Marketing* **3**, 8–20.

DeSarbo, W.S. and Manrai, A.K. (1992) A new multidimensional scaling methodology for the analysis of asymmetric proximity data in marketing research. *Marketing Science* **11**, 1–20.

DeSarbo, W.S., Manrai, A.K. and Burke, R.R. (1990) A non-spatial methodology for the analysis of two-way proximity data incorporating the distance-density hypothesis. *Psychometrika* **55**, 229–53.

De Soete, G., Hubert, L. and Arabie, P. (1988) On the use of simulated annealing for combinatorial data analysis. In W. Gaul and M. Schader (eds) *Data, Expert Knowledge and Decisions.* Berlin: Springer.

Fraser, C. and Bradford, J.W. (1983) Competitive market structure analysis: principal partitioning of revealed substitutabilities. *Journal of Consumer Research* **10**, 15–30.

Fraser, C. and Bradford, J.W. (1984) Competitive market structure analysis: a reply. *Journal of Consumer Research* **11**, 842–7.

Gallant, St.I. (1993) *Neural Network Learning and Expert Systems.* Cambridge, MA: MIT Press.

Ghose, S. (1994) Visually representing consumer perceptions. Issues and managerial insights. *European Journal of Marketing* **28**, 5–18.

Glazer, R. and Nakamoto, K. (1991) Cognitive geometry: an analysis of structure underlying representations of similarity. *Marketing Science* **10**, 205–28.

Grover, R. and Srinivasan, V. (1987) A simultaneous approach to market segmentation and market structuring. *Journal of Marketing Research* **24**, 139–53.

Haywood, K.M. and Muller, T.E (1988) The urban tourist experience: evaluating satisfaction. *Hospitality Education and Research Journal* **12**, 453–9.

Holbrook, M., Moore, W. and Winer, R.S. (1982) Constructing joint spaces from pick-any data: a new tool for consumer analysis. *Journal of Consumer Research* **9**, 99–105.

Johnson, M.D., Lehmann, D.R., Fornell, C. and Horne, D.R. (1992) Attribute abstraction, feature-dimensionality, and the scaling of product similarities. *International Journal of Research in Marketing* **9**, 131–47.

Kannan, P.K. and Sanchez, S.M. (1994) Competitive market structures: a subset selection analysis. *Management Science* **40**, 1484–99.

Katahira, H. (1990) Perceptual mapping using ordered logit analysis. *Marketing Science* **9**, 1–17.

Laroche, M., Hui, M. and Zhou, L. (1994) A test of the effects of competition on consumer brand selection processes. *Journal of Business Research* **31**, 171–81.

Lefkoff-Hagius, R. and Mason, C. (1993) Characteristic, beneficial, and image attributes in consumer judgements of similarity and preference. *Journal of Consumer Research* **20**, 100–10.

MacKay, D.B. and Zinnes, J.L. (1986) A probabilistic model for the multidimensional scaling of proximity and preference data. *Marketing Science* **5**, 325–44.

Mayerhofer, W. (1994) Die Erlebniswelten europäischer Metropolen. *Werbeforschung & Praxis* **5/94**, 194–6.

Mazanec, J.A. (1995a) Competition among European tourist cities: a comparative analysis with multidimensional scaling and self-organizing maps. *Tourism Economics* **1**, 283–302.

Mazanec, J.A. (1995b) Positioning analysis with self-organizing maps. An exploratory study on luxury hotels. *Cornell Hotel and Restaurant Administration Quarterly* **36**, 80–95.

Moore, W.L. (1990) Factorial preference structures. *Journal of Consumer Research* **17**, 94–104.

Nishisato, S. (1994) *Elements of Dual Scaling. An Introduction to Practical Data Analysis.* Hillsdale, NJ: Lawrence Erlbaum.

Page, S. (1995) *Urban Tourism.* London: Routledge.

Pal, N.R., Bezdek, J.C. and Tsao, E.C.-K. (1993) Generalized clustering networks and Kohonen's self-organizing scheme. *IEEE Transactions on Neural Networks* **4**, 549–57.

Sambandam, R. and Lord, K.R. (1995) Switching behaviour in automobile markets: a consideration-sets model. *Journal of the Academy of Marketing Science* **23**, 57–65.

Shimp, T.A., Samiee, S. and Madden, T.J. (1993) Countries and their products: a cognitive structure perspective. *Journal of the Academy of Marketing Science* **21**, 323–30.

Shocker, A.D., Zahorik, A.J. and Stewart, D.W. (1984) Competitive market structure analysis: a comment on problems. *Journal of Consumer Research* **11**, 836–41.

Srivastava, R.K., Alpert, M.J. and Shocker, A.D. (1984) A customer-oriented approach for determining market structures. *Journal of Marketing* **48**, 32–45.

Steenkamp, J.-B.E.M., Van Trijp, H.C.M. and Ten Berge, J.M.F. (1994) Perceptual mapping based on idiosyncratic sets of attributes. *Journal of Marketing Research* **31**, 15–27.

Torgerson, W.S. (1986) Scaling and psychometrika: spatial and alternative representations of similarity data. *Psychometrika* **51**, 57–63.

Uysal, M., Marsinko, A. and Barrett, R.T. (1995) An examination of trip type switching and market share: a Markov chain model application. *Journal of Travel & Tourism Marketing* **4**, 45–55.

van der Kloot, W. and van Herk, H. (1991) Multidimensional scaling of sorting data: a comparison of three procedures. *Multivariate Behavioral Research* **26**, 563–81.

Woodside, A.G. and Carr, J.A. (1988) Consumer decision making and competitive marketing strategies: applications for tourism planning. *Journal of Travel Research* **26**, 2–7.

Woodside, A.G., Pearce, B. and Wallo, M. (1989) Urban tourism: an analysis of visitors to New Orleans and competing cities. *Journal of Travel Research* **27**, 22–30.

Zahorik, A.J. (1994) A nonhierarchical brand switching model for inferring market structure. *European Journal of Operational Research* **76**, 344–58.

Part V

Strategic market evaluation

5.1

Strengths and weaknesses of the growth-share matrix approach

Karl Wöber

For a city tourist office operating in a changing environment, management is required to assess how these changes and its own organizational dynamics affect future prospects. According to Henshall and Roberts (1985) strategic decisions in the tourism industry include such issues as which markets are most attractive (e.g. which markets have the highest visitor expenditure potential); in which markets a country's products are most competitive; how promotional budgets should be allocated for greatest effectiveness; and what the promotional message should convey.

The most widely used methods of strategic planning techniques are portfolio models where a company is viewed as a portfolio of individual businesses or products and brands. The simplest model is the growth-share matrix which was developed by the Boston Consulting Group and particularly noticed by Day (1977), Wind and Mahajan (1981) and Aaker (1992). This model enables diversified companies to maximize the performance of their product portfolio by comparing the performance of their own products with the market share and growth rate prospects of their dominant competitor. The growth share matrix consists of three assessment criteria for products:

- the market growth rate, which describes the attractiveness of a market;
- the relative market share, which represents the company's performance measure;
- the contribution to overall sales. This criterion can be interpreted as the 'importance value' of a product within a company's product mix.

In this approach the company classifies each of its strategic business units (SBUs) in the business portfolio matrix. If adopted for strategic planning support for tourism organizations, the assessment criteria are portrayed along the vertical axis as growth rate and the horizontal axis as relative share, with the diameters of circles representing the importance value for each major generating country. The Austrian National Tourist Office, for instance, uses this approach of portfolio presentation as its basic managerial communication interface (Wöber, 1993). Calantone and Mazanec (1991) also demonstrate a practical example of the growth share matrix applied to tourist receiving countries.

The various attractions a city offers to tourists resemble the SBUs of a company. Depending on the position of a business unit, it is usually called a dog, question mark, cash cow or star product. Each quadrant represents a distinct type of success situation (stars are high growth, high share SBUs; cash cows are low growth, high share SBUs; question marks are low share, high growth SBUs; and dogs are low share, low growth SBUs). McKercher (1995) argues that tourism marketers face different challenges as they have no direct financial interest in the specific products their regions offer and even less control over the product mix and new product development. As a result, their function becomes one of matching markets that best fit with the region's product offerings, rather than designing products specifically for various markets as is the case with traditional product development. For them their strategic marketing requirements become one of managing the market portfolio rather than the product portfolio.

Indeed, the marketing function of a city's tourist office includes promoting the city both internationally and nationally as a tourist destination. Further marketing activities undertaken by tourist offices include the provision of appropriate marketing research studies and the maintenance of information centres (see Part II). Only a few CTOs manage individual tourist attractions themselves and open new or close less attractive sites (e.g. the Dublin Tourist Office; see also Magee, 1995). Recommendations and strategies for products and markets in the various quadrants of the matrix are therefore only suggestive and not prescriptive. Also, the primary utility of the growth-share matrix, as adapted to strategic tourism marketing, is the ability to identify and analyse the performance of individual markets, to identify those needing support, those with potential to be developed and those which need no significant support. Normally, it is not the task to eliminate or develop tourist attractions or to interfere in the tourist service delivery.

The adoption of the growth-share matrix for city tourism marketing planning is conceptually simple. It is frequently assumed that European cities base their marketing effort on a geographical segmentation approach. This simplification corresponds to many tourist offices' strategy by allocating their budget by attractive countries of origin (see Mazanec, 1986, for an Austrian case study). Market share calculations (Part II) show that it is apparently possible for many small cities to be profitable in large markets. In reality they have a large share of a smaller market segment which they are sometimes not aware of. This is another reason why understanding market segmentation is the key to successful marketing. Therefore, as a first step, CTO management has to be certain that the market has been carefully defined. In Part IV the comparison of different guest mix structures was identified to be an appropriate way to find subgroups of competitive European cities out of more than 40 locations. The cities of Amsterdam, Brussels and Lisbon were found to be under mutual competitive pressure and were chosen for a pictorial presentation in a growth-share matrix.

The measure of market share used is the city's bednight[1] share relative to its largest competitor. This is important because it reflects the degree of dominance the city exerts in the market. For example, if a city has 20 per cent market share and its biggest competitor also has 20 per cent, this position is usually less favourable than the biggest competitor having only 10 per cent market share. The relative ratios would be 1:1 compared to 2:1. It is this ratio, or measure of market dominance, that is denoted by the horizontal axis. The difference between absolute and relative market shares is demonstrated for Amsterdam, Brussels and Lisbon in Table 5.1.

Turning now to the vertical axis of the matrix, the market growth rates for

Table 5.1 Absolute and relative market shares for Amsterdam, Brussels and Lisbon

	Bednights* 1994					
	Absolute market share			Relative market share		
Market/destination	Amsterdam	Brussels	Lisbon	Amsterdam	Brussels	Lisbon
Australia/NZ	77.9	11.6	10.5	6.70	0.15	0.13
Austria	35.7	35.9	28.3	0.99	1.01	0.79
Germany	41.8	31.7	26.4	1.32	0.76	0.63
Belgium/Luxembourg	27.1	55.8	17.1	0.49	2.06	0.31
Canada	55.1	24.4	20.5	2.26	0.44	0.37
Switzerland	51.1	23.3	25.6	1.99	0.46	0.50
Denmark	38.4	44.7	17.0	0.86	1.16	0.38
France	30.0	46.6	23.4	0.64	1.55	0.50
United Kingdom	55.3	31.3	13.4	1.77	0.57	0.24
Greece	19.4	64.3	16.3	0.30	3.33	0.25
Italy	43.5	26.6	29.9	1.46	0.61	0.69
Japan	39.6	40.0	20.4	0.99	1.01	0.51
Netherlands	47.2	38.0	14.8	1.24	0.80	0.31
Finland	32.9	48.8	18.3	0.67	1.49	0.38
Spain	24.8	18.9	56.3	0.44	0.34	2.27
Sweden	35.0	46.4	18.7	0.75	1.33	0.40
USA	53.1	28.4	18.5	1.87	0.54	0.35

* Bednights in all accommodations (*Source*: Grabler and Wöber, 1995).

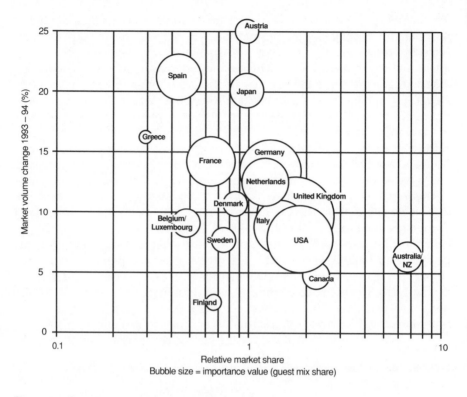

Figure 5.1 Growth/share matrix for Amsterdam 1994

the various generating markets have to be estimated. The general assumption is that the market growth rate is of particular importance because in markets growing at a very low rate, it is extremely difficult to increase market share. Possibly due to the fact that the market is in the saturation phase of the product life cycle, it is dominated by a few major cities which have reached a stage of equilibrium.

The market growth rates for seventeen generating European countries have been calculated in Part II. Markets which are going through a period of high growth face either an increase in travel propensity for city trips or a significant growth in population. This situation offers the opportunity to tourism marketers to gain market share by taking a bigger proportion of the growth than their competitors. However, such a policy is very costly in promotional terms. If a city experiences growth rates lower than the market rate, then the destination is in fact losing market share. This means cost advantages for the competitors. The portfolio diagram in Figure 5.1 summarizes market growth and relative market share data for Amsterdam in 1994.

For Amsterdam, British guests contribute the largest proportion of bednights to the overall inbound volume. The diameter of the circle representing the Dutch market clearly shows the minor importance of domestic tourism and the high internationality of the city. Besides the British market, the United States, Germany, Italy, France and Spain are of particular importance for Amsterdam.

Firms are headed for a balanced portfolio of strategic business units under the growth-share matrix approach. In the field of tourism, managers are typically facing market share and guest mix problems. The presence of a fair number of business units in the star and cash cow categories is a sign of a healthy and balanced portfolio. Assuming a large number of SBUs in the cash cow section, but very few in the star section might be an indication that – with respect to tourism development – a city is currently successful, but has an uncertain future. As the market evolves over time, declining market growth rates would shrink the size of the market for today's 'cash cows'. As high growth markets become mature low growth markets over time, a city lacking strategic business units in the star section is likely to make up without cash cows in the future.

The diagram shows that in 1994 Amsterdam had a relatively balanced portfolio. Austria, Spain and Japan were the most attractive generators of city tourists in 1994. Investments into more aggressive market operation in these markets could result in a more favourable competitive position. As the competitive position of each destination in the major generating countries (particularly UK and USA) is fairly good, there will be a tough and continued struggle for building market share in the future. A considerable proportion of the promotional budget will have to be allocated to these markets. It is obvious that the Australia/New Zealand market is located in the cash cow segment. In 1994 this market was relatively unattractive, and it is very unlikely that competing destinations will be able to threaten Amsterdam's position in this market. A maintenance strategy, implying a moderate promotional budget, would be appropriate here.

According to Day (1977) the desirability of pursuing these suggestions can be examined through two additional kinds of portfolio analysis, namely:

• product portfolio trajectory analysis
• analysis of major competitors' portfolio.

Product portfolio trajectory analysis

The analysis of a firm's portfolio at a given point in time provides only a static view. The development of portfolio matrices for previous time periods using historical data to track the portfolio trajectory (the progression or movement of SBUs over a period of time) helps to analyse trends and introduces a dynamic perspective. Portfolio matrix scenarios can be

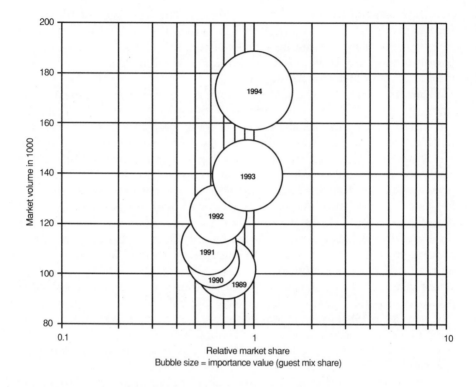

Bubble size = importance value (guest mix share)

Figure 5.2 Example for portfolio trajectory analysis: Brussels' success in the Austrian market segment between 1989 and 1994

developed for future years on the basis of projected market growth rates and tentative decisions regarding the market share strategies for the various SBUs. Tracing the trajectory of individual SBUs in previous years and projecting into future years informs about the successful or disastrous paths taken by SBUs in the past, the prospects for maintaining a balanced portfolio in the future and the need to develop new SBUs to overcome present or imminent imbalances.

Wöber (1994) demonstrates how a marketing information system can be employed to evaluate the success or failure of marketing actions by deviation analysis based on the sequential presentation of portfolio diagrams and by comparing the development with the major competitors' product portfolios. For instance, Figure 5.2 clearly shows Brussels' success in the Austrian market between 1989 and 1994. During a period of stable growth of the Austrian market Brussels conquered additional market share and reached the market leadership in this segment.

This type of framework is particularly useful to demonstrate to senior management the implications of different marketing strategies. For instance,

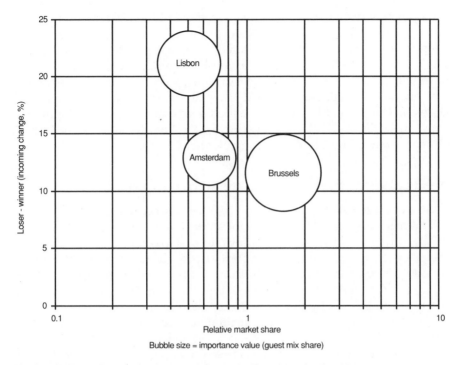

Bubble size = importance value (guest mix share)

Figure 5.3 Three European cities competing in the French market in 1994

it easily helps to explain the impracticality of targets such as 'Our goal is to achieve 5 per cent more bednights than last year . . .'. Such an objective, while fine as an overall policy, clearly becomes meaningless and self-defeating if applied to individual products in the portfolio. For example, aiming at a 5 per cent growth in a market which is growing at 10 per cent per annum is likely to prove disastrous in the long run. Likewise, to go for much higher than market growth rate in a low growth market is certain to be very cost intensive and risky.

Analysis of major competitors' portfolios

The success in attracting more business from specific market segments will depend to a great extent on competitors' marketing tactics. To outperform the competitors, city tourism managers must make more compelling offers or pre-empt their market offer. Hence, a tourism organization should not base its strategic marketing planning decisions solely on its own portfolio of businesses. Efforts should be made to develop similar matrices for the major competitors. Imbalances in the portfolios of some competitors and strengths in the portfolios of others may reveal the strategies they are likely to pursue.

Day (1977) argues that an additional gain and loss analysis for important

SBUs can be advantageous. Adapted to the field of tourism marketing, the period performance and destination preferences of various generating countries could be constantly monitored on the basis of bednights sold. For the Amsterdam tourist office, for example, comparison with other major European receiving cities might give a proxy for relative tourism performance. With this approach it is possible to monitor the competitive success or failure within a certain market segment. For instance, Figure 5.3 shows three European cities competing for the French market from 1993 to 1994 measured by nights in all accommodations.

Weaknesses of the growth-share matrix approach

While the Boston matrix is widely recognized as being important (Brown, 1992) it has a number of limitations for strategic planning utility. Wind *et al.* (1983) notice that there is considerable disagreement concerning the adequacy of the growth-share matrix approach using single factors as indicators of industry attractiveness and a firm's competitive position. In particular, Calantone and Mazanec (1991) demonstrate that the Boston matrix is constrained by the limited number of evaluation criteria utilized and by its inability to incorporate qualitative data. To overcome this defect and to provide a more flexible approach, multifactor portfolio models seek improvements in perspective, methodology, assumptions, data, conclusions and implications. All of these approaches allow for two or more assessment criteria to be condensed into each of the two dimensions named market attractiveness and business or competitive position. An adaptation of these models to the city tourism case is carried out in the following section.

Furthermore, the growth-share model is oriented to a firm's product mix rather than its market mix. The growth-share matrix was designed as an introspective analytical tool to let businesses assess the performance of their own products in the marketplace and to help them decide which products to support, build, milk or drop. Imagine for a moment a city with 80 per cent of its generating countries in the low growth markets, and only a few of them where the city is a market leader. The city's matrix would look unevenly distributed and almost all generating countries would be described as dogs. To divest in these markets may well be tantamount to throwing the baby out with the bath water!

The growth-share matrix contributes to a better understanding of the performance of an urban destination, but it has limited practical applicability in strategic tourism marketing. The Boston Matrix is conceptually appealing but it is product-oriented, rather than market-focused.

Note

[1] Counted in all accommodations.

References

Aaker, D. (1992) *Strategic Market Management*, 3rd edn. Brisbane: John Wiley and Sons.

Brown, L. (1992) *Competitive Marketing Strategy*. South Melbourne: Nelson.

Calantone, R.J. and Mazanec, J.A. (1991) Marketing management and tourism. *Annals of Tourism Research* **18**, 101–19.

Day, G.S. (1977) Diagnosing the product portfolio. *Journal of Marketing* **41**, 29–38.

Grabler, K. and Wöber, K.W. (1995) *City Tourism in Europe: Results of the 1995 FOTVE/FECTO Survey*. Unpublished research report, Institute for Tourism and Leisure Studies, Vienna University of Economics and Business Administration.

Henshall, B.D. and Roberts, R. (1985) Comparative assessment of tourist generating markets for New Zealand. *Annals of Tourism Research* **12**, 219–38.

Magee, F. (1995) *The Structures of Tourism in Dublin*. MBS thesis, Dublin: University College Dublin.

Mazanec, J.A. (1986) Allocating an advertising budget to international travel markets. *Annals of Tourism Research* **13**, 609–34.

McKercher, B. (1995) The destination-market matrix: a tourism market portfolio analysis model. *Journal of Travel & Tourism Marketing* **4**, 23–40.

Wind, Y. and Mahajan, V. (1981) Designing product and business portfolios. *Harvard Business Review* Jan–Feb, 155–65.

Wind, Y. Mahajan, V. and Swire, D.J. (1983) An empirical comparison of standardised portfolio models. *Journal of Marketing* **47**, 89–99.

Wöber, K.W. (1993) Entwicklung von Wettbewerbsstrategien mittels verschiedener Portfolioansätze im Verbund. In A. Zins (ed.) *Strategisches Management im Tourismus*. Vienna, New York: Springer.

Wöber, K.W. (1994) Strategic planning tools inside the marketing-information-system in use by the Austrian national tourist office. In W. Schertler *et al.* (eds) *Information and Communication Technologies in Tourism*. Vienna, New York: Springer.

5.2

Introducing multifactor portfolio models

Josef A. Mazanec

Basics of multifactor portfolio analysis

The multifactor approach to portfolio analysis is appealing to the management of a city tourist office (CTO) in charge of analysing tourist demand and promoting a tourist-receiving city. Unlike the growth-share matrix (Calantone and Mazanec, 1991; Mazanec, 1994) the multifactor concept is not restricted in its number of evaluation criteria for the tourism-generating countries. These countries corresponding to the 'markets' in conventional portfolio terminology are again the objects to be evaluated in a multifactor portfolio matrix or diagram. The diagram portrays the overall attractiveness of the markets and the competitive positions an urban destination occupies in each market. An innovative feature of the method demonstrated here is implemented in the computation of attractiveness and competitive position scores. The aggregate values will not be determined by a simple weighting model as usual. Instead, they will be inferred from pairwise comparison data. This approach allows the consistency of the managerial judgements to be checked. It helps to train managers in making consistent assessments of the relative importance of the attractiveness and the competitive strength criteria.

A manager prepared to accept the 'company view' for a CTO will benefit from the visualization properties of portfolio analysis. It seeks to represent complex relationships in an easy-to-read visual display. A multifactor model for assessing tourist markets will be tailored to serve this purpose. The cities of Budapest, Prague and Vienna have been found to be under mutual competitive pressure (see Part IV). They have been chosen for a sample demonstration.

Compared to the simple growth-share matrix a multifactor approach is expected to allow for a refined evaluation of the tourism-generating countries (the 'markets') and of the competitive position of an urban destination. One or more experienced managers of a CTO are responsible for making this assessment. The most popular criticism brought forward against the growth-share matrix (Day, 1986) refers to the limited number of factors entering the evaluation (i.e. market growth rate, relative market share and contribution to overall sales volume). With the multifactor approach there should be ample possibilities for the CTO managers to include more assessment criteria they deem important.

The business management practice and the literature offer a number of multifactor proposals for industry effectiveness analysis (IAA) such as the

Table 5.2 Market attractiveness and competitive position factors

---

Market attractiveness

Market factors:
     size (in dollars and/or units)
     annual growth rate (total, segments)
     diversity of market
     sensitivity to price
     cyclicality, seasonality
Competition factors:
     degree of concentration
     entries and exits
     changes in share
Financial and economic factors:
     contribution margins
     economies of scale, experience
     capacity utilization
Technological factors
Sociopolitical factors:
     social attitudes and trends
     laws and regulations

Your competitive position

Market factors:
     your share
     your annual growth (total, segments)
Competition factors:
     how you compare in terms of service, marketing capability,
     financial strength, management
     segments you have entered or left
     your relative share change
Financial and economic factors:
     your margins
     your capacity utilization
     your scale and experience
Technological factors:
     depths of your skills
Sociopolitical factors:
     your company's ability to cope with
     social change and trends

General Electric/McKinsey business screen portfolio matrix, the Arthur D. Little life cycle portfolio matrix or the Shell directional policy matrix. All of these approaches share one common feature: they allow for two or more assessment criteria to be condensed into each of the two dimensions termed 'market attractiveness' and 'business' or 'competitive position'. Table 5.2 enumerates examples for such assessment criteria (simplified from Abell and Hammond, 1979, p. 214, and Kerin *et al.*, 1990, pp. 75–6).

Given this list of examples it will be one of the first steps to detect and to operationalize factors suitable for a CTO. What makes tourism-generating countries (the objects which are going to be evaluated as 'markets') attractive for the tourism manager in a tourist city? How might a city characterize its own competitive position within a group of rivalling urban destinations? Besides looking into tourism statistics and economic data the city tourism managers may want to exploit their experience about 'qualitative' criteria.

Ratings and weights in multifactor portfolio analysis

The factors employed to determine market attractiveness or business position are not of equal importance. In order to attain a compound score for each factor a weighting scheme is necessary. It is common practice to use a simple scoring model where management has to deliver ratings for the factor values and weights for their relative importance. Ratings may be 'hard' data (e.g. a growth percentage figure) or subjective judgements (e.g. on a scale where 5 means 'highly attractive' and 1 denotes 'very unattractive'). Weights are judgmental data in most instances. Consider the example of computing a compound attractiveness score for market X and a position score for competitor Y in Table 5.3.

Table 5.3 Ratings and weights

Criteria	Criteria rating	Weight	Rating×weight
Market attractiveness			
market size (units)	2	0.40	0.80
growth rate	3	0.20	0.60
seasonality	5	0.15	0.75
price level	4	0.25	1.00
Overall attractiveness of X			3.15
Competitive position			
market share	1	0.50	0.50
availability	2	0.15	0.30
advertising pressure	2	0.20	0.40
image	3	0.15	0.45
Position of Y			1.65

The weights assigned to the factors should add up to 1.00. The quality of the weight estimates fully depends on the managers making the judgements, on their competence, experience and willingness to cooperate. To exert some control over the 'soft' data, a more sophisticated procedure of deriving ratio-scaled weights will be employed here. It is based on Thomas Saaty's eigenvector method (1977) and offers two major advantages (Hwang and Yoon, 1981; Dyer and Forman, 1991):

- It includes a measure to check the internal consistency of the managerial judgements. The factual knowledge on real-world market situations must be acquired in business practice. The ability to make logically consistent judgements, however, can be improved through trial and error.
- It facilitates the rating task for managers as it operates in a paired comparison format prompting ratings only for two criteria at a time. Cardinal weights are thus computed indirectly. (The reader interested in the algorithmic details is referred to the Appendix.)

During the rating process the manager is confronted with each pair of attractiveness (or competitive position) criteria on which he has to take two decisions:

- identifying the more important factor (unless the two criteria are considered to be of equal importance);
- assessing the difference in importance by attaching a rating scale value.

The Saaty scale allows integer ratings between 1 and 9 with the uneven values being verbalized: 1 = equal importance, 3 = weak importance, 5 = essential or strong importance, 7 = demonstrated importance, 9 = absolute importance of one factor over the other. Given a number of n criteria the assessor works through a series of $n(n-1)/2$ steps each time deciding first whether factor number one is more important than factor two (unless they have equal importance), and second, determining the perceived difference in importance on the 1–9 scale. The rating task, of course, needs some PC assistance. The following sample application for the tourist-receiving cities of Budapest, Prague and Vienna include a number of screenshots from a PC session. Figure 5.5, for example, demonstrates how a manager produces weight estimates for three market attractiveness criteria.

Multifactor portfolio analysis applied to tourist cities

In international city tourism the city tourist offices (CTOs) are responsible for strategic market planning. A city's portfolio consists of a mixture of travellers arriving from various generating countries. The CTO management has to evaluate the tourism generators in order to decide on how much marketing effort should be directed to each of these markets. A CTO's market operation in most cases is restricted to advertising and public and industry relations. The amount of advertising dollars invested into the generating countries, however, has a 'signal' effect for the tourist businesses of the destination city. The CTO may operate as a non-profit organization expecting no direct financial response for itself. Instead, the CTO considers the total influx of tourists into the municipality as a relevant basis to express the performance of a tourist city. The absolute and relative number of 'bednights sold' or the amount of tourist expenditure are appropriate measures for the size of a market and the strength of a destination.

Working steps

At first the manager has to determine the generating countries from where he expects a significant number of visitors. The volume of outbound tourism varies greatly between generating countries. But there are a number of economic and social criteria one may choose in order to come to a conclusion on how attractive these countries are for a city as a tourist destination. However, the managers must not exaggerate in finding assessment criteria. Too large a number of criteria raises serious doubts concerning the face validity of the judgements given. The New Zealand case by Henshall and Roberts (1985) may serve as an example where the two sets of attractiveness and competitive position criteria become too bulky and redundant.

Three to five criteria should be sufficient for deriving plausible and reproducible attractiveness results. The IAAWIN program (freely available through the World Wide Web page http://www.wu-wien.ac.at/inst/tourism/software) was employed for the following sample application. A rating of 5 denotes the best value indicative of the highest contribution to market attractiveness. Criteria inversely related to attractiveness (e.g. rate of unemployment, inflation rate) must be given low ratings if they reach a high level for a particular generating country. IAAWIN will transform all ratings to normalized values with the highest rating equalling unity. The same principles apply for the competitive position criterion (Mazanec, 1986). In each of the generating countries a tourist city occupies a more or less successful position. Eventually there are two compound values assigned to each generating country. There is a very useful third measure called the 'importance value'. It denotes the proportion of bednights sold to a particular generating country of the bednight total of guests recorded in the tourist city. The IAAWIN program then produces the usual pictorial representation where market attractiveness is portrayed along the vertical axis, competitive position along the horizontal axis and the importance value through the diameter of the circles for the generating countries. A tourist city's competitive strengths and weaknesses become apparent from this portfolio plot.

A sample application to the cities of Budapest, Prague and Vienna

Market attractiveness

Parts I and II commented on a recent research project commissioned by the Federation of European City Tourist Offices (FECTO). A major effort in this project regards basic data collected from more than 60 receiving cities in Europe. The data were harmonized and made comparable (Grabler and Wöber, 1995). Table 5.4 shows 1985–94 bednight figures for those countries of origin of the city travellers who are paramount for the three central European cities. For most of the generating countries the city market volume reached a peak value in 1990 and 1991 and then dropped to the level of the mid-1980s.

According to the more instructive line chart in Figure 5.4 there are no growth markets among the twelve generators. Germany appears to have a moderate long-term growth momentum. The UK market volume has shrunk considerably in the middle of the decade and seems to stabilize on the 30 million level.

Market size and market growth certainly are elementary assessment criteria. However, no experienced manager would like to compare tourist nationalities unless more is known about their spending patterns. It is a minimum requirement to perceive the 'market attractiveness' of a generating country as being made up of at least three criteria: market size (SIZE), growth rate (GROWTH) and daily expenditure (DAILY EXP). Imagine an international consultant rating the same set of attractiveness criteria for each of the three cities. According to the response given in Figure 5.5 he attaches a significantly higher importance to market size compared to growth (a rating of 5). Obviously, the main concern is about cherishing large and established markets rather than emphasizing potential growth. The consultant also rates size moderately higher than daily expenditure (a scale

Table 5.4 Leading city tourism generators for Budapest, Prague and Vienna (million bednights generated in European cities)

Generating country	1985	1986	1987	1988	1989	1990	1991	1992	1993	1994
Austria (A)	3.4	3.5	3.6	3.9	4.3	4.2	4.2	4.2	4.2	4.3
Denmark (DK)	3.0	3.3	3.4	3.3	3.3	3.4	3.0	3.4	3.3	3.4
France (F)	29.9	28.7	31.2	32.2	33.5	33.9	32.7	32.4	31.2	31.2
Germany (D)	32.6	33.7	35.5	37.6	38.6	40.6	40.5	41.5	41.0	41.3
Hungary (H)	4.1	4.0	3.8	3.6	3.4	2.5	1.7	1.5	1.4	1.4
Italy (I)	20.9	21.1	22.4	25.6	26.7	24.8	24.4	25.1	23.0	22.9
Japan (J)	5.3	4.5	5.8	6.6	8.4	8.9	7.5	9.2	9.0	9.3
Netherlands (NL)	5.1	5.0	5.4	5.6	5.8	6.0	5.9	5.6	5.8	5.8
Spain (E)	15.3	15.1	16.4	17.0	18.0	18.9	18.8	17.3	16.7	17.3
Switzerland (CH)	5.9	5.7	5.7	6.1	6.4	6.4	6.0	5.9	5.8	5.8
UK (UK)	50.5	47.4	49.4	44.9	38.6	33.5	32.2	33.2	33.4	33.5
USA (US)	34.0	24.9	28.5	27.1	28.4	29.7	24.1	27.3	27.2	27.4

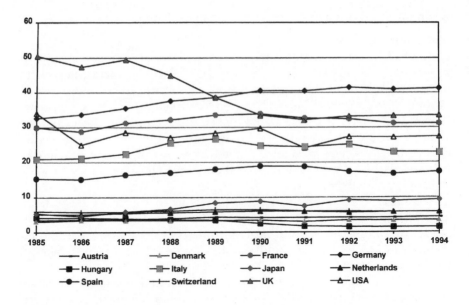

Figure 5.4 The trend during the decade 1985–1994 (*Source*: OECD, WTO.)

value of 3). The central European cities are forced to rely on the 'mass' markets. Larger numbers of visitors from European countries – though they may not belong to the big spenders' segment – cannot easily be replaced by more spendthrift long-haul travellers. The expenditure level, however, is considered slightly more important than the growth rate (scale value 2). Treating these pairwise judgements with the eigenvector method (see Appendix) results in a weight vector of 0.65, 0.12 and 0.23 for the three attractiveness criteria. The judgements are highly consistent (with a consistency coefficient of 0.001 where 0 indicates perfect consistency).

The assessment of each of the major generating countries in terms of market size and market growth exploits the information in the time series in Figure 5.4. Austria (A), Denmark (DK), Hungary (H), the Netherlands (NL), Switzerland (CH) and Japan (J) are the smallest (rating 1); Germany (D) is the largest in size (rating 5); France (F) and the UK are of approximately equal size (rating 4); Italy (I) and the USA (US) are in between (rating 3); and Spain (E) is best represented by a value of 2. As all the markets have been stagnant during the second half of the decade a uniform and neutral rating of 3 is justified for the growth criteria. From what is internationally known about the spending patterns of various nationalities within the urban destinations (Grabler and Wöber, 1995) ratings of 2 are applied to half the nations. Japan (5), Spain, Switzerland and the USA (4) are rated highest (Table 5.5). The European average and not the particular destination value is relevant here as the rating should refer to the spending potential of the origin country in general.

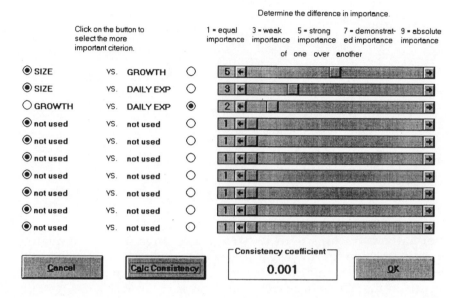

Figure 5.5 Weight judgements and consistency for the market attractiveness criteria

Table 5.5 Daily expenditure (in ECU)

Generating country	Budapest survey 1993	Vienna survey 1994	Average for European cities	Rating
Austria (A)	44	–	61	2
Denmark (DK)	44	–	57	2
France (F)	86	98	72	2
Germany (D)	44	124	74	2
Hungary (H)	–	–	34	1
Italy (I)	58	114	82	3
Japan (J)	66	356	158	5
Netherlands (NL)	44	–	68	2
Spain (E)	–	124	92	4
Switzerland (CH)	64	–	99	4
UK (UK)	88	–	69	2
USA (US)	90	120	114	4

Table 5.6 combines these intermediate results. Note that the number of the nationalities will be restricted to the eight or nine leading generators for each destination (marked by B – Budapest, P – Prague, V – Vienna). The attractiveness scores are computed by multiplying each of the three

Table 5.6 Generating country scores on the attractiveness dimension

Generating country	SIZE (weight = 0.65) rating	GROWTH (weight = 0.12) rating	DAILY EXP (weight = 0.23) rating	Attractiveness score = normalized rating×weight for B, P, V
A	1	3	2	0.37, 0.37, 0.37
DK	1	3	2	—, 0.37, —
F	4	3	2	—, 0.76, —
D	5	3	2	0.89, 0.89, 0.86
H	1	3	1	0.31, —, —
I	3	3	3	0.68, 0.68, 0.65
J	1	3	5	—, —, 0.48
NL	1	3	2	0.37, 0.37, —
E	2	3	4	—, 0.57, 0.61
CH	1	3	4	0.48, —, 0.44
UK	4	3	2	0.76, 0.76, 0.73
US	3	3	4	0.74, 0.74, 0.69
Maximum for B	5	3	4	
P	5	3	4	
V	5	3	5	

(normalized) ratings with its weight and subsequent summation. Normalization means dividing by the maximum rating value attained by a generating country in a city's portfolio. Hence, to calculate the score for Austria in the Budapest portfolio the sum is $(1/5)\times0.65 + (3/3)\times0.12 + (2/4)\times0.23 = 0.37$.

The three cities' competitive positions
Budapest recorded 9.1 million bednights during the peak year 1987, but this figure dropped to 4.3 million in 1993. Prague reached a record high of 4.7 million in 1991 when the European city tourism was booming and then followed the overall trend down to 3.5 million in 1993. With 7.5 million in 1990 and 6.9 million in 1994 (6.6 in 1993) Vienna seems to be less vulnerable to the overall trend. One fifth of the bednight volume in Budapest but only one eighth of Vienna's bednight total is of domestic origin making the Austrian capital less dependent on domestic travel (no data are available for Prague). The guest mix is fairly balanced in each of the three destinations with the major guest nation being Germany (holding shares between 19 and 24 per cent).

To portray the cities' competitive positions the managers and their consultants in this demonstration study also define three assessment criteria. Number one, market share (SHARE), and number two, relative prices (REL PRICES), are standard assessment factors in international tourism. Share ratings are based on the relative number of bednights attracted from a generating country's total volume. Various indicators may be employed to assess the relative level of prices in a destination vis-à-vis an origin. Relative 'tourist' prices would require a special index based on a typical traveller's 'basket' of goods and services purchased while on a trip. With the exception of Germany this information is not periodically available for the European generating countries. The second-best approximation an economist is likely to recommend is purchasing power parity based on exchange rate adjusted indices of consumer prices. The REL PRICES, therefore, are based on indices where 100 denotes perfect parity and a value > 100 (< 100) means a purchasing power (dis)advantage for the tourists. Market shares (Grabler and Wöber, 1995) and purchasing power parities (ÖGAF, 1995) for 1994 are listed in Table 5.7.

The three cities involved are not equally attractive for long-haul travellers. Therefore, a third criterion suggested is cost of transport. A stronger force of 'pull factors' is required to overcome the travel barrier of 'transport cost' and to capture a significant share in overseas markets. To facilitate the data collection effort the 'transport cost' may be represented by 'travel distance' (DISTANCE) with a sufficient degree of precision. Transforming these pieces of information into five-point ratings is a straightforward procedure (Table 5.8).

The past market share, the purchasing power (dis)advantages and the travel distance determine a destination's chance to capture a larger or smaller portion from a generating country's overall demand for city trips. If econometric results on the strength of these influential factors are not immediately to hand, subjective estimates may step in. In judging the weights of the competitive position criteria the managers in this case example trust more in the market share already attained compared to the relative purchasing power (scale value 4). The current share is considered to be significantly more indicative of the cities' competitive (dis)advantages than travel distance (value 8). The relative prices also dominate the barrier of travel distance (value 3). The resulting criteria weights are obtained with

Table 5.7 European city travel market shares and purchasing power parities

Generating country	SHARE (%)			REL PRICES (index points (100))		
	Budapest	Prague	Vienna	Hungary	Czech Republic	Austria
A	5.5	4.5	27.2	134.5	126.9	100.0
DK	0.1	5.3	1.6	151.2	143.1	112.8
F	0.6	0.8	1.1	118.1	111.8	88.1
D	3.6	3.8	7.7	119.6	113.2	89.2
H	62.7	1.8	6.3	100.0	94.7	74.6
I	2.1	1.8	3.5	102.9	97.5	76.8
J	<0.1	0.4	4.1	241.6	228.7	180.2
NL	2.4	3.8	2.9	111.8	105.8	83.4
E	<0.1	0.9	1.9	104.2	98.6	77.7
CH	3.2	1.4	7.0	156.2	147.8	116.5
UK	0.6	0.4	0.8	107.9	102.2	80.5
US	1.2	0.7	2.4	116.9	110.7	87.2

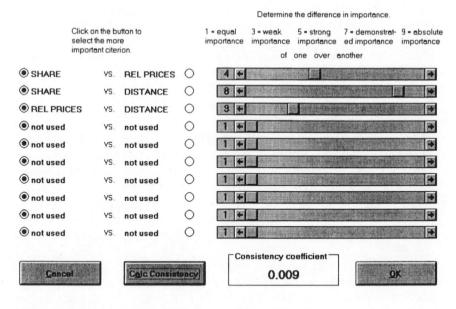

Figure 5.6 Weight judgements and consistency for the competitive position criteria

a high consistency index (0.009) and amount to 0.71, 0.21 and 0.08 (see Figure 5.6).

Besides a dominant share in the home market (63 per cent, rating 5), the city of Budapest holds about 5.5 per cent in the Austrian city tourism market (rating 3) and smaller shares in the other generating countries (ratings of 1 or 2). For Prague the share of the Czech city travel demand is not known; the largest shares, therefore, result for Denmark (5.3 per cent), Austria (4.5 per cent), Germany and the Netherlands (3.8 per cent). Vienna holds 27.2 per cent of the home market and reaches shares up to 7.7 per cent in Germany, 7 per cent in Switzerland and 6.3 per cent in Hungary. Almost all nations have a purchasing power advantage vis-à-vis Budapest and Prague, while most of the city travellers to Vienna – except the Japanese, Swiss and Danish – suffer from the relative weakness of their currency. Travel distance does not vary too much for the three cities; of course, the distance is least comfortable for long-haul tourists from Japan and the US (ratings of 1), slightly better for the British or the Spaniards (2), and much better for the other European countries of origin (3–5). Table 5.8 presents the resulting competitive position scores.

Table 5.8 Competitive position scores

Generating country selected	SHARE (weight = 0.72) rating			REL PRICES (weight = 0.21) rating			DISTANCE (weight = 0.08) rating			Competitive position score = normalized rating×weight		
	B	P	V	B	P	V	B	P	V	B	P	V
A	3	3	5	4	4	3	5	5	5	0.67	0.78	0.92
DK	-	4	-	-	5	-	-	3	-	-	0.97	-
F	-	1	-	-	3	-	-	3	-	-	0.35	-
D	3	3	4	3	3	2	4	5	4	0.66	0.74	0.72
H	5	-	-	3	-	-	5	-	-	0.92	-	-
I	2	2	3	3	3	1	4	3	4	0.47	0.53	0.53
J	-	-	3	-	-	5	-	-	1	-	-	0.65
NL	2	3	-	3	3	-	3	3	3	0.46	0.71	-
E	-	1	1	-	3	1	-	2	-	-	0.33	0.22
CH	3	-	4	5	-	3	3	-	3	0.68	-	0.74
UK	1	1	1	3	3	2	2	2	2	0.30	0.51	0.26
US	1	1	1	3	3	2	1	1	1	0.28	0.32	0.24
Maximum	5	4	5	5	5	5	5	5	5			

Importance values

Germany contributes the largest portion of bednights to the overall inbound volume of each of the cities. Besides the home markets (no data for Prague) Italy is of particular importance for each destination. Italians and also Americans are typical city travellers. In spite of the fact that only the eight or nine leading generators for each city's inbound tourism have been selected, the importance values drop to 3–4 per cent (Table 5.9). They will be visualized by the relative size of the bubbles in each city's IAA diagram.

Table 5.9 The nations' importance for the cities' inbound tourism

Generating country	Importance value % (rounded)		
	Budapest	Prague	Vienna
A	4.0	4.0	13.0
DK	-	4.0	-
F	-	6.0	-
D	18.0	23.0	24.0
H	19.0	-	-
I	9.0	10.0	9.0
J	-	-	5.0
NL	3.0	5.0	5.0
E	-	4.0	-
CH	3.0	-	4.0
UK	4.0	4.0	4.0
US	7.0	5.0	8.0

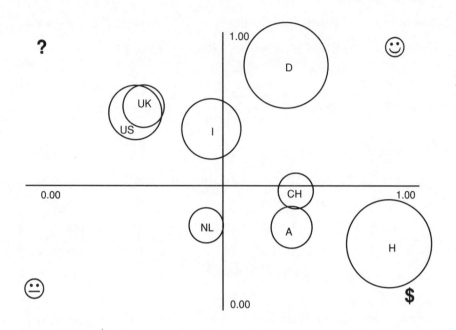

Figure 5.7 IAA diagram for Budapest

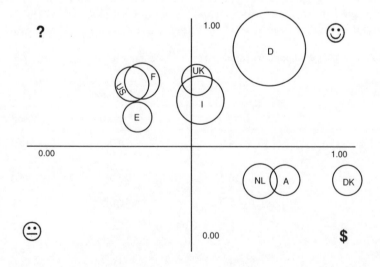

Figure 5.8 IAA diagram for Prague

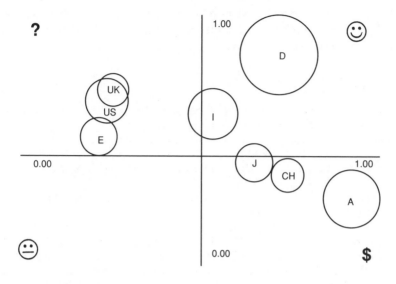

Figure 5.9 IAA diagram for Vienna

Commenting on the three cities' IAA diagrams (Figures 5.7–5.9)
Germany, France, the UK and the USA are the most attractive generators of city tourists (in the upper hemisphere of the diagram), indicating that investments into more aggressive market operation should be allocated there – provided that a destination city occupies a favourable competitive position (far right on the horizontal axis). None of the three cities enjoys a notable competitive advantage in these priority markets. As the competitive position in the major generating country (Germany) is fairly good for each destination there will be a tough and continued struggle for building market share in future. A large appropriation of the promotional budget will have to go there.

The home markets, Austria, Switzerland (for Budapest and Vienna) or the Netherlands (for Prague) correspond to the 'cash cows' in ordinary portfolio jargon. At this particular time (1993–94) these generators are relatively unattractive; on the other hand, it is unlikely that competing destinations will be able to threaten the three cities' positions in these markets. A maintenance strategy implying a moderate promotional budget will be appropriate there.

According to the size of the country circles relative to each other the overall guest mix appears to be well balanced. There is no single dominant market making any of the cities dependent on just one guest nation. The situation is quite different in other European cities as a strong home market is normal for most of the cities in northern and southern Europe (see Part IV). The portfolio diagrams in Figures 5.7, 5.8 and 5.9 summarize the 'status quo'. The multifactor approach may be extended to visualize the future objectives of the CTOs (e.g. shifting some of the bubbles to the right, increasing their size) and, later on, to relate the objectives to the actual results.

References

Abell, D.F. and Hammond, J.S. (1979) *Strategic Market Planning: Problems and Analytical Approaches*. Englewood Cliffs, NJ: Prentice Hall.

Calantone, R. and Mazanec, J.A. (1991) Marketing management and tourism. *Annals of Tourism Research* **18**, 101–19.

Day, G.S. (1986) *Analysis for Strategic Market Decisions*. St Paul, MN: West Publishing Co.

Dyer, R.F. and Forman, E.H. (1991) *An Analytic Approach to Marketing Decisions*. Englewood Cliffs, NJ: Prentice Hall, 87–114.

Grabler, K. and Wöber, K. (1995) *City Tourism in Europe: Results of the 1995 FOTVE/FECTO Survey*. Unpublished research report, Institute for Tourism and Leisure Studies: Vienna University of Economics and Business Administration.

Henshall, B.D. and Roberts, R. (1985) Comparative assessment of tourist generating markets for New Zealand. *Annals of Tourism Research* **12**, 219–38.

Hwang, Ch.L. and Yoon, Kw. (1981) *Multiple Attribute Decision Making, Methods and Applications, A State-of-the-Art Survey*. Berlin, Heidelberg, New York: Springer, 41–7.

Kerin, R.A., Mahajan, V. and Varadarajan, P.R. (1990) *Contemporary Perspectives on Strategic Market Planning*. Boston: Allyn and Bacon, 71–113.

Mazanec, J.A. (1986) *How to Evaluate a Travel Market, Econometric Modeling vs. Multiattribute Decision Making with Management Estimates*. Les Cahiers du Tourisme, Série C, nr. 48, Aix-en-Provence: Centre des Hautes Etudes Touristiques.

Mazanec, J.A. (1994) International tourism marketing: adapting the growth-share matrix. In J. Montana (ed.) *Marketing in Europe, Case Studies*. London: Sage, 184–203.

ÖGAF (1995) *TourMIS: BUDOPT '96, Verteilungsempfehlung für das Budget 1996 der Österreich Werbung*. Unpublished report for the Austrian NTO, Vienna: Austrian Society for Applied Research in Tourism.

Saaty, Th.L. (1977) A scaling method for priorities in hierarchical structures. *Journal of Mathematical Psychology* **15**, 234–81.

Part VI

Exploiting new media: city tourism and the data highway

Gunther Maier

Introduction

Since the 1992 US presidential elections 'data-highway', 'information-superhighway' and 'national information infrastructure' have become constant topics in the popular press in the US and Europe and buzzwords for the industry. Although the proposal of the Clinton–Gore administration is quite vague in many respects, it has shaken the industry and triggered a series of joint ventures, mergers and takeovers in the US computing, telecommunications and entertainment industries.

While a national information infrastructure now 'lies within striking distance of becoming a reality' (National Research Council, 1994), it is still little more than a set of inspiring ideas. In the meantime, its predecessor, the Internet, is taking the world by storm and reshaping our economy. In Part VI we want to show how the Internet is used and how it can be used in city tourism. We will describe the fundamental characteristics of the Internet and some of the services it offers, and we will also look at cities and city tourism. We will discuss the potential of information technology for the tourism sector in general and for city tourism in particular. As it turns out, because of the large number of actors, a global market with many potential customers, the need for fast response and a complex product, the (city) tourism sector is very sensitive to new developments in information technology. We next turn to the question of how the Internet is used and how it can be used in the context of city tourism. We start this section by discussing the potential value of traditional Internet services like e-mail, newsgroups and file transfer. A special subsection is devoted to World Wide Web (WWW), where we review city information systems that are currently available on this system, as well as discuss some basic aspects of WWW use in a city tourism context. We touch security issues as well as important new developments in WWW-based communication and close with some concluding statements.

The Internet and Internet services

The Internet started more than a quarter of a century ago with a defence project of the Advanced Research Projects Agency. In 1969 the first node of the ARPANET, the first packet-switching network, was installed at the University of California at Los Angeles. The definition and publication of TCP/IP, a set of protocols that define how information is put on the network and how this information travels from one computer to another, has laid the foundation for the enormous growth of the Internet that we observe today. By mid-1995, the number of computers connected to this network had reached 6.6 million. and it doubles every year. The basis for this enormous growth lies in the basic characteristics of the Internet.

- First, and most important, the Internet allows for the exchange of information in digital form. Therefore, the information can be duplicated indefinitely without loss of quality, and it can be processed by computer programs. The information can be stored, indexed, retrieved, restructured, redistributed, matched with other information, etc., automatically by software and without human intervention. The digital form is also important for transferring information over the network because it allows for mechanisms to check the correct transmission.
- The Internet connects computers in all continents (including Antarctica) and can transfer information from one to another in seconds. It allows for very fast global communication. What type of information is transferred is decided by the users. In a business context it may be product information, orders, customer support information or information to coordinate with a distantly located part of the company. In any case, this information can be sent across borders and time zones, thus allowing companies to operate on a global scale.
- The Internet is based on packet-switching technology, which means that when one computer sends information to another computer, this information is broken down into small packets. As each packet carries – among other information – the address of the recipient, the packets can travel through the network independently. The software at the receiving computer reassembles the original information from the incoming packets. The routes by which packets travel on the Internet are determined by the networking software based on the condition of the network at that moment. The packets of a single piece of information may travel via a number of different routes between the sending and the receiving computer. Because of packet-switching the Internet is very stable against failure of individual links of the network. If one link fails or is congested, the networking software sends the packets through other links. This technology also uses the individual links very efficiently, because they can be used by many different users at the same time. Therefore, communication over the Internet is usually much cheaper than over leased communication lines.

- The Internet is based upon published communication standards. All basic definitions are available in publicly accessible documents. Because of this open structure, new Internet services can easily be developed. Their success will depend upon their usefulness to other Internet users. This structure generates continuous competition of ideas on a global scale, which has already resulted in a number of outstanding services and software products. This structure is necessary because there is no single organization that controls the Internet as a whole. The Internet is made up of individual, interconnected local or regional networks, and is therefore often called a network of networks. The rules and regulations of these individual networks are coordinated by public discussions that lead to Internet standards.
- Internet technology does not differentiate between senders and recipients of information. Each Internet user may be a consumer and a provider of information. This can be in many different forms ranging from messages sent to e-mail discussion lists and articles posted in newsgroups to pages on a web server. In any case, the information is accessible for all other Internet users much like information on traditional broadcast media (radio, TV, etc.). Therefore, the Internet can tap into the accumulated knowledge of its user community which really represents the distributed knowledge-base of the Internet.

These characteristics stimulate the fast growth of the Internet in two ways. First, they generate strong network economies that make it more attractive for new users to connect to the network, the more users are already connected. Second, they support some general development trends in economy and society, namely:

- the transition from the industrial society to the information society;
- the globalization of the economy;
- the transition toward more flexible, demand-triggered production processes.

As will be argued below, tourism is particularly affected by these development trends. Therefore, the Internet is of particular importance to the tourism sector.

Originally, the Internet was intended to provide just two services. First, to allow researchers to run programs on a remote computer, and second, to let them transfer data to and from this remote computer. Internet users soon realized that more could be done with this infrastructure and they developed additional services that operate over the network. Today, a broad range of Internet-based services is available. We will briefly describe the most important ones below.

All Internet services make use of a client-server structure: two programs, a client and a server, usually running on different computers, communicate in a standardized way in order to provide the service. The server has access to some information and makes it available over the Internet. The client knows how to request this information from the server, issues a standardized request, receives the server's reply and makes it available to the user. The standardized form of communication between the server and the client is called 'protocol'.

Internet services fall into two broad categories: communication services and information services (for more detailed descriptions see, for example, Maier and Wildberger, 1995; Krol, 1992; LaQuey, 1992). Communication services allow the direct exchange of ideas and arguments between two or more Internet users. Information services allow Internet users to access information that has been made available by some other user.

The most important communication service is electronic mail (e-mail), where an electronic message is sent from one user to another. E-mail is a very basic service that is available on many computer networks other than the Internet. Those networks are usually connected to the Internet through gateways so that e-mails can be exchanged between users on these different networks. So, the virtual community of e-mail users extends considerably beyond the Internet.

This holds also for e-mail discussion lists which are based on e-mail communication and for netnews. These services extend the one-to-one communication of regular e-mail to group discussions. While with discussion lists the messages are delivered to the mailbox of each subscriber, netnews articles are temporarily stored on the hard disks of news servers. Users interested in these discussions can connect to one of these servers and select the articles they want to read.

Discussion lists and newsgroups in netnews are devoted to certain topics. Their numbers go into the thousands and they cover practically any topic that may come up in human conversation. Discussion lists and netnews are also used intensively to discuss the development of the Internet, propose and discuss new standards, support new Internet users, etc. They are the most important means for forming 'virtual communities'.

Over time these virtual communities have developed rules for proper behaviour in their virtual world. However, as in any human society, most of these rules are unwritten and have developed out of tacit understanding among the members of the community. Therefore, a newcomer is well advised to observe the behaviour of other members before taking an active profile. Moreover, the implicit rules may differ from one part of the Internet to another. What is perfectly acceptable in one e-mail discussion list may be considered rude in another newsgroup.

Traditional information services on the Internet were Telnet and anonymous FTP. They allowed users to log into remote computers and to download files from these machines. Telnet (remote login) was mainly used for access to databases, particularly electronic library catalogues. With anonymous FTP, Internet users built up large archives of public domain software and made it available for other net users.

In recent years, these traditional information services have been surpassed by a very attractive new information service, the World Wide Web (WWW), which was so successful that it changed the appearance of the Internet and for some even became synonymous with the Internet. While some WWW clients, like Netscape, can be used as general front-end programs to all major Internet services, the World Wide Web as a service offers only part of the flexibility of the Internet. This is particularly important for suppliers of information.

As we will describe the WWW in more detail below, we will only give a brief description here. WWW integrates text, pictures, sounds, video sequences, etc., into multimedia documents. Embedded into these documents are hyperlinks, pointers to other resources on the Internet. When the user clicks on a hyperlink, his/her client software issues a request for this other Internet resource and displays the result on the screen. Hyperlinks are the innovative element of the WWW. They allow the author of one document to integrate the work of others into one virtual document. The user may explore the document in a way never expected by any one of the authors.

The WWW integrates all other information services of the Internet like Telnet, anonymous FTP and Gopher.[1] Moreover, the WWW allows forms that the user can fill in and send back to the server, and a programmable gateway for interfacing with other services. These important features are discussed below.

Cities, city tourism and information technology

But, why are we discussing information technologies and the Internet at all in a book on city tourism? The answer to this question is quite simple: tourism and city tourism in particular is to a large extent an 'information business' (Schertler, 1994a, p. 20). 'If you look at tourism as a service industry you can understand that information is one of the most important quality parameters for servicing actions. The wrong departure time information or the fact that you didn't know that all hotel rooms or cars are rented are influencing the consumer behaviour significantly because they determine the value of the service provided by tour operators, travel agencies, hotel room or car renting' (Schertler, 1994a, p. 23).

Approaching the question from an information systems management perspective, Cash *et al.* (1988) list characteristics of enterprises for which information technology will be of particular importance. It almost reads like a description of tourism. In their marketing those companies will be particularly influenced by information technology that answer the following questions with 'yes':

- Does the business require a large number of routine customer interactions per day with vendor for either ordering or information?
- Is product choice complex?
- Do customers need to compare competitors' product/service/price configuration simultaneously?
- Is a quick customer decision time necessary?
- Is accurate, quick customer confirmation essential?

- Would an increase in multiple ordering or service sites provide value to the customer?
- Are customer tastes potentially volatile?
- Do significant possibilities exist for product customization?
- Is pricing volatile (can/should salesman set price at point of sale)?
- Is the business heavily regulated?
- Can the product be surrounded by value-added information to the customer?
- Is the real customer two or more levels removed from the manufacturer?' (Cash *et al.*, 1988, p. 19).

Most managers in the tourist industry will probably answer the majority of these questions positively (Schertler, 1994b). Therefore, information technology has been used intensively in the tourist industry; in tourism agencies, hotels, by travel agents, etc. Most of them, however, are standalone – predominantly database – applications that support the management and information processing of the respective organization. Telecommunication was used only by very large corporations who had the capacity to develop, operate and maintain a proprietary telecom-munications network. Air carriers like United Airlines and American Airlines developed their own booking and reservation system with terminals in all airports linked to a central computer system. The immediate information flow through these systems allowed them to implement more differentiated pricing systems and frequent flyer programmes for loyal customers. The high investment cost of such proprietary systems, however, created a high entry barrier for competitors that smaller companies in particular found hard to overcome.

With the existence of a public telecommunication network these entry barriers lost importance. Because of the cost-sharing of the Internet and its efficient use of telecommunication links, even very small tourism companies can afford to connect to the network and use telecommunication services. With the dramatic growth of the Internet more and more users can be accessed through this network, making use of telecommunication more valuable for tourism companies.

Promoting city tourism and presenting a city's most attractive aspects to tourists can be seen in the broader context of city marketing, a 'new paradigm (that is a new approach) structuring the way the complex functioning of the city is viewed' (Ashworth and Voogd, 1988, p. 65). Kotler *et al.* (1993) see visitors (business visitors, tourists and travellers) as just one of the target markets of city marketing. Others are '(2) residents and workers, (3) business and industry, and (4) export markets' (Kotler *et al.*, 1993, p. 23). That city marketing is to a large extent an information activity becomes clear when we look at its major activities:

- designing the right mix of community features and services
- setting attractive incentives for the current and potential buyers and users of its goods and services
- delivering a place's products and services in an efficient, accessible way

- promoting the place's values and image so that potential users are fully aware of the place's distinctive advantages (Kotler *et al.*, 1993, p. 18).

All these activities contain components where information needs to be distributed to current or potential users of the city.

One of the main problems of city marketing lies in the many actors who need to be part of this activity. Kotler *et al.* (1993, p. 34) list a total number of 24 'major actors in place marketing' in five categories:

1. public sector actors at the local level
2. private sector actors at the local level
3. regional actors
4. national actors
5. international actors.

Coordination at the conceptual as well as at the operational level between them is essential for a successful city marketing initiative. Insufficient coordination may lead to 'one of the major problems associated with the marketing of places: place marketers adopt a composite view of the place-product with little real understanding of the diversity of the services and products being sold by the tourism industry within the locality' (Page, 1995, p. 195).

This argument applies not only for city marketing in general, but also for the promotion and marketing of city tourism. City tourists consume a highly complex composite good, the elements of which are provided by different actors: hotels, restaurants, theatres, museums, shop owners, travel agents, transportation authorities, etc. Continuous coordination and communication between all the actors is needed for the creation of an attractive product. Information technology should be quite instrumental for this complex task. The ways in which the Internet and its services can be used in this context are discussed below.

Internet services in city tourism

Currently, Internet access is still more common in urban areas than in rural areas because of the high density of potential users. Therefore, using Internet services seems better suited to city tourism than tourism in rural areas.

In general, Internet services can be used in three fundamental relations of a commercial operation:

- in internal communication and flow of information
- in its communication and exchange of information with suppliers and customers
- in its need to observe the development of markets and activities of competitors.

The Internet offers particular advantages in all three areas for tourism.

Much of the public discussion of the Internet in recent years has focused on the World Wide Web. Because of its attractive features and multimedia capabilities, 'the Web' has become the Internet service that inspired managers and received most attention. Although the WWW is an important service, other Internet services are better suited for certain tasks. Therefore, before discussing the WWW we want to briefly describe how other Internet services can be used for tourism.

E-mail, netnews and file transfer

The most important alternative services are e-mail and netnews. As described above, they are mainly used for exchanging messages and articles. E-mail-based discussion lists and netnews newsgroups are forums where opinions are expressed and exchanged. Many such forums are devoted to general discussions of certain countries, regions, sports and other leisure time activities. Examples are *soc.culture.*[*2], *alt.bacchus*, *alt.restaurants*, *alt.travel.**, *rec.arts.theatre*, and *rec.travel*. They frequently discuss topics that are of relevance to city tourism or to the general image of a city as tourist destination. Tourist agencies should follow these discussions and provide specific information when needed or correct erroneous or misleading statements by other users about their city. In any case, the agency needs to be aware of the culture and customs of newsgroups and discussion lists: information needs to be accurate and unsolicited advertising may severely backfire. In contrast to other media, on the Internet the tourist agency has no privileged access to information channels. All the recipients of the information in a discussion list or newsgroup can express their opinion equally well. Therefore, the provision of biased information may trigger negative responses from other users that can accumulate to severely negative publicity.

The tourist agency will most likely generate a positive image in these communication media, when it acts like a good citizen of cyberspace. It should be honest and supportive to other users and respect their opinion. The tourist agency does not have to provide any infrastructure or make any special arrangements for such discussions to happen but, on the other hand, it cannot control the discussions and should not even try to do so. Irrespective of whether the tourist agency gets involved or not, Internet users will discuss certain aspects of the city and its image in the respective newsgroups and discussion lists. The tourist agency can only choose to be part of these discussions or not.

Discussions in discussion lists and newsgroups tend to jump from one topic to another and often discuss various topics in parallel. These discussions carry a lot of information about the preferences of the potential customers and how they perceive certain characteristics of cities. Information that otherwise needs to be collected in expensive surveys, comes free of charge on Internet communication services.[3] Discussion lists and newsgroups allow the tourist agency to constantly monitor the market.

As new ideas travel particularly fast on the Internet, these services also provide an early warning system about new trends and fashions in the behaviour of customers.

Open public discussion is the most common form of communication services on the Internet. E-mail-based discussion lists can also be used in a more restrictive and controlled way as a mechanism for delivering information. A tourist agency may decide to collect e-mail addresses of customers in a discussion list that is not open for public access. It can then be used to distribute information to all those customers at once at the cost of one e-mail message. A more sophisticated version may be a customer database that generates individual and individualized e-mail messages to all customers.

Besides mass delivery of information through discussion lists and newsgroups, plain e-mail offers many additional opportunities for the management of city tourism. It allows for a more efficient way to provide individual customers with information than the telephone, simply because the requests do not have to be answered immediately when they come in. E-mail may also reduce telephone costs considerably, in particular in those organizations that tend to get requests that require long distance answering calls.

At the same time, e-mail can be helpful for internal communication as well as for the coordination with other actors in the city. All text information that is currently faxed between tourist agencies, travel agents, hotels, ticket offices, etc. can be handled more efficiently through e-mail. E-mails come in machine readable form and can be stored, indexed and retrieved electronically. Moreover, e-mails can be generated automatically by programs, for example as a reminder when the program detects that information, that should have been provided by some other organization, is missing at a certain date.

When information is exchanged between two partners on a regular basis, they should probably establish some file transfer procedure. It is superior to e-mail in the sense that the information is always received in the same format as it was sent, so it can be directly read by some programs. Establishing such a procedure usually requires one of the partners to operate a file server and to allow the other partner to access it.

World Wide Web

As already mentioned above, the World Wide Web has been the hottest and most inspiring Internet service of the last few years. It is powerful and flexible as far as generating applications is concerned, but on the client side extremely easy to use. Thousands of users worldwide, from individual students to large corporations, have designed and published their Web-pages, some of them becoming professional information providers. New, technically advanced client software made surfing the Web an easy and enjoyable activity that has led to a sharp rise in the share of WWW-related traffic on the Internet. The Web's ability to integrate multimedia elements like pictures, sounds and video clips has added considerably to its attractiveness.

One of the reasons for the success of the WWW is its use of the 'uniform resource locator' (URL). The URL identifies information resources on the Internet in a consistent way and makes it possible, therefore, to integrate different Internet services into one environment and make them accessible through a single software tool. The URL typically defines

- which type of Internet service should be used;
- which server provides the resource; and
- where on this server the information can be found (for more information see, for example, December and Randall, 1994; Maier and Wildberger, 1995; Magid *et al.*, 1995).

By using URLs, the WWW packs all the necessary information into its hyperlinks and can therefore allow the user to access information from different Internet services as well as from different parts of the world. The WWW not only integrates other file transfer protocols like Gopher and FTP, but also allows the user to access hosts through Telnet, read newsgroups and send e-mail.

In addition to integrating such Internet services, the WWW provides another feature of its own that makes it a very flexible tool for both information retrieval and communication. Through the Common Gateway Interface (CGI) users can pass requests through the server to small programs on the host computer and thus initiate special activities like querying a database, passing information to a database, adding to an information file, etc. Often, the information that is passed to the CGI comes from WWW forms the user has filled in.

WWW-based city information systems
From early on, information about cities and tourist-related information appeared on the World Wide Web. Students who tried to become familiar with this new technology often compiled information about their hometown or about their favourite travel location from brochures and guidebooks and put it on the Web. Today, the number of such virtual destinations probably goes into the thousands and there are web sites that compile the respective links in long lists or searchable databases (see, for example, Grabig, 1995).

Schmalzhofer (1996) analyses a sample of 231 tourist information sites and draws the following conclusions:

- This part of the Internet is dominated by US sites. Only about one third of the visited sites are located outside the US.

- The largest number of sites only provides information about a city, a region or a special touristic service. Systems that allow booking or provide another more sophisticated service are relatively rare.
- As far as hotels and accommodation are concerned, the sites display an interesting dichotomy. Most offers belong either to the highest (first class hotels) or to the lowest (youth hostels, etc.) end of the segment. This seems to reflect the perceived structure of Internet users (high income business people and low income students).

Maier (1995) looks at city information systems and distinguishes three types:

1. ad-hoc systems
2. sector information systems
3. integrated city information systems.

Ad-hoc systems are by far the most common category. They have often been created by individuals in the above-mentioned way. Although their development was rarely supported by significant financial resources, some of them provide a quite attractive and complete overview of what the respective city has to offer. Frequently, ad-hoc systems adopt a more creative and general perspective than systems from the other categories.

Sector information systems concentrate on a certain sector of the city (tourism, business location, real estate, museums, specific events, etc.). They are usually set up and operated by a specialized agency and therefore go deep in this one aspect, but lack information about other segments of the city and of city life.

Integrated city information systems try to be both broad and deep. They are usually not the result of a single information provider, but of a coordinated endeavour of numerous agents and organizations. Each one of them supplies and maintains information from its own realm, but takes into account links to other information and the need for overall coordination. Of course, creating an integrated city information system is quite demanding; therefore, their number is limited. Maier (1995) mentions just two: Portland, Oregon[4] and Blacksburg, Virginia.[5]

WWW-based meta city information systems and search engines
The Web's ability to link to resources anywhere on the Internet makes it easy to combine existing information systems into meta information systems. They usually try to collect links to all the Web pages that are of relevance for the respective topic. Meta information systems do not collect the information themselves, only the links to the information. They differ by the number of links they contain, how frequently the information is updated and how the meta information is structured. In the context of city tourism two meta information systems are of particular importance: City.Net and GNN Traveler's Center.

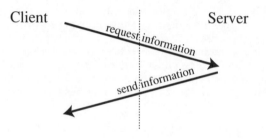

Figure 6.1 Standard communication between server and client

By early November 1995 City.Net contained links to 1126 cities and to 557 other destinations. The information typically comes from the providers of the city information. City.Net is updated on a daily basis and is one of the most visited sites on the World Wide Web.

GNN Traveler's Center is more a travel magazine than a meta index. It was founded in 1993 as a marketing instrument by O'Reilley & Associates, a Californian publishing company, and was sold to America Online Incorporated in 1995. GNN Traveler's Center combines a broad set of travel and tourist information. In doing so, it intends to explore the many different ways in which the Internet can be used as a tool for travel research, as a vehicle for travel journalism and as a forum for information exchange and personal networking.

While meta information systems are topic-oriented, search engines collect links with a broad scope of content and allow the user to search for the type of information he or she needs. Search engines are based on databases that can be queried by WWW users through the CGI interface. The search engines use different database software and different strategies for collecting information. Because of this they may react quite differently to a certain query. Important search engines are Lycos,[6] Yahoo,[7] and World Wide Web Worm[8] (for a more complete discussion see, for example, December and Randall, 1994; Maier and Wildberger, 1995; Magid *et al.*, 1995).

Providing information on the World Wide Web
In order to make information available on the World Wide Web, it must be in a certain format and stored on a computer where a Web server can access it. A Web server (also called HTTP server) is a program that understands the hypertext-transfer-protocol (HTTP) and makes Web pages available. The Web server gets a request for a certain document (described by its URL) from a Web client and responds to the request by transmitting the document (Figure 6.1). In the course of this process the server checks whether the client is allowed to receive the document, may ask for a username and password and may encrypt the document before sending it.

The text documents on the WWW are plain ASCII texts – called HTML files – with embedded tags that describe the form of the document. When a Web page is requested, the server simply sends the plain ASCII text. The client program displays the document according to the formatting described by the embedded tags.

The language used for describing the format of the document on the WWW is 'hypertext markup language' (HTML). HTML tags are enclosed in '<' and '>' and either describe a certain event, like a paragraph, the location of an image or a horizontal rule, or mark the beginning and the end of certain formatting elements in the text, like headlines, ordered and unordered lists, hyperlinks, etc. End tags have the same name as the corresponding beginning tag, preceded with a '/'. So, for example, <H1> and </H1> mark the beginning and the end of a first level headline.

HTML has evolved considerably over the last few years. Today, there are three versions of the standard and different flavours. The details are described in the respective online documents[9] and in various printed publications (for example, Stanek and Purcell, 1995; Graham, 1996; Chu and Chin, 1996). Just to give an impression of how HTML formats web pages, Figure 6.2 shows the original HTML file and how it is presented by the Web client. HTML describes web pages in a logical way, not in terms of its physical characteristics. The interpretation of the tags and their translation into physical characteristics (e.g. font type, font size, position on the screen) is left to the Web client. By enclosing it in <H1> and </H1> the author of a web page defines that a certain line is a first level headline. However, he/she has no control over how a first level headline should be displayed. This is to be decided by the web client, maybe based on parameters set by the user.

The most important element of hypertext documents is hyperlinks.[10] They provide connections to other resources on the Internet. These resources can be other HTML documents, pictures, sounds, movies, terminal connections, newsgroups, etc. Everything that can be described by a URL can become the target of a hyperlink. In some cases, the client may need additional software or hardware (e.g. a soundcard) in order to display the resource correctly. When the user clicks on the hyperlink, the client program connects to the respective server, downloads the resource and presents it in the appropriate way.

It is the responsibility of the author of a hyperdocument to include the appropriate HTML tags and hyperlinks. Because URLs can point to resources anywhere on the Internet, a hyperdocument may include documents and resources from all over the world. HTML documents can be created either 'by hand', through special HTML editors, or by converting a standard wordprocessor file by use of a converter program. Numerous HTML editors and converter programs can be found on the Internet.

The World Wide Web is the ideal medium for presenting information, locations, events, etc. As compared to other media, pages on the WWW can

```
<html>
<head>
<title>Demo File</title>
</head>
<body>
<H1>HTML-Tags</H1>
<H2>Examples</H2>
This page demonstrates some important HTML-tags. Probably the most frequently used tag is the one
for ending a paragraph <P>
Here comes an unordered list <UL>
<LI> one list item, and <LI> another list item.
</UL>
Numbered (ordered) lists are created like this:
<OL> <LI> first list item <LI>second list item </OL>
Note that formatting is done with tags. Carriage return and empty lines have no effect.<P>
Here is a Hyperlink <a href="URL">to another page</a>.
```

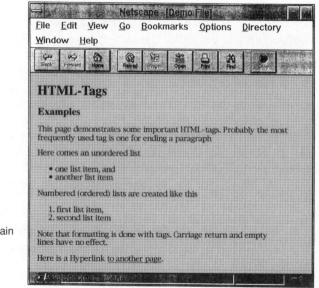

Figure 6.2 HTML-file in plain ASCII (above) and as displayed by web browser (right)

be changed and updated continuously. Because of transmission over the Internet, the information is distributed automatically. Because of this high speed, however, Web pages become outdated very quickly. Users expect to see new and up-to-date information whenever they visit a Web page. An organization that announces events on its Web page that have already passed may develop a rather bad reputation. Therefore, when a tourist agency or any other city tourism organization decides to step into the WWW, it should have efficient mechanisms in place for getting the newest information into its Web pages. While the distribution costs are minimal on the Internet, without the appropriate mechanisms the costs of collecting the information may grow quite high.

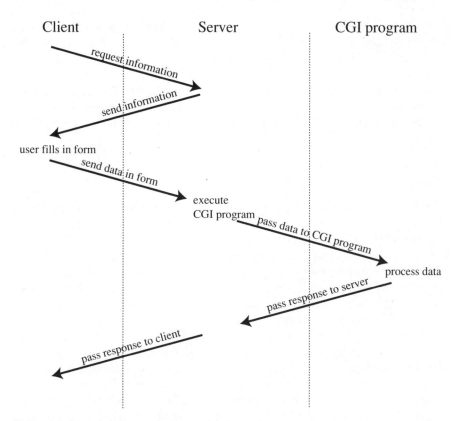

Figure 6.3 Communication between client and server in case of forms

Web pages are ideal for transporting information to a global audience. However, unless the author of the web pages provides for it, this technology lacks the immediate feedback option of other Internet services. The easiest form to allow for feedback is through a hyperlink with a 'mailto' URL.[11] When the user clicks on such a hyperlink and the client program supports this feature, a window opens up where the user can type a message that is then mailed to the recipient specified in the URL. It is good practice on the WWW to allow for e-mail feedback.

A more sophisticated way to allow for feedback is via WWW forms. Forms are generated through special HTML tags and are part of a regular HTML file. By filling in a WWW form the user can send information from his/her client program to the server. The communication between client and server in this case is shown in Figure 6.3.

Each form begins with the '<FORM>' tag that has to include an 'action' statement. The action statement includes the URL of a program on the server machine, which is supposed to process the incoming information.[12] Usually in addition to processing the incoming information, the CGI program also generates some message that is passed to the server and sent back to the client program. This message typically informs the user that the information has been received or about the result of the computations of the CGI program.

As there are no limitations on the CGI program, this mechanism is very flexible and allows for different types of communication between the client and the server. HTML allows one to construct forms with:

- radio buttons
- checkboxes
- menus to select from
- single and multiline text fields.

The minimum activity of the CGI program is to append the information it received from the user to a file. Before doing so, the program may check the information for consistency and completeness and reject it when it fails the test. More sophisticated CGI programs may query (or update) a database (e.g. for vacant hotel rooms or for available tickets), send an e-mail, initiate validation of credit card information, etc. However, HTML forms have two important limitations: they are static, and the communication in the WWW between a client and a server is stateless.

The first limitation means that HTML forms cannot change according to the user's selections. The form is transmitted from the server to the client and displayed completely before the user inputs any information. All the information provided by the user is transmitted back to the server at once when the user clicks on a certain button – usually called the 'submit' button.

The statelessness of the communication means that every single communication between client and server is treated separately. The server does not keep a record of earlier communication with a certain user and therefore cannot respond differently depending on earlier activities of the user. This would be necessary, for example, for a system where the user looks at various services, marks those that interest him/her, and later gets an order form based on the collected elements. Because of the statelessness of the WWW communication, either the user would need to order each element separately, or the author of the system would need to design mechanisms that overcome this limitation. This is usually done such that when he/she enters this area on the web, the user gets a randomly generated ID assigned that is used to tie the various orders together. In order to support this, HTML allows for hidden fields in forms that can carry the necessary information.

The power of CGI programs can also be used without forms. Forms are only needed when the user has to provide information or has to make complex choices. CGI programs can also be started through regular hyperlinks, where parameters can be passed as part of the URL. This can be used, for example, in the context of predefined queries of a database. A hyperlink like 'get a list of all hotels with vacancies' that looks to the user like a link to a file that lists the respective hotels may actually be a link to a CGI program that queries a database. The CGI program would reformat the output of the database and thus return a nicely formatted HTML file. The user would not immediately see that this file has been created 'on the fly' by the CGI program.

Security issues

In the popular press the Internet has a bad reputation as far as security is concerned. Security is of particular importance for commercial applications as they would typically be used in the context of city tourism and city marketing.

Although the security problems of the Internet are often exaggerated, especially as compared to the security hazards of competing technologies, there is always some risk involved in being connected to a public infrastructure like the Internet. As perfect security is impossible, the real question is how much risk a company or tourist agency is willing to accept in return for the benefits of the technology.

The level of risk can be adjusted considerably by use of special hardware, software or organizational strategies. As the literature on Internet security is already quite voluminous (e.g. Baker, 1991; Brand, 1990; Cheswick and Bellovin, 1994; Farrow, 1991; Hughes, 1995) we will briefly discuss only those aspects that are somewhat specific to tourist organizations on the World Wide Web.

As long as the WWW is used only for distributing information, security problems are limited and basically consist of keeping hackers and viruses out of the system. As the information on the WWW server is intended for the general public, there is no incentive for any hackers to tamper with this information. The situation changes when the Web is used for commercial transactions such as reserving rooms, ordering tickets or even making payments. In these cases both parties involved have an interest that the information is received in the same form as it was sent, that the information really comes from the party from which it appears to come and that it is received only by the intended recipient.

All these problems can be solved with encryption. Instead of sending information in its plain form, the server or the client (in the case of HTML forms) transforms the information according to some algorithm and by use of a certain key before sending it. While it is travelling over the public network the information appears like a random stream of bytes and is useless to anyone intercepting it. The original information can be extracted only with the corresponding key. Particularly promising for secure communication on the Internet in general seem to be public–private key systems (see, for example, Zimmerman, 1995). They are based on pairs of keys where information that is encrypted with the one key can only be decrypted with the other. Each user of such a system keeps one key secret (private key) and makes the other key known to as many people as possible (public key). So, when someone intends to send a secret message to this user, he/she uses the user's public key to encrypt the message before sending. So, he/she can be sure that only the intended recipient (the only one who holds the corresponding private key) can extract the original information from the message. In the same way, if a user wants to assure another user that a certain message was sent by him or her, the user encrypts the message by use of his/her private key. The recipient then needs to use the user's public key to extract the information and knows that only the holder of the corresponding private key could have sent it.

A number of Web servers and clients are available in commercial versions that support encryption. They differ in the encryption technique they use and how they derive their keys (Magid *et al.*, 1995). Some use session-specific keys, others a system of public–private keys. Since client and server must cooperate in the case of encrypted communication, different standards on the World Wide Web pose a certain threat for the open structure of the technology as well as for the ease of communication. The problem of competing standards also hampers the adoption of encryption techniques in WWW communication. Once one of these standards has succeeded in the marketplace, encrypted communication will probably become the default mode of operation on the web.

High security standards are a fundamental requirement for financial transactions on the Web. Here too, various competing standards have evolved over recent years. They typically use encryption techniques to transfer information about transactions and to protect both the merchant and the customer. Two examples are CyberCash and DigiCash. They both use their own client and server software that cooperates with Web programs and are designed to make electronic payment on the Internet as secure as bank transfer and as easy as cash payment. Here, too, the technology is readily available and awaiting its breakthrough in the market. One of the currently available standards for electronic payment will probably move ahead in the next years and become the generally accepted standard.

However, not all commercial transactions require such high levels of security. Many companies are willing to accept orders or reservations over the telephone. It would be quite exaggerated for them to require user authentication through a public–private key system when they do the same transactions over the WWW. But, as many WWW users surf around the Web and often just try things out, some protection against false requests may be in order. The company may ask the potential customer to confirm his or her request with an additional step, preferably by use of another communication channel. A very simple technique is that the CGI program behind an order form does not initiate the respective processes in the company directly, but generates a fax page as response that the user may print out of his/her WWW client, sign and fax to the company. A slightly more complicated procedure would require the user to specify an e-mail address. The CGI program would generate an e-mail to the user and ask him/her to return this message that contains the order information. In both procedures the WWW communication is used only to initiate the order process. The information received by the CGI program does not need to be stored or processed in any other way. Another procedure would store the information in some temporary location and generate a random code that is sent to the user via e-mail. The user would need to return the mail with the secret code for confirmation. Upon receipt of the code a program would activate the temporarily stored information and initiate the steps that are necessary to fulfil the customer's requests. These procedures differ in their level of automation. Whereas a response via fax usually needs to be processed by a human operator, e-mail response can be treated by a program. On the other hand, a fax response can also be sent to a service provider (hotel, ticket office, etc.) without an Internet access. The two e-mail-based procedures differ in that in the first case all the relevant information needs to be extracted from the incoming e-mail and in the second case only the secret code needs to be extracted. The first case may be considerably more demanding because the e-mail message may have been reformatted by the user or by any intermediate host.

Important new developments
The standards of the WWW and the software that implements it are improved constantly and interactively. On the one hand, new features are suggested by newly proposed standards and gradually find their way into the software. On the other hand, software developers react to the needs of their customers and implement hot new features into their programs that later are absorbed by some standard. HTML 3, for example, includes definitions for much more sophisticated text formatting, maths, tables and style sheets for separating formatting and content of a page.

One of the features that will allow communication over the WWW to evolve considerably is the ability of many clients to make use of other programs. Just like a Web server can start a CGI program and have it perform certain tasks, so can most clients use other programs for certain types of information. As with each file the WWW client receives information about its type, it can pass certain files on to add-on programs. This special file is then typically displayed by the specialized program.[13] Two interesting such developments are Java and 'virtual reality modelling language' (VRML).

Java (see, for example, Flanagan, 1996), developed by Sun Microsystems, takes a radically new approach to networked computing. Instead of requiring the user to install different kinds of programs, suited for the respective processor and operating system, with Java the user only needs a general purpose interpreter and gets specialized small programs over the network when they are needed. Since these 'applets' are executed by the user's interpreter program, the same applets can be used for all computer systems and operating systems that support the standard. Java is in its early stage of development and is currently used for animating WWW presentations.

Although Java has high potential in the long run, VRML is of greater relevance for city tourism at the moment. VRML combines the ideas of virtual reality and hyperlinks and allows the user to enter interlinked virtual worlds. VRML defines how such a world needs to be described, namely by three-dimensional geometrical shapes (for a detailed presentation of VRML see Pesce, 1995). These descriptions are stored in plain ASCII files on Web servers and transferred to the user upon request just like HTML files. The world is recreated from this description on the user's screen. This is typically done by a specialized VRML browser. Just as the user can scroll through an HTML document, so he/she can move through the virtual world displayed by the VRML-browser. Instead of a two-dimensional picture the VRML browser presents one or more three-dimensional objects such as a building, a landscape or a room that the user can twist around and view from different angles. In VRML certain objects such as doors, windows or books on a bookshelf can be defined as hyperlinks that lead to another world (actually its description on a WWW server) or a hypertext document. When the user clicks on a hyperlink, the respective file is retrieved from the server and displayed; in the case of a description of another VRML world by the VRML browser.

VRML has obvious potentials in city tourism applications. It can allow the user to 'explore' the city before getting there, to 'walk into' museums, art galleries and historical buildings, 'stroll' through recreation areas etc. Various such places can be integrated into a virtual city tour, where imbedded hyperlinks transport the user from one sight to another.

Although VRML is fairly new and in an early stage of development, first attempts at such applications can already be found on the web. Figure 6.4 shows the example of the CN Tower in Toronto. Other examples can be found in various VRML repositories (e.g. http://www.sdsc.edu/vrml/, http://webspace.sgi.com/Repository/indexch.html, http://www.vir.com/~farid/ctrepos.htm).

Conclusions

The emerging data highway is a new infrastructure of tremendous importance and high potential impact. As we have argued above, this technology will particularly influence those sectors of the economy that –

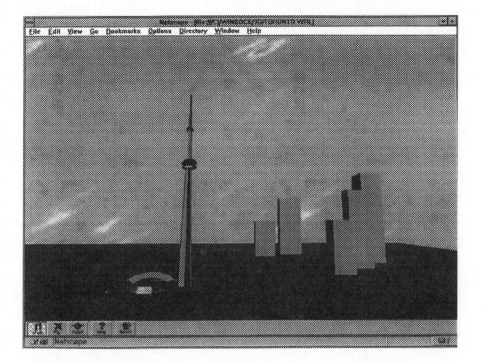

Figure 6.4 VRML example

among other characteristics – consist of many interdependent actors who sell a complex product in a global market. The tourism sector in cities is almost a prototype for a sector with a high need for Internet technology. It can be expected that this sector will be strongly influenced by the further development of information technology.

Because of its peculiarities, Internet technology is sometimes hard to understand and difficult to judge from a traditional business perspective. The open discussions on the Internet are accompanied by a loss of control, and its level of connectivity is sometimes more frightening than fascinating. Therefore, administrators and managers of city tourism agencies may tend to 'wait and see' and stay away from the global network until it has become more mature and more controllable. They may even be able to justify this strategy by pointing to one of their current markets that may be hard to reach via Internet.

Such a conservative approach overlooks the fact that the Internet may be the ideal technology for reaching new customers and new market segments. As we have shown in the above discussion, a large number of cities are already present on the Internet and 'staking their claims in Cyberspace'. It may well be that those who choose to stay out may fall behind permanently in the global competition of cities, in the same way as those who once decided to stay off the railroad network.

We have shown that Internet technology can be used for city tourism in a number of ways. It can help coordinate the many actors of city tourism, support the distribution of information and improve the communication with potential customers, and it can help managers to observe the market and get a better understanding of emerging new trends and fashions. The necessary tools for tapping this rapidly growing global market are available. They only need to be applied in the correct way.

Notes

[1] Gopher offers similar features to the WWW, but distinguishes strictly between links, which are collected in menus and documents. Therefore, it does not allow such smooth integration of information as in the WWW.

[2] An asterisk indicates that various subgroups exist.

[3] Of course, in much lower quality and without adequate sampling.

[4] URL: http://city.net/countries/united_states/oregon/portland.

[5] URL: http://www.bev.net/.

[6] URL: http://lycos.cs.cmu.edu.

[7] URL: http://www.yahoo.com.

[8] URL: http://www.cs.colorado.edu/home/mcbryan/WWWW.html.

[9] The official definition of HTML can be found at URL http://www.w3.org/-hypertext/WWW/MarkUp/MarkUp.html.

[10] The general form of a hyperlink is: <a href="URL">hyperlink</a>.

[11] A 'mailto' URL has the form mailto:user@host.

[12] The server starts this program through the CGI interface. Therefore, we call it CGI program. The minimum version of the <FORM> tag is therefore: <FORM ACTION="URL-CGI">, where URL-CGI is the URL of the CGI program.

[13] When an emerging new file type becomes very popular, the routines for displaying it may be included into later versions of WWW clients.

References

Ashworth, G.J. and Voogd, H. (1988) Marketing the city: concepts, processes and Dutch applications. *Town Planning Review* 59, 65–80.

Baker, R.H. (1991) *Computer Security Handbook*. Blue Ridge Summit: Professional and Reference Books.

Brand, R.L. (1990) *Coping with the Threat of Computer Security Incidents, A Primer from Prevention to Recovery*. Available via anonymous FTP from various sources, e.g. (ftp://ftp.univie.ac.at/security/cert/info/primer).

Cash Jr, J.I., McFarlan, F.W. and McKenney, J.L. (1988) *Corporate Information Systems Management*. Homewood, IL: Dow Jones-Irwin.

Cheswick, B. and Bellovin, S.M. (1994) *Firewalls and Internet Security*. Englewood Cliffs, NJ: Prentice Hall.

Chu, K. and Chin, F. (1996) *HTML Publishing in the Internet*. New York: McGraw-Hill.

December, J. and Randall, N. (1994) *The World Wide Web Unleashed*. Indianapolis: Sams Publishing.

Farrow, R. (1991) *UNIX System Security: How to Protect Your Data and Prevent Intruders*. Reading, MA: Addison Wesley.

Flanagan, D. (1996) *Java in a Nutshell*. Sebastopol: O'Reilly & Associates.

Grabig, J. (1995) *Reiseplanung im Internet*. Düsseldorf: Sybex.

Graham, I.S. (1996) *HTML Sourcebook*, 2nd edn. New York: Wiley.

Hughes Jr, L.J. (1995) *Actually Useful Internet Security Techniques*. Indianapolis: New Riders.

Kotler P., Haider, D.H. and Rein, I. (1993) *Marketing Places: Attracting Investment, Industry, and Tourism to Cities, States, and Nations*. New York: The Free Press.

Krol, E. (1992) *The Whole Internet User's Guide & Catalog*. Sebastopol: O'Reilly & Associates.

LaQuey, T. (1992) *The Internet Companion: A Beginner's Guide to Global Networking*. Reading, MA: Addison Wesley.

Magid, J., Matthews, R.D. and Jones, P. (1995) *The Web Server Book: Tools & Techniques for Building Your Own Internet Information Site*. Chapel Hill: Ventana Press.

Maier, G. (1995) Städte präsentieren sich im Internet. In E. Schifferl (ed.) *Österreichs Tourismuswirtschaft auf dem Info-Highway: Kriech- oder Überholspur?* ÖGAF-Protokolle, Band 8, Vienna: Österreichische Gesellschaft für Angewandte Fremdenverkehrswirtschaft.

Maier, G. and Wildberger, A. (1995) *In 8 Sekunden um die Welt: Kommunikation über das Internet*, 4th edn. Bonn: Addison-Wesley.

National Research Council (1994) *Realizing the Information Future: The Internet and Beyond*. Washington: National Academy Press.

Page, S. (1995) *Urban Tourism*. London: Routledge.

Pesce, M. (1995) *VRML: Browsing & Building Cyberspace*. Indianapolis: New Riders.

Schertler, W. (1994a) Tourism 2000 – an information business. In W. Schertler, B. Schmid, A.M. Tjoa and H. Werthner (eds) *Information and Communication Technologies in Tourism: Proceedings of the International Conference in Innsbruck, Austria, 1994*. Vienna: Springer.

Schertler, W. (1994b) Informationssystemtechnologie und strategisches Tourismusmanagement. In W. Schertler (ed.) *Tourismus als Informationsgeschäft: Strategische Bedeutung neuer Informations- und Kommunikationstechnologien im Tourismus*. Vienna: Ueberreuter.

Schmalzhofer, W. (1996) *Tourismusinformation am Internet als Instrument der Regionalentwicklung*. Master's thesis, Vienna: Vienna University of Economics and Business Administration.

Stanek, W.R. and Purcell, L. (1995) *Electronic Publishing Unleashed*. Indianapolis: Sams Publishing.

Zimmerman, P.R. (1995) *The Official PGP User's Guide*. Cambridge, MA: MIT Press.

Appendix: Advanced methodology for detecting competitors, mapping destinations, constructing tourist types and analysing competitive positions

Josef A. Mazanec

Collecting and preprocessing grouping data

The analysis of competitive relationships between product and service alternatives sometimes relies on the degree of similarity and substitution perceived by consumers. The 'evoked set' of purchasing alternatives (Howard and Sheth, 1969) has been known since long before the concepts of the consideration and choice sets were adopted by travel behaviour research (Crompton, 1992). It is reasonable to assume that two cities, like any products or services, are subject to tough competition if many travellers take both of them into consideration when planning a trip. But competitive relationships are not restricted to pairs of objects. A typical set size may be up to five or even more alternatives. A measure of the intensity of competition, therefore, should exploit the set size information. Two cities are tougher rivals in a smaller set of alternatives of comparable attractiveness than in a larger one.

There are many ways of collecting similarity and 'likelihood-of-substitution' data. They range from paired comparisons and triads and tetrads of objects to (conditional) rank orders and grouping tasks. In terms of respondents' effort the grouping of alternatives into purchasing options of comparable attractiveness is most convenient, particularly if the number of groups is left to the respondent's discretion. The procedure generates dichotomous information (two alternatives are in the same group or not) which may be adjusted for the group size. An appropriate psychometric indicator was proposed by Burton (1975) and implemented for competitor analysis by Mazanec (1976).

Formally, the grouping performed by a particular respondent leads to a partition of a set M of n objects (stimuli) into T disjunctive subsets M_t, t = 1, . . .,T, where

$$M_t \neq \emptyset, \text{ where } \sum_{t=1}^{T} n_t = n \text{ and } n_t \text{ is the number of elements in } M_t \tag{1}$$

$$M_t \cap M_{t'} = \emptyset, \text{ where } t \neq t' \tag{2}$$

$$\bigcup_{t=1}^{T} M_t = M. \tag{3}$$

One respondent may build a 'coarse' partition with few subsets while another more discriminating one may construct a 'subtle' partition with many groups. To account for these differences Boorman and Arabie (1972, p. 234) developed a measure named 'height of partition':

$$\text{hop} = \sum_{t=1}^{T} \left(\binom{n_t}{2} / \binom{n}{2} \right) = \sum_{t=1}^{T} \frac{n_t! / (2! / (n_t-2)!)}{n! / (2! / (n-2)!)} = \sum_{t=1}^{T} n_t (n_t-1) / (n(n-1)), \tag{4}$$

where $0 \leq \text{hop} \leq 1.0$.

n(n−1)/2 pairs of objects can be formed out of the total number of n. $n_t (n_t - 1)/2$ pairs can be formed in a subset of size n_t . Hence the height of partition is the number of all pairs to be built within the subsets divided by the number of pairs that can be formed out of the whole set of objects. Consider the partition (A,B,C), (D,E), (F), (G,H) as an example. It allows for

$$\binom{3}{2} + \binom{2}{2} + \binom{2}{2} = 5$$

pairs. In total $\binom{8}{2}$ = 8×7/2 = 28 pairs are possible. The height of partition then amounts to 5/28 = 0.184. An extremely discriminating respondent (a 'splitter' in psychometric jargon) who forms a group for each individual object, i.e. (A), (B), . . ., (H), generates a hop of 0/28 = 0; an extremely indifferent person satisfied with just one big group (a 'lumper') gets a hop of 28/28 = 1. The Burton measure uses the hop concept to compute proximity values that:

- define a metric
- may be accumulated over a sample of respondents
- give more weight to the dissimilarity of a pair of stimuli in a larger subset than to those in a smaller subset
- give more weight to the dissimilarity of a pair of objects in different subsets if fewer subsets are available.

In more rigorous terms these requirements imposed on the desired dissimilarity measure $d_{i,j}$ for a pair of stimuli i and j means:

$$d_{i,j} = \sum_{k=1}^{m} d_{i,j}^{(k)}, \text{ with m = sample size} \tag{5}$$

$$d_{i,j}^{(k)} = a_t^{(k)}, \text{ if respondent k attributes objects i and j to the same subset } M_t \tag{6}$$
$$= b^{(k)}, \text{ if respondent k attributes objects i and j to different subsets}$$
$$= 0, \text{ if i=j}$$

$$b^{(k)} \geq \max(a_1^{(k)}, \ldots , a_T^{(k)}) \tag{7}$$
$$a_t^{(k)} > 0. \tag{8}$$

It is also desirable that $a_t^{(k)}$ depends on the number of stimuli $n_t^{(k)}$ in the tth group formed by respondent k. $b^{(k)}$ should depend on the number of pairs of stimuli which never appear together in any group formed by respondent k. The height of partition according to (4) denotes the probability of finding two randomly selected stimuli in the same group. Reasoning in analogy to the information-theoretic measure of entropy (Attneave, 1969) leads to the similarity (substitutability) $s_{i,j}^{(k)}$ for stimuli i and j as seen by respondent k:

$$s_{i,j}^{(k)} = -\text{ld } H_t^{(k)}, \text{ if stimuli i and j are in group t} \tag{9}$$
$$(\text{ld denotes the dyadic log and } -\text{ld } H = \text{ld} \frac{1}{H}$$
$$= \text{ld } (1-H^{(k)}), \text{ if i and j are in different groups}$$
$$= \text{ld } (\binom{n}{2} + \varepsilon), \varepsilon > 0, \text{ if i = j.}$$

Setting ε arbitrarily to 1.0 leads to a constant $C = \text{ld}((n \times (n-1)/2) + 1.0)$ which denotes maximal similarity. Then

$$d_{i,j}^{(k)} = C - s_{i,j}^{(k)} \tag{10}$$

with the possible values according to (6)

$$a^{(k)}_t = C + \text{ld } H^{(k)}_t \qquad \text{for } H^{(k)}_t > 0$$

$$a^{(k)}_t = C \qquad\qquad \text{for } H^{(k)}_t = 0$$

$$b^{(k)} = C - \text{ld } (1 - H^{(k)})$$

where H is the hop for respondent $k = \sum_{t=1}^{T} H^{(k)}_t = \sum_{t=1}^{T} \binom{n^{(k)}_t}{2} \bigg/ \binom{n}{2}$

$0 \le H^{(k)}_t, H^{(k)} \le 1.0$

is the desired measure of dissimilarity. The smaller $n^{(k)}_t$ the more $d^{(k)}_{i,j}$ diminishes for i and j in this group. For i and j sorted into different groups $d^{(k)}_{i,j}$ increases faster with a growing height of partition (i.e. a shrinking $H^{(k)}$).

The dissimilarities $d^{(k)}_{i,j}$ are accumulated over the whole sample of respondents. To keep the result comparable for varying sample sizes it is recommended to compute the mean values. In addition it is most unlikely that each respondent qualifies for judging the same number of alternatives. The total number of possible pairs and, therefore, the constant C must be given a person-specific value. The dissimilarity value $b^{(k)}$ is also assigned to the ungrouped stimuli outside the respondent's set of alternatives. Obviously these choice alternatives cannot compete with each other. The derivation of dissimilarities from grouping data is implemented in the FORTRAN77 programs DIGROUP/GROUPB for interactive or batch processing obtainable from the author.

Consider an example with two respondents R1 and R2 sorting seven choice alternatives into two and three subsets:

- R1: (A,B,C,D,E), (F,G)
- R2: (A,B), (C,D), (E,F), G unknown/ungrouped.

Constant C is $\text{ld}((7 \times 6/2) + 1) = 4.46$ for R1 and $\text{ld}((6 \times 5/2) + 1) = 4.00$ for R2. R2 makes finer distinctions (hop = 0.20) than R1 (hop = 0.52). The following (symmetric) dissimilarity matrices result for R1 (and for R2). They demonstrate the influence of the height of partition on the d-values. The stimuli in the large subgroup coarsely formed by R1 attain rather high dissimilarities of 3.39; the stimuli accurately sorted into pairs by R2 exhibit very small dissimilarity values of 0.09.

$d_{i,j}$	A	B	C	D	E	F
A	0					
B	3.39 [0.09]	0				
C	3.39 [4.32]	3.39 [4.32]	0			
D	3.39 [4.32]	3.39 [4.32]	3.39 [0.09]	0		
E	3.39 [4.32]	3.39 [4.32]	3.39 [4.32]	3.39 [4.32]	0	
F	5.53 [4.32]	5.53 [4.32]	5.53 [4.32]	5.53 [4.32]	5.53 [0.09]	0
G	5.53 [4.32]	5.53 [4.32]	5.53 [4.32]	5.53 [4.32]	5.53 [4.32]	0.07 [4.32]

Hierarchical non-disjunctive clustering

The individual or aggregate dissimilarity data of the above outlined grouping procedure may be analysed further with multidimensional scaling (MDS) or clustering procedures to visualize the competitive relationships. The strength of competition is conceived as a continuous variable. New competitors enter the consumer's choice set if the competitive intensity is gradually relaxed. This points to using a hierarchical clustering procedure.

Owing to the limited rationality of consumer decision-making it is unlikely that consumers build crisp and mutually exclusive groups of choice alternatives based on a transitive order of preference (Kroeber-Riel, 1992). In contrast with the majority of well known numerical taxonomy methods the desired clustering procedure should not enforce a partition of exhaustive and mutually exclusive clusters. In the consumer's mind a brand, a company or a destination may rival different competitors in more than one competitive group at the same time. This rationale leads to combining the preprocessing of grouping data with subsequent hierarchic non-disjunctive clustering (Mazanec, 1976).

An appropriate clustering algorithm was developed by Peay (1975). It rests on the graph-theoretic concept of the 'clique'. A 'clique of level d' is defined as a subset of distinct elements C_d out of a set Q, where

$$C_d \subseteq Q \text{ and } d_{i,j} \leq d \ \forall \ i, j \in C_d.$$

$d \geq 0$ is a predetermined upper limit of dissimilarity. A clique is called 'maximal' if there is no element in $Q - C_d$ that may be added to C_d while satisfying the inequality $d_{i,j} <= d$ (Bock, 1974, p. 318; Peay, 1975, p. 300):

$$\max_{i \in C_d} (d_{i,k}) > d, \ \forall \ k \in Q{-}C_d. \tag{11}$$

A 'maximal clique' with the number of elements $| C_d | \geq 1$ is called a 'group of level d' (Bock, 1974). This mathematical concept corresponds perfectly with the notion of a highly competitive choice set where the inequality $d_{i,j} <= d$ holds for each pair of alternatives.

The 'group' concept easily lends itself for a graph-theoretic interpretation. A set of n elements allows for $n \times (n-1)/2$ pairwise connections. These connections represent a complete, undirected graph joining n nodes via $n \times (n-1)/2$ edges. Erasing some of these edges gives a 'partial graph' and further skipping of all unconnected nodes gives a 'subgraph'. A graph G is evaluated by assigning a distance or dissimilarity value $d_{i,j}$ to the edge between i and j. Introducing a limit for d leads to a partial graph G(d) consisting only of the dissimilarities $d_{i,j} <= d$. Each 'group of level d' is then equivalent to a subgraph of G if only the nodes connected by edges $d_{i,j} <= d$ are considered (Bock, 1974, pp. 300ff.; Harary 1974, p. 21).

Graph theory defines the 'group' (or 'maximal clique') as a maximal and complete subgraph (Harary, 1974, pp. 21, 30). It contains only immediately adjacent nodes (connected via edges). The 'group' concept was generalized by Peay (1975) by permitting indirectly adjacent nodes which are mutually 'reachable' via r intermediate nodes. Two points connected by a path of length r are called 'r-reachable'.

$$\forall \ i, j \in C_d^{(r)} \ \text{are mutually r-reachable, and} \tag{12}$$

$$\neg \ \exists \ k \in Q - C_d^{(r)} \ \text{where i and k are r-reachable } (\forall \ i \in C_d^{(r)}) \tag{13}$$

hold for the generalized r-reachable group ('r-group') of level d (Peay, 1975, p. 301).

If the search for competitive alternatives is to proceed hierarchically the limit d must be increased stepwise under a predetermined reachability parameter r. The Peay clustering procedure employs a recursive method which rests on the principle that a new dissimilarity matrix $D^{(r)} = (d_{i,j}^{(r)})$ is constructed for each level of d and a predetermined r ($1 <= r <= n-1$). The immediately reachable ('1-reachable') groups of level d of this matrix simultaneously are r-reachable groups of level d of the initial dissimilarity matrix $D^{(1)}$. According to Hubert (1974, p. 289) and Peay (1975, p. 302) the recursion formula is

$$d_{i,j}^{(r)} = \min \ _{1 \le k \le n} (\max (d_{i,k}^{(r-1)}, d_{i,j}^{(1)})), r \ge 2.$$

By choosing a value for r the analyst determines the permitted level of 'indirectness' for the path between i and j. In cluster-analytic jargon this means that (s)he seeks a result lying between the two extremes of 'single linkage' and 'complete linkage' clustering. If r = 1 the inequality condition $d_{i,j} <= d$ applies to all pairs of elements of a group ('complete linkage'). For r = n−1 it is sufficient if each pair of elements is indirectly connected via a path of edges < d ('single linkage'). For the purpose of competitor detection a 'complete linkage' effect is desirable. The conventional complete linkage methods are sometimes criticized because they do not produce strictly determined solutions but depend on the idiosyncrasies of the particular clustering algorithm (Johnson, 1967; Jardine and Sibson, 1971, p. 56). As the r-group method does not enforce mutually exclusive (disjunctive) clusters it is not subject to these criticisms. By permitting partly overlapping clusters it also avoids an irreversible allocation of elements to a cluster on a particular hierarchical level (Sodeur, 1974, p. 159).

The r-group procedure is implemented in the CLIP clustering program. In the version modified by and obtainable from this author the CLIP program also accepts profile data for input where distances in general Minkowski space (for arbitrary p)

$$d_{i,j} = (\sum_{g=1}^{n} | x_{ig} - x_{jg} | P)^{1/P} \tag{15}$$

still have to be computed. It is recommended to set the reachability parameter r to 1 (Mazanec, 1976). As a consequence the CLIP program outputs a large number of hierarchical levels. The marketing manager looking into competitive relationships, however, will be satisfied with a very limited number of the lowest d-levels where the toughest competition occurs.

Consider the example of the two respondents R1 and R2 above. The CLIP clustering processes the average dissimilarity matrix for seven stimuli A, ..., G. The dissimilarity values range between 1.74 (e.g. for $d_{A,B}$ or for $d_{C,D}$) and 4.92 (e.g. for $d_{A,F}$ or for $d_{B,G}$). In total there are five d-levels; the reachability parameter is set to 1:

d-level	Non-disjunctive clusters				
4.92		(A,B,C,D,E,F,G)			
3.85	(A,B,C,D,E)		(E,F)	(F,G)	
2.81	(A,B)	(C,D)	(E,F)	(F,G)	
2.19	(A,B)	(C,D)	(E)	(F,G)	
1.74	(A,B)	(C,D)	(E)	(F)	(G)

Both respondents had the stimuli (A,B) and (C,D) either in one large subgroup (R1) or in two pairs (R2). R2 also formed one pair (F,G). Given his less discriminating sorting behaviour, however, this response only becomes effective on the next highest distance level. As the aggregate response of R1 and R2 is taken into account F is similar to E as well as to G and to the whole remainder of the stimuli. None of the solutions to be obtained with ordinary disjunctive clustering – (A,B,C,D,E) and (F,G), or (A,B,C,D,E,F) and (G), or (A,B,C,D) and (E,F,G) – would correctly reflect the sorting data of both respondents R1 and R2.

Partitioning, non-hierarchical cluster analysis for binary data

The BINCLUS clustering method will be outlined in some detail. It has been fairly successful in solving a posteriori segmentation tasks in hundreds of market research projects. BINCLUS is tailored to handle binary data and to cope with a large sample size. The method was cross-validated with the advanced probabilistic model of latent class analysis, proving that in spite of being much simpler it could detect 'structure' in the data quite reliably (Formann *et al.*, 1979; Mazanec, 1980, 1984). The raw data usually arrive in multidimensional scale batteries or item lists from questionnaires or personal interviews. Dichotomous data do not imply a complicated scale for data collection. A simple response such as 'yes/no', 'agree/disagree', 'important/unimportant' that is coded into unity and zero is sufficient.

Variables with more than two categorical values (polytomous data) and ordinal data are easily transformed into a binary format. For example, a variable like 'country of origin' with values 'UK', 'France' and 'Germany' becomes a set of three 'artificial' binary variables 'UK', 'France' and 'Germany' each with values 1 = 'yes' or 0 = 'no'. Each respondent generates a 0-1 vector as his/her response pattern. Identical patterns gathered from two or more respondents are weighted by their frequency and treated jointly during the clustering procedure. Depending on the number of variables this data collapsing helps to reduce computing time.

A partition into exhaustive and mutually exclusive clusters is constructed by sorting respondents according to their pairwise similarity. Similar cases become members of the same cluster, dissimilar ones are attributed to different clusters. BINCLUS offers four options to compute (dis)similarity measures for binary data:

- the matching coefficient and distance
- the Tanimoto coefficient and distance
- the Dice coefficient and distance
- the binary Euclidean distance.

A similarity measure is needed to express the information about respondents' homogeneity given their data vectors of 0-1 reactions. Among a variety of similarity measures for binary data (Anderberg, 1973, pp. 83ff.; Bock, 1974, pp. 48ff.; Späth, 1975, pp. 24ff.; Späth, 1976; Vogel, 1975, pp. 93ff.) the matching coefficient and the Tanimoto measure are intuitively understood. The first measure counts all 1 and 0 matches as a proportion of the total number of variables. The Tanimoto coefficient derives the similarity of a pair of respondents from 1-1 matches but not from 0-0 matches. If, for example, both tourists i and j want to visit the opera on a city trip they are considered to be similar (at least in this individual item). If neither of them is interested in opera performances this is not taken to add to their similarity. Consider a sample computation of the similarity coefficients from ten items in response patterns of two respondents R_i and R_j, i.e. two data vectors x_i and x_j:

• item number:	1	2	3	4	5	6	7	8	9	10
• x_i of R_i:	1	1	1	0	0	1	0	0	1	0
• x_j of R_j:	1	1	0	1	0	1	1	1	1	0

The matching coefficient equals the number of matches divided by the number of items. The Tanimoto coefficient counts the number of 1-1 matches divided by the number of items not tied in zero matches. A third measure, the Dice coefficient, doubles the 1-1 matches. This is necessary to avoid an implicit double weighting of the non-matches b + c in cases where polytomous variables have been converted to zero-one dummy variables (Anderberg, 1973, p. 89). All these measures are bound to vary between the upper and lower limits of 1.0 and 0.0:

R_j:

$$\begin{array}{cc} 1 & 0 \end{array}$$

(1') matching coefficient $M_{i,j} = a/m =$
$$= (4+2)/10 = 0.60$$

R_i:
$$\begin{array}{ccc} 1 & a = 4 + & b = 1 = 5 \\ & + \quad + & + \\ 0 & c = 3 + & d = 2 = 5 \\ & 7 & 3 \quad m = 10 \end{array}$$

(1") Tanimoto coefficient $T_{i,j} = a/(a+b+c) =$
$$= 4/(10-2) = 0.50$$

(1''') Dice coefficient $D_{i,j} = 2a/(2a+b+c) =$
$$= 8/11 = 0.73. \tag{16}$$

Computationally, the absolute frequencies a, b, c, and d are obtained from summation, multiplicative and min-functions applied to each pair of data vectors x_i and x_j:

$$a = \sum_{l=1}^{m} \min (x_{il}, x_{jl}) = \sum_{l=1}^{m} x_{il}\, x_{jl} \tag{17}$$

$$b = \sum_{l=1}^{m} x_{il} - a = \sum_{l=1}^{m} x_{il}\, (1 - x_{jl}) \tag{18}$$

$$c = \sum_{l=1}^{m} x_{jl} - a = \sum_{l=1}^{m} x_{jl}\, (1 - x_{il}). \tag{19}$$

For (1') and (1") a transformation of 1.0 less the similarity value defines a metric. The distance functions

$$d^{(M)}_{i,j} = 1 - M_{i,j} = 1 - \frac{a+d}{a+b+c+d} = \frac{b+c}{m} \quad \text{and} \tag{20}$$

$$d^{(T)}_{i,j} = 1 - T_{i,j} = 1 - \frac{a}{a+b+c} = \frac{b+c}{a+b+c} \tag{21}$$

denote the dissimilarity of a pair of response patterns.

$$d^{(E)}_{i,j} = \sqrt{m\, d^{(M)}_{i,j}} \tag{22}$$

is the binary Euclidean distance, while d_E^2 corresponds to the so-called 'city-block' metric

$$\sum_{l=1}^{m} | x_{il} - x_{jl} | = b + c \tag{23}$$

except for the scaling factor $1/m$ as can be seen in (20).

For a number of n response patterns there are $n \times (n-1)/2$ pairwise distances $d_{i,j}$. The sum of distances portrays within-cluster heterogeneity. One obtains an overall measure of heterogeneity by accumulating the sum of distances over the clusters. Average distances may be used for comparing between different cluster solutions. The objective function seeks to minimize the overall heterogeneity:

$$\sum_{s=1}^{q} \frac{1}{n_s} \sum_{i \epsilon C_s} \sum_{j \epsilon C_s, j \rangle i} d_{i,j} \;\rightarrow\; \text{min!} \tag{24}$$

where n_s is the number of elements in cluster C_s (s = 1, ..., q).

The BINCLUS clustering program implements a partitioning (not a hierarchical) procedure. This means that a number of clusters has to be tentatively fixed in advance. The optimization process starts with an initial random grouping of the response patterns. The patterns are systematically reallocated and exchanged between the clusters until the overall heterogeneity (24) reaches a minimum (Späth, 1975, 1977; Steinhausen and Steinhausen, 1977). A series of consecutive solutions is produced for an increasing number of clusters in a feasible range depending on the empirical problem and on the sample size. The heterogeneity of the cluster solutions is bound to decrease with the growing number of clusters. Sometimes a marked decline (an 'elbow' kink) in the heterogeneity graph indicates that the improvement of homogeneity is levelling off after a certain number of clusters has been formed. Given no such indication one has to rely on the face validity of the frequency distributions of the cluster defining variables. The experience from numerous clustering studies tells that an inconclusive situation rarely occurs, unless the variables have been compiled 'ad hoc'. The most efficient computational procedure cannot compensate for a lack of theory.

A subsequent discriminant analysis is recommended to examine the statistical meaningfulness of the cluster solution. In the DA the x_{il} are the predictors and the cluster affiliation becomes the group-defining dependent variable. The DA reveals the amount of information extracted from the x-variables regarding a respondent's membership in a specific cluster. In case of a poor predictive power it is imperative to replicate the clustering for several randomly generated initial partitions. The repetitive computation checks the robustness of the cluster solution. As the exchange algorithm does not warrant a global optimum the final result depends on the starting partition and may get trapped in a particularly unsatisfying local minimum.

Self-organizing feature mapping

Compared to the old and established clustering procedures outlined above the self-organizing feature map is a new and fascinating method taken from the neurocomputing toolkit. The early applications of neurocomputing (or neural network) models in business and marketing research have focused on 'supervised learning' (Curry and Moutinho, 1993; Hruschka and Natter, 1992, 1993; Hruschka, 1993; Mazanec, 1990, 1992, 1993a, b). Learning in supervised mode implies prior knowledge about the correct output expected from a network model. Estimating market response functions or classifying consumers into predetermined segments are typical examples. But business and marketing managers also deal with exploratory problems where the desired model output is not known in advance. A posteriori market segmentation ('similarity segmentation'; Bagozzi, 1986, p. 229) is an excellent example. The concept of 'self-organizing (feature) maps' (SO(F)M) was introduced by Teuvo Kohonen of the Helsinki Technology University. It represents an elegant version of 'unsupervised learning'. The process is unsupervised as the SOM model learns to extract stable features or 'prototypes' from a database without correction and assistance from an 'outside teacher' (Kohonen, 1982, 1990). SOMs have been successfully applied to many categorization and pattern recognition issues, e.g. for speech and images (Aleksander and Morton, 1990, p. 152; Chappell and Taylor, 1993; Sabourin and Mitchie, 1993), for decoding signals from radiotelescopes (Hiotis, 1993), or for solving the popular travelling salesman problem (Hertz *et al.*, 1991, pp. 244–6; Maren, 1990, pp. 150–1). SOM computation is 'adaptive' in the sense that it functions online by processing one data point at a time. The data manipulation may be directly implemented in VLSI, i.e. very large-scale digital circuits (Thiran *et al.*, 1994) for extremely fast processing. In tourism or retail research this technology is attractive for processing a continuous influx of new data (such as automated check-in/check-out systems and scanner data).

An intriguing characteristic of SOMs is their topology-preserving property (Kohonen, 1984, p. 133; Pao, 1989, pp. 182–96; Freeman and Skapura, 1991, pp. 263–89; Gallant, 1993, p. 136). This means that input vectors of arbitrary dimensionality (e.g. consumers' evaluations of choice alternatives on multiattribute lists) become associated with the nodes in a two-dimensional grid (the map) in such a way that more similar data vectors get associated with nodes lying closer to each other than less similar ones. The 'objective is to extract and visually display hidden topological structure' in the multidimensional data. This 'feature mapping' (Pal *et al.*, 1993) may now be added to the more traditional data reduction techniques.

The SOM model for a 'toy' problem is shown first. SOM learning (or 'training') is discussed afterwards. The SOM operation is demonstrated with a small set of artificial data. Assume that a number of 27 profiles of three attributes each are to be condensed into a smaller number of nine 'typical' companies, brands or cities ('prototypes') in only two dimensions. Figure A.1 contains these data. They are 'artificial' because the profiles – unlike real-world data – are represented by equally spaced points in a three-dimensional attribute space. As the distances between two adjacent data points along each dimension are all equal there are several ways of replacing neighbouring points by a prototype. The SOM is expected to detect one 'intelligent' solution subject to the constraint that the nine prototypes should conform with the topology of a two-dimensional grid. The prototypes are arranged as nodes in a grid with three rows and three columns. The grid defines the topology in terms of neighbourhood relations. 'Neighbourhood' has an ordinal meaning. First-order neighbours are adjacent to each other, second-order neighbours are separated by one intermediate node, third-order neighbours by two intermediate nodes etc. In theory, the grid should be as 'flat' as possible to fit into a two

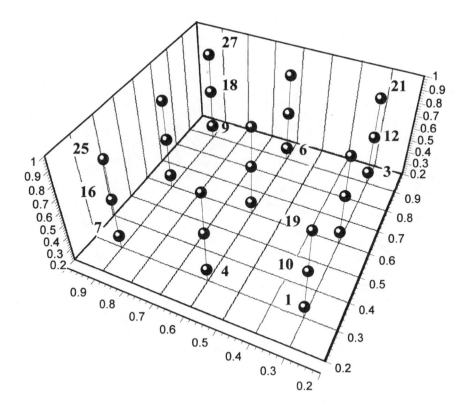

Figure A.1 Artificial data points

dimensional plane. In practice, it will be folded and distorted as a consequence of dimensionality reduction. But contrary to principal components analysis the SOM also approximates non-linear principal surfaces in a multidimensional data distribution (Ritter *et al.*, 1992, pp. 244ff.).

Figure A.2 portrays the grid or 'map' after about 2700 training iterations. It is a fairly flat and roughly two-dimensional structure of nine prototypes within the data space of Figure A.1. Each of the nine prototypes in Figure A.2 represents a subset of the observed data points in Figure A.1 (Table A.1).

The coordinates of the prototypes in the map are called 'weights'. Figure A.2 shows the 'true' locations of the prototypes in the dataspace. The grid is needed to determine the neighbourhood relationships among the prototypes. While seeking the optimal positions of the prototypes in the dataspace the SOM training must respect these neighbourhood restrictions. Thus the three data points captured by, say, prototype #2 are more similar to prototype #5 (one 'neighbour' away) and its data point #14 than to

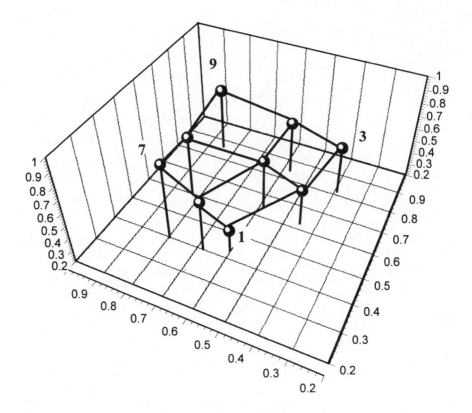

Figure A.2 The two-dimensional grid ('map') in data space

Table A.1 Prototypes and data points

Prototype #	Represent the data points #				
1	1	4	5	7	8
2	2	10	11		
3	3	12	20	21	
4	13	19			
5	14				
6	6	15	24		
7	16	22	25		
8	17	23	26		
9	9	18	27		

prototypes #7 or #9 (two 'neighbours' away) and their associated data points.

The topological properties of the 27-point raw data cube are nicely preserved, though not perfectly recovered by the prototypes. The grid (or map) 'forms some kind of projection image' (Kohonen, 1984, p. 135) on a planar surface. The 'map' in Figure A.2 appears to be an 'artificially' flattened grid imposed on a higher-dimensional structure. It is evident, however, that there must be some sacrifice for condensing a higher-dimensional dataset into a sparse two-dimensional representation (Ritter and Schulten, 1988; Martinetz and Schulten, 1994).

The prototypes in an SOM may be considered to be cluster centroids for their respective data points where the centroids themselves are ordered according to their similarity in two dimensions. Thus the prototype system of the SOM preserves most of the topological properties of the data. If the data are of higher dimensionality than the number of dimensions chosen for the grid of prototypes the mapping becomes 'asymmetric': data points must be similar to get associated with adjacent prototypes, but data points not belonging to neighbouring prototypes need not necessarily be dissimilar. In mathematical terminology SOMs perform an inversely continuous mapping. If '$\cong$' ('$\neq$') denotes 'similar' or 'adjacent' ('dissimilar' or 'not adjacent') and x and y denote data points and p(x) or p(y) are their respective prototypes the following two implications hold true:

$$x \neq y \Rightarrow p(x) \neq p(y) \qquad \text{and } p(x) \cong p(y) \Rightarrow x \cong y, \tag{25}$$

but vice versa,

$$x \cong y \Rightarrow p(x) \cong p(y) \qquad \text{and } p(x) \neq p(y) \Rightarrow x \neq y \tag{26}$$

do not. Like in any other data reduction technique there is a trade-off for squeezing dimensionality.

In principle, ordered prototypes can also be found with conventional methodology (e.g. nearest-centroid clustering and subsequent sorting of centroids by their similarity). But the ordering soon becomes analytically intractable as the number of prototypes increases. SOM models are restricted neither by the size of the map nor by the sample size. Like most neural networks they are adaptive as they operate online and learn through exposure to individual examples. Mathematically, SOMs can be entirely treated in concise matrix notation. But before outlining SOM operation in greater detail it may be appropriate to demonstrate how SOMs are presented in the neural networks literature.

Figure A.3 displays the architecture of another simple SOM network in standard neural networks style and terminology. NeuralWorks Professional II/PLUS by NeuralWare (1991a, b) is chosen as an example. Each 'processing unit' (node, prototype) in a two-dimensional 'layer' (the grid or map with three rows and three columns of elements in Figure A.3) is

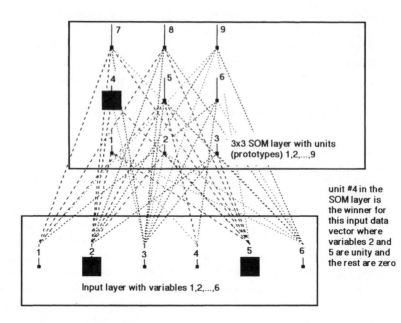

Figure A.3 The SOM architecture

connected to a multidimensional input data vector (comprising the six variables 1,2,. . . 6 in Figure A.3). There are as many data vectors as objects (companies, brands, retail outlets, destinations, etc.). Each object has been evaluated in six attributes. These attributes may be measured on a ratio or interval scale or they may represent binary variables. They originate from rating scales or from easily collected 'yes-no' reactions from individual respondents. The units in the SOM (or Kohonen) layer 'compete' with each other. This means that only one SOM unit (prototype) is allowed to respond to the activation aroused by a particular data vector (see unit #4 in Figure A.3). It depends on the 'similarity' of the weight vector $\mathbf{w}$ (represented by the connecting lines in Figure A.3) and the data vector $\mathbf{x}$ which SOM unit will qualify as the 'winner'. 'Similarity' in this example is measured by the Euclidean distance d between the i-th SOM unit's weight vector $\mathbf{w}_i$ and a data vector $\mathbf{x}$ with values x_k arriving at the input layer:

$$d_i = \|\mathbf{x} - \mathbf{w}_i\| = (\sum_{k=1,\ldots,m} (x_k - w_{ik})^2)^{\frac{1}{2}} \qquad (27)$$

with $\mathbf{x} = (x_1, \ldots, x_m)$
and $\mathbf{w}_i = (w_{i1}, \ldots, w_{im})$.

During the training process the network is repeatedly exposed to input vectors randomly selected from the dataset. Starting from an initial weight distribution of small random weights it learns to adapt its weight structure according to the distribution pattern of the input data. Each of the SOM units becomes a prototype by taking responsibility for a homogeneous set of data vectors. The weight update follows the learning rule (Kohonen, 1984, p. 138; Caudill, 1993a, p. 19)

$$w_{ij\,new} = \begin{cases} w_{ij\,old} + \lambda\,(x_j - w_{ij\,old}), \text{ if } i\,\epsilon N\,(i') \\ w_{ij\,old} \text{ otherwise} \end{cases} \tag{28}$$

with the learning constant $0 < \lambda < 1$. As the nodes in the SOM layer compete with each other only the 'winner' i' and the units in its neighbourhood $N(i')$ are allowed to (further) improve their fit (i.e. reduce distance) by a weight update. The Kohonen feature map manages to preserve the topological order of the input data through a mechanism called 'lateral interaction' (Kohonen, 1984, p. 129) or 'lateral inhibition' (Caudill, 1993b, p. 41). This means that the elements in the vicinity of the winning unit participate in the updating process producing an 'activity bubble' (Kohonen, 1984, p. 131). In a biologically consistent model of activation in the cortex the other units may be 'punished for having lost' the competition the farther away they are from the bubble centre. In the previous examples the neighbourhood of an SOM unit is defined by the rectangle of eight units surrounding a winning element.

Some refinements are useful in optimizing SOM operation. The major ones are implemented in the author's SOMnia program that may be downloaded free from the Internet (http://www.wu-wien.ac.at/inst/tourism/software/). To prevent the nodes from becoming inactive the process may keep track of the excitation frequency of each node. This is implemented in the NeuralWorks Professional (NeuralWare, 1991a). If the winning frequency of an SOM unit increases too fast (depending on the initialization with random weights) some other nodes may stop learning. Then the network runs the risk of degeneration resulting in a poor representation of the input data and of their topological properties. As an alternative to frequency-tracking, the neighbourhood of the winning unit in the map may vary during the unsupervised training process. This is implemented in the NeuroWindows NNW dynamic link library (Ward Systems Group, 1993). If the size of the neighbourhood is large in the beginning and then shrinks gradually during the SOM training, a degenerate solution with poor prototypes is unlikely to occur (Ahalt et al., 1990). Subject to training with a decreasing learning rate and a frequency-of-winning or a neighbourhood control bias, the SOM layer is bound to settle down after a finite number of training cycles (Cherkassky and Mulier, 1994). The required number of cycles is rather small compared to other neural network paradigms such as backpropagation learning (Rumelhart et al., 1986).

Saaty scaling

Multifactor portfolio models may use a simple scoring method to calculate a weighted sum of 'market attractiveness' and of 'competitive position' criteria. The manager is then asked to make direct weight judgements. But there is a more sophisticated way of prompting these judgements. Condensing n attractiveness or competitive position criteria into one single value for each of the two axes in the portfolio plot requires a set of cardinal weights w_i (i = 1, . . . ,n). Saaty's (1977) eigenvector method transforms a manager's importance judgements for $n(n-1)/2$ pairwise comparisons of criteria into n ratio-scaled weights (Hwang and Yoon, 1981; Dyer and Forman, 1991). Two judgements are elicited for each pair of attractiveness (or competitive position) criteria:

- Select the more important criterion (unless the two are considered equal).
- Evaluate the difference in importance by attaching a value between 1 and 9 (where 1 means 'equal importance' and 9 denotes 'absolute importance of one over the other').

For a number of, say, five criteria an assessor works through a series of ten steps deciding first, whether criterion i is more important than j or vice versa and second, how the difference in importance is reflected in a rating a_{ij}. These ratings expressing the differences in importance are arranged in matrix form $\mathbf{A} = (a_{ij})$, where $a_{ji} = 1/a_{ij}$ and the main diagonal values $a_{ii} = 1$. Table A.2 lists the sample judgements of a manager for five criteria depicting the attractiveness of a tourism-generating country: market size (number of trips), growth rate, seasonality, share of package tours and average tourist spending. Two out of ten paired comparisons end up in a tie. $a_{ij} > 1.0$ denotes a row criterion dominating the column criterion and vice versa for $a_{ij} < 1.0$. Thus, the manager attaches great importance to market size over seasonality or to growth rate over seasonality; the seasonal demand fluctuations seem to come off worst, whereas the average tourist spending and the market size are dominant.

The Saaty scale is based on the fact that the normalized eigenvector pertaining to the largest (and real) eigenvalue of $\mathbf{A}$, λ_{max}, contains unique and ratio-scaled importance weights $w_1, . . . ,w_n$ ($\Sigma w_i = 1.0$). With complete

Table A.2 Sample judgements for market attractiveness

Criterion	Size	Growth	Seasonality	Share	Expenditure
Size	1	1	7	5	1
Growth	1	1	7	3	1/3
Seasonality	1/7	1/7	1	1/3	1/5
Share	1/5	1/3	3	1	1/5
Expenditure	1	3	5	5	1
Weight	0.296	0.221	0.041	0.077	0.365

consistency of the $\mathbf{A}$ matrix λ_{max} equals n, the number of criteria to be weighted. Deviations from n, $(\lambda_{max} - n) > 0$, indicate the extent of perturbation in the judgemental data. Accounting for the size of the square matrix $\mathbf{A}$, $(\lambda_{max} - n)/(n-1)$ serves as a measure of consistency. Returning to the sample judgements in Table A.2 demonstrates that the manager weights tourist spending highest ($w_5 = 0.365$) and seasonality lowest ($w_3 = 0.041$). Growth rate ranks five times as important ($w_2 = 0.221$) as seasonality. A consistency coefficient of $(5.241 - 5)/(5 - 1) = 0.06$ is highly satisfactory. A matrix filled with random numbers would have generated a coefficient value of 1.12.

In more rigorous terms, the square matrix of weights $\mathbf{A} = (a_{ij})$ is reciprocal ($a_{ji} = a_{ij}^{-1}$, $a_{ii} = 1$). As the elements a_{ij} constitute a manager's pairwise comparison ratings of the relative importance of criteria i over j they may be written as $a_{ij} = w_i/w_j$ $(i,j = 1, \ldots ,n)$. Suppose for a moment that the ratings arranged in $\mathbf{A}$ are noisefree data and perfectly consistent. Hence postmultiplying $\mathbf{A}$ by the weight vector $\mathbf{w}' = (w_1, \ldots ,w_n)$ renders

$$\mathbf{Aw} = n\mathbf{w}. \tag{29}$$

Solving (29) for the unknown $\mathbf{w}$ leads to the eigenvalue problem

$$(\mathbf{A} - \lambda\mathbf{I})\mathbf{w} = 0, \tag{30}$$

where λ stands for an eigenvalue of $\mathbf{A}$ and $\mathbf{w}$ for the corresponding eigenvector. Given the linear dependencies of the rows in $\mathbf{A}$ (any row is a multiple of the first one) rank($\mathbf{A}$) = 1 and thus all but one eigenvalues λ_i, $i = 1, \ldots ,n$, of $\mathbf{A}$ vanish. Since trace($\mathbf{A}$) = $\Sigma\lambda_i$ = n the one and only non-zero eigenvalue λ_{max} = n.

Consider now that the ratings a_{ij} are not free from error. In this case perturbations in the eigenvalues will occur in such a way that λ_{max} is still real and positive while λ_i, $i = 2, \ldots ,n$, may become complex. $(\lambda_{max} - n)/(n-1)$ increases with growing inconsistency of the managerial judgements. If one wants to check whether some degree of inconsistency in a rating dataset $\mathbf{A}$ is rather 'normal' or spurious, average consistency values may be calculated for reciprocal random data matrices of the same dimensionality. Given an $\mathbf{A}$ of order 3 to 15 and integer scale values $1 <= \max(a_{ij}, a_{ji}) <= 9$ the consistency coefficient attains values rising from 0.42 to 1.47. This means that a satisfactory degree of consistency for the portfolio weight judgements should not exceed a coefficient of 0.05 (for three criteria) and 0.10 or 0.15 (for four or five criteria).

References

Ahalt, St C., Krishnamurthy, A.K., Chen, P. and Melton, D.E. (1990) Competitive learning algorithms for vector quantization. *Neural Networks* **3**, 277–90.
Aleksander, I. and Morton, H. (1990) *An Introduction into Neural Computing*. London: Chapman and Hall.

Anderberg, M.R. (1973) *Cluster Analysis for Applications*. New York: Academic Press.

Attreave, F. (1969) *Informationstheorie in der Psychologie*, 2nd edn. Berne: Huber.

Bagozzi, R.P. (1986) *Principles of Marketing Management*. Chicago: Science Research Associates.

Bock, H.H. (1974) *Automatische Klassifikation, theoretische und praktische Methoden zur Gruppierung und Strukturierung von Daten (Cluster-Analyse)*. Göttingen: Vandenhoeck & Ruprecht.

Boorman, Sc.A. and Arabie, Ph. (1972) Structural measures and the method of sorting. In R.N. Shepard, A.K. Romney and S.B. Nerlove (eds) *Multidimensional Scaling, Theory and Application in the Behavioral Sciences* vol. 1. New York: Seminar Press, 225–45.

Burton, M.L. (1975) Dissimilarity measures for unconstrained sorting data. *Multivariate Behavioral Research* 10, 409–22.

Caudill, M. (1993a) A little knowledge is a dangerous thing. *AI Expert* 8, 16–22.

Caudill, M. (1993b) *Neural Networks Primer*, 3rd edn. Published by *AI Expert*, San Francisco: Miller Freeman, Inc.

Chappell, G.J. and Taylor, J.G. (1993) The temporal Kohonen map. *Neural Networks* 6, 441–5.

Cherkassky, V. and Mulier, F. (1994) Self-organizing networks for nonparametric regression. In V. Cherkassky, J.H. Friedman and H. Wechsler (eds) *From Statistics to Neural Networks, Theory and Pattern Recognition Applications*. Berlin: Springer, 188–212.

Crompton, J. (1992) Structure of vacation destination choice sets. *Annals of Tourism Research*, 19, 420–34.

Curry, B. and Mountinho, L. (1993) Neural networks in marketing: modelling consumer responses to advertising. *European Journal of Marketing*, 27, 5–20.

Dyer, R.F. and Forman, E.H. (1991) *An Analytic Approach to Marketing Decisions*. Englewood Cliffs, NJ: Prentice Hall, 87–114.

Formann, A.K., Mazanec, J.A. and Oberhauser, O.C. (1979) *Numerische Klassifikationsprobleme in 'großen' Datensätzen der demoskopischen Marktforschung: Ein empirischer Methodenvergleich von Latent Class- und Cluster-Analyse*. Arbeitspapiere der absatzwirtschaftlichen Institute der Wirtschaftsuniversität Wien, Vienna: Orac.

Freeman, J.A. and Skapura, D.M. (1991) *Neural Networks, Algorithms, Applications, and Programming Techniques*. Reading, MA: Addison-Wesley.

Gallant, St. I. (1993) *Neural Network Learning and Expert Systems*. Cambridge, MA: MIT Press.

Harary, F. (1974) *Graphentheorie*. Munich: Oldenbourg.

Hertz, J., Krogh, A. and Palmer, R.G. (1991) *Introduction to the Theory of Neural Computation*. Reading, MA: Addison-Wesley.

Hiotis, A. (1993) Inside a self-organizing map. *AI Expert* 8, 38–43.

Howard, J.A. and Sheth, J.N. (1969) *The Theory of Buyer Behavior*. New York: Wiley.

Hruschka, H. (1993) Determining market response functions by neural network modelling: a comparison to econometric techniques. *European Journal of Operations Research* 66, 27–35.

Hruschka, H. and Natter, M. (1992) *Using Neural Networks for Clustering-Based Market Segmentation*. Research Memorandum. no. 307. Vienna: Institute for Advanced Studies.

Hruschka, H. and Natter, M. (1993) Analyse von Marktsegmenten mit Hilfe konnexionistischer Modelle. *Zeitschrift für Betriebswirtschaft* **63**, 425–42.

Hubert, L.J. (1974) Some applications of graph theory to clustering. *Psychometrika* **39**, 283–309.

Hwang, Ch.L. and Yoon, Kw. (1981) *Multiple Attribute Decision Making, Methods and Applications, A State-of-the-Art Survey*. Berlin, Heidelberg, New York: Springer.

Jardine, N. and Sibson, R. (1971) *Mathematical Taxonomy*. New York: Wiley.

Johnson, St.C. (1967) Hierarchical clustering schemes. *Psychometrika* **32**, 241–54.

Kohonen, T. (1982) Self-organized formation of topologically correct feature maps. *Biological Cybernetics* **43**, 59–69. Reprinted in J.A. Andersen and E. Rosenfeld (eds) (1988) *Neurocomputing: Foundations of Research*. Cambridge, MA: MIT Press, 511–21.

Kohonen, T. (1984, 3rd edn 1988) *Self-Organization and Associative Memory*. New York: Springer.

Kohonen, T. (1990) The self-organizing map. In *Proceedings of the IEEE* **78**, 1464–80. Reprinted in P. Mehra and B.W. Wah (eds) (1992) *Artificial Neural Networks: Concepts and Theory*. Los Alamitos: IEEE Computer Society Press, 359–75.

Kroeber-Riel, W. (1992) *Konsumentenverhalten*, 5th edn. Munich: Vahlen.

Maren, A.J. (1990) Vector-matching networks. In A.J. Maren, C.T. Harston and R.M. Pap (eds) *Handbook of Neural Computing Applications*. San Diego: Academic Press, 141–53.

Martinetz, Th. and Schulten, K. (1994) Topology representing networks. *Neural Networks.* **7**, 507–22.

Mazanec, J. (1976) *BMDIC – ein demoskopischer Indikator zur Messung der Intensität der Substitutionskonkurrenz zwischen Produktmarken*. Arbeitspapiere der absatzwirtschaftlichen Institute der Wirtschaftsuniversität Wien, Vienna: Orac.

Mazanec, J. (1980) Deterministische und probabilistische Klassifikation in der Konsumverhaltensforschung: Ein empirischer Anwendungsversuch der Quervalidierung clusteranalytischer Verfahren für qualitative Daten mit der Latent Class-Analyse. In G. Fandel (ed.) *Operations Research Proceedings 1980*. Berlin, Heidelberg, New York: Springer, 296–305.

Mazanec, J.A. (1984) How to detect travel market segments: a clustering approach. *Journal of Travel Research* **23**, 17–21.

Mazanec, J.A. (1990) Market segmentation once again: exploring neural network models. In Association Internationale d'Experts Scientifiques du Tourisme, *Tourist Research as a Commitment*. St Gall: AIEST, 36–53.

Mazanec, J.A. (1992) Classifying tourists into market segments: a neural network approach. *Journal of Travel & Tourism Marketing* **1**, 39–59.

Mazanec, J.A. (1993a) Apriori and aposteriori segmentation: heading for unification with neural network nodeling. In *Proceedings of the 22nd EMAC Conference, European Marketing Academy* vol. 1. Barcelona: ESADE, 889–917.

Mazanec, J.A. (1993b) Exporting the EUROSTYLES to the USA. *International Journal of Contemporary Hospitality Management* **5**, 3–9.

NeuralWare Inc. (1991a) *Neural Computing, NeuralWorks Professional II/Plus*. Pittsburgh: Technical Publications Group.

NeuralWare Inc. (1991b) *Reference Guide, NeuralWorks Professional II/Plus*. Pittsburgh: Technical Publications Group.

Pal, N.R., Bezdek, J. C. and Tsao, E.C.-K. (1993) Generalized clustering networks and Kohonen's self-organizing scheme. *IEEE Transactions on Neural Networks* **4**, 549–57.

Pao, Y.-H. (1989) *Adaptive Pattern Recognition and Neural Networks*. Reading, MA: Addison-Wesley.

Peay, E.R. (1975) Nonmetric grouping: clusters and cliques. *Psychometrika* **40**, 297–313.

Ritter H. and Schulten, K. (1988) Convergence properties of Kohonen's topology conserving maps: fluctuations, stability, and dimension selection. *Biological Cybernetics* **60**, 59–71.

Ritter, H., Martinetz, Th. and Schulten, K. (1992) *Neural Computation and Self-Organizing Maps*. Reading, MA: Addison-Wesley.

Rumelhart, D.E., Hinton, G.E. and Williams, R.J. (1986) Learning internal representation by error propagation. In D.E. Rumelhart and J.L. McClelland (eds) *Parallel Distributed Processing*, vol. I (*Foundations*). Cambridge, MA: MIT Press, 318–62.

Saaty, Th.L. (1977) A scaling method for priorities in hierarchical structures. *Journal of Mathematical Psychology* **15**, 234–81.

Sabourin, M. and Mitchie, A. (1993) Modeling and classification of shape using a Kohonen associative memory with selective multiresolution, *Neural Networks* **6**, 275–83.

Sodeur, W. (1974) *Empirische Verfahren zur Klassifikation*. Stuttgart: Teubner.

Späth, H. (1975) *Cluster-Analyse-Algorithmen zur Objektklassifizierung und Datenreduktion*. Munich, Vienna: Oldenbourg.

Späth, H. (1976) Tanimoto-Koeffizient. *WiSt–Wirtschaftswissenschaftliches Studium* **5**, 328–9.

Späth, H. (1977) Partitionierende Cluster-Analyse für große Objektmengen mit binären Merkmalen am Beispiel von Firmen und deren Berufsgruppenbedarf. In H. Späth (ed.) *Fallstudien Cluster-Analyse*. Munich, Vienna: Oldenbourg, 63–80.

Steinhausen, D. and Steinhausen, J. (1977) Cluster-Analyse als Instrument der Zielgruppendefinition in der Marktforschung. In H. Späth (ed.) *Fallstudien Cluster-Analyse*. Munich, Vienna: Oldenbourg, 9–36.

Thiran, P., Peiris, V., Heim, P. and Hochet, B. (1994) Quantization effects in digitally behaving circuit implementations of Kohonen networks. *IEEE Transactions on Neural Networks* **5**, 450–8.

Vogel, F. (1975) *Probleme und Verfahren der numerischen Klassifikation*. Göttingen: Vandenhoeck & Ruprecht.

Ward Systems Group (1992) *NeuroWindows, Neural Network Dynamic Link Library*. Frederick: Ward Systems Group, Inc.

Name index

Subject index